WITNESS TO ANNIHILATION

WITNESS TO ANNIHILATION

Surviving the Holocaust
A Memoir

SAMUEL DRIX, M.D.

BRASSEY'S
Washington

Brassey's, Inc.

Editorial Offices
Brassey's, Inc.
8000 Westpark Drive
First Floor
McLean, Virginia 22102

Order Department
Brassey's Book Orders
c/o Macmillan Publishing Co.
100 Front Street, Box 500
Riverside, New Jersey 08075

Brassey's books are available at special discounts for bulk purchases for sales promotions, premiums, fund-raising, or educational use.

Library of Congress Cataloging-in-Publication Data

Drix, Samuel.
  Witness to annihilation: Surviving the Holocaust—a memoir/Samuel Drix.
    p. cm.
  Includes index.
  ISBN 0-02-881087-2
  1. Jews—Ukraine—Lwów—Persecutions. 2. Holocaust, Jewish (1939–1945)—Ukraine—Lwów—Personal narratives. 3. Drix, Samuel. 4. Janowska (Ukraine: Concentration camp) 5. Lwów (Ukraine)—Ethnic relations. I. Title.
DS135.U42L8535 1994
940.54'18'092—dc20
                                                                    [B] 93-48943
                                                                         CIP

Designed by Lisa Chovnick

10 9 8 7 6 5 4 3 2

Printed in the United States of America

CONTENTS

ACKNOWLEDGMENTS

I would like to express my deep gratitude to Professor Roger Hilsman for his encouragement and advice given to me in editing and publishing my book. I am deeply thankful to Mr. Don McKeon, associate director of publishing at Brassey's, and to my editor, Mr. Andy Ambraziejus, for their help and suggestions. Their perseverance has allowed me to tell my story much more clearly and fully. I wish also to thank Mrs. Irene Tannen and her nephew, Professor Dr. Slominski in Warsaw, for the transcription and translation of the audiotapes with which I began to record my memoir. Lastly, my profound gratitude to my dearest son and daughter-in-law, Severin and Pamela, for their tremendous help in all the stages of editing the manuscript, and to my beloved wife, Alice, for her moral support in the long years of writing this book.

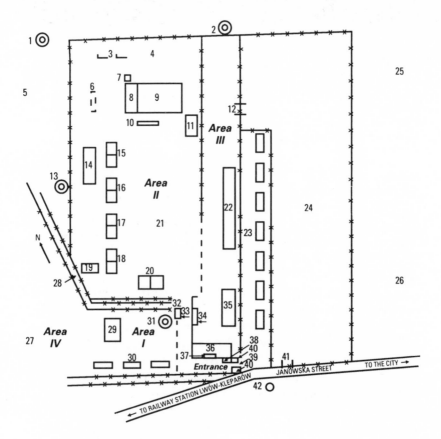

1. Turret
2. Turret
3. Two gallows
4. Old assembly ground
5. To the Sands
6. Old latrine (pit with a wooden beam across it)
7. Wooden platform
8. Kitchen
9. Old Barracks (#1 and #2 a two-story building)
10. Water trough
11. New washroom (built in early November 1942; it had earlier been a shack for interrogation)
12. Entrance to D.A.W.
13. Turret
14. New latrine (built in November 1942)
15. New Barracks #3 and #4 (built in Fall 1942)
16. New Barracks #5 and #6 (built in Fall 1942)
17. New Barracks #7 and #8 (built in Fall 1942)
18. New Barracks #9 and #10 (built in Fall 1942)
19. Brewery barrack (built in Winter/Spring 1943)
20. New Barracks #11 and #12 (built in Winter/Spring 1943)
21. New assembly ground (built in November 1942)
22. Laundry and workshops
23. Houses for SS-men, Askaris, and camp police
24. D.A.W. (German Armament Workshops—contained a complex of buildings, not shown)

25. To the Jewish cemetery
26. Christian cemetery
27. Vegetable gardens
28. "Behindwire"
29. Women's camp (built in January 1943)
30. Garage, shops, and stables
31. Turret
32. Entrance to "behindwire"
33. Orchestra platform
34. Exit and entrance control booth (with table inside)
35. Infirmary (two floors: first—for emergencies; second—twelve beds)
36. Willhaus's villa
37. Admissions office
38. Guard house
39. Main gate and main entrance to Janowska Camp
40. Bunkers
41. Street entrance to D.A.W.
42. Hydrant

KEY

✳✳✳✳ barbed wire

– – – – grass line

———— road or building

Note

It is assumed: a) Areas I and IV were closed off on the west end with barbed wire, although I never actually saw this part of the camp; b) the section containing the SS houses probably had barbed wire running along the south end bordering Janowska Street.

PREFACE

I am dedicating this book to my beloved family, which I lost entirely in the Holocaust, and to the hundreds of thousands of martyrs of Janowska camp and of the city of Lwów, the forgotten people.

The city of Lwów was the third largest city in Poland before World War II, after Warsaw and Łódz, and was inhabited by the third largest Jewish community in the country. Now part of Ukraine, Lwów at that time was in the southeast part of Poland. The Jewish community of Lwów was politically, culturally, and economically a vibrant community. Between World War I and World War II, this community's representatives played a significant and prominent role in Jewish political life in Poland—and in the Polish parliament, the Sejm. They often led the club of Jewish parliament members called the Jewish Circle.

The Jewish community of Lwów was hit more viciously by the Nazis than any other. The extermination process started early, soon after the city was occupied by the Germans, and was completed as early as November 1943—that is, one and a half years before the end of the war. In the western and central parts of Poland the SS took women and sometimes children to the concentration camps; however, in Lwów the SS sent all women, young or old, healthy, skilled, professionals, and also all children, directly to the gas chambers in Bełzec during the so-called actions starting in 1942. Only for a short period of time, beginning in January 1943, did some women have the "luck" to be admitted to Janowska camp instead. They were all killed there four months later, in May 1943.

In any Jewish community or ghetto the *Judenrat* (Jewish Council) was the official representative of the Jewish population, the ones to whom the Germans gave their orders and whose job it was to enforce them (although it tried, where possible, to soften the impact of these orders). The first chairman of the *Judenrat* of Lwów, Dr. Parnas, was arrested and murdered for his refusal to obey the orders of the Nazis; the second, Dr. Rothfeld, died—allegedly of leukemia; the third, Dr. Landesberg, was hanged by the SS from a balcony on Łokietka Street in Lwów as a penalty for some Jewish resistance during the August 1942 "action" in the city. (Dr. Landesberg was hanged together with eleven other men, among them members of the *Judenrat* and the Jewish police. Afterward the German security police sent a bill to the *Judenrat* for the six ropes used in hanging its members!) The last chairman of the *Judenrat*, Dr. Eberson, was appointed by the Germans; he was murdered a few months later, with most of the *Judenrat*. After that, there was no longer any *Judenrat* in Lwów, no intermediary, however minimal the protection it could offer, between the Jewish population and the German authorities.

The Jewish population of Lwów was about 160,000 before World War II. It fluctuated early in the war, for many reasons. The largest single change came in 1939, when many Jews arrived from the western part of Poland, fleeing the Germans.

Immediately after liberation about 700 Jews registered as having survived. This represents under one half of one percent of the Jews of Lwów, using any of the estimates of the prewar population. A few more survived elsewhere (for example, in Russia) and were not among the early registered survivors, but not enough to significantly alter the figures. In short, virtually all of the Jews of Lwów were annihilated.

Some of these were among the roughly 200,000 murdered in Janowska camp, the death mill where the Jews of Lwów and eastern Galicia were concentrated. Janowska was officially a forced labor camp, but the usual life expectancy there was about six weeks, unless one had help from outside. Unlike Bełzec, which, like Treblinka, served only for annihilation, with Jews there going to the gas chambers as quickly as they could be processed, Janowska was like Auschwitz and Majdanek, using inmates as a labor force for the German army and related private firms. At the same time, inmates regularly died through executions, disease, and malnutrition. Periodically, large numbers were sent to Bełzec. New inmates provided replacements for the many who died.

The destruction was made even more complete when the Nazis, trying to erase the evidence of their crimes, formed a death brigade in Janowska camp whose function was to dig up the mass graves in Lwów and burn the remnants of the victims into ashes.

In November 1943 SS General Katzmann, who was chief of the SS and the police in District Galicia (the German term for eastern Galicia), reported to Hitler: "*Galizien ist judenrein* [Galicia is cleansed of Jews]." For his perfect job of extermination he was promoted by Hitler from major general of the police to lieutenant general of police and from SS-Brigadeführer to SS-Gruppenführer, the highest SS rank below Himmler, who was chief of both SS and the police. Meanwhile, in western and central Poland, in Germany and in Austria, concentration camps continued to exist until 1945. The very few Jews who survived in eastern Galicia were those who managed to hide until the arrival of the victorious Soviet army.

It is therefore very strange and painful that I have noticed hardly any mention of the Jews of Lwów and Janowska camp in the annual memorial celebrations of Holocaust survivors in New York that I have attended or read accounts of. There are very few books on the topic, and even less in the mass media. Neither Lwów nor other cities of eastern Galicia with substantial Jewish populations have been mentioned in the Jewish press or in the general press, or in television documentaries I have seen in New York. Nor has Janowska camp been mentioned in any of the innumerable articles and features I have read.

The same happened, unfortunately, in Jerusalem in 1981, when I participated in the First World Gathering of the Survivors of the Holocaust: many ghettos and camps were mentioned in all the speeches, but not one word about Lwów or Janowska camp. Most probably this is because so few Jews from that area remain, but that is even more reason to remember them in events that claim to commemorate all the victims of the Holocaust.

There was a film some years ago, *Image Before My Eyes*, which described Jewish life in Poland prior to World War II; it was shown on television (PBS) twice. There was nothing said in it about Lwów or eastern Galicia, nothing about the more than half million Jews in southeastern Poland. The film included a map of Jewish settlements in Poland before 1939 on which southeastern Poland (eastern Galicia) was blank, as if there were no Jewish settlements there. Again, in a documentary about the history of Jews in Poland, shown on PBS television in May 1992, there was a description of Jewish life in Warsaw, Wilno, Łódz, Białystok, Kraków, and a small town named Maków, but nothing about the city of Lwów or any other city of eastern Galicia.

In the annual memorial celebrations no prayers were said for the martyrs of Lwów and Janowska camp, no candles were lit for them. They are forgotten by their own brothers as though they had never existed. In Janowska camp they were singing, "The world will someday know about us." The world? Their own brothers from other parts of Poland don't know about them. The souls of these forgotten hundreds of thousands of martyrs are crying, "Remember us, don't kill us for the second time, putting us into oblivion! Remember! *Zachor!*"

When I was in Janowska camp I vowed to myself that if I should survive I would tell the world of all the horrors we had experienced under the Nazis' inhuman occupation. I hoped also that one day I would be able to testify against the SS murderers from Janowska, if they were caught and brought to trial for their crimes.

In the history of mankind there have been many mass murders of civilians committed by barbaric armies. But this holocaust happened in the twentieth century and was committed by a highly civilized nation, famous for its philosophers, writers, composers, poets, and scientists. It combined brutal force with modern technology, psychology, and hate propaganda. The torture and murder of millions of innocents, including old people, women, and children, was well planned and efficiently executed. This was a uniquely horrible experience in human history—and a serious warning for the future, demanding to be understood.

In 1946 I met the historian and Holocaust author Dr. Philip Friedman in Munich. His books, especially his main work, *Roads to Extinction—Essays on the Holocaust,* are the sources for many of the statistics and historical details cited in this book. When we met he urged me to write my memoirs as one of the very few of the intelligentsia to have survived Janowska camp. All these years I have realized that this is my sacred duty, which I owe to the martyrs of Janowska camp and the Lwów ghetto; however, I postponed it over and over because of my professional work. But in the last few years we have seen more frequently published declarations, by pseudohistorians and Nazi activists, that the Holocaust is a hoax, that it never happened. This puts a profound obligation on all survivors still living to come out with their stories, to share their experiences. With this book I am fulfilling my sacred duty, and I hope not in vain.

INTRODUCTION

I was born in the city of Lwów. This beautiful city was located in the southeastern part of prewar Poland, and was its third largest city. It was the main city of a region then called eastern Little Poland but most commonly known as eastern Galicia, a much-contested land on the northern slopes of the Carpathian Mountains that changed hands many times.

Lwów was established by a Ruthenian prince in the thirteenth century, and the surrounding countryside was primarily Ruthenian. It was later incorporated into Poland under King Casimir the Great, who expanded and modernized the city. When Poland formed a union with Ruthenia and Lithuania in 1569, this included all of eastern Galicia as well. Poles eventually dominated this union to a large extent, in effect making it a greater Poland, so that the Ruthenians, though they remained a majority in eastern Galicia, were largely unrepresented in the ruling class.

In the late eighteenth century, Poland was partitioned among Russia, Germany (Prussia), and Austria. The southern part of Poland became an Austrian province and was given the name Galicia. Its capital was Lwów, which was renamed Lemberg. In the eastern half of Galicia the Ruthenians, who began to call themselves Ukrainians, were the vast majority in the countryside, while the Poles outnumbered them in the cities and towns, with Jews the largest minority there. Poles continued to dominate culturally and politically, however. As the region attained some autonomy, this amounted to de facto Polish rule, and Polish became the official language. There was growing antagonism between Poles and Ukrainians, and many Ukrainians demanded their own independent state. With the collapse of the Austrian monarchy at the end of World

One of the main squares in Lwów, named Plac Marjacki, before the war. In the fore-
ground is a monument to Adam Mickiewicz, Poland's greatest poet. *Courtesy of the Josef
Piłsudski Institute of America.*

War I, fierce fighting broke out between these peoples, and the
Ukrainians briefly took over Lwów before its recapture by the Poles. All of
Galicia became part of the new state of Poland. The eastern part was now
called eastern Little Poland.

When World War II started, eastern Galicia was taken over by the
Soviet Union and became incorporated into the Ukrainian Soviet
Republic. It was now called western Ukraine and Lwów was called Lvov
by the Russians. In 1941 the Germans occupied eastern Galicia, wel-
comed by the Ukrainians as allies against both the Poles and the Russians.
The region was then called District Galicia (western Galicia was not part
of this district, for it was included in the portion of Poland that Germany
had occupied since 1939). Lwów was again called Lemberg. In 1944,
when the Soviet army retook the region, the situation was restored to
what it was before 1941. With the recent collapse of the Soviet Union, an
independent Ukraine was formed, and Lwów, now called Lviv, is the main
city of the western part of Ukraine.

Witness to Annihilation

CHAPTER 1

THE WAR BEGINS

Lwów, Poland, March 1939

In March of 1939 I was finishing my one year of internship at the second largest hospital in Lwów and starting my residency in internal medicine there. It was the Hospital of Social Insurance (in prewar Poland the state-assisted social insurance system also ran dispensaries and hospitals). One day, about eight or ten of us were sitting at breakfast in a small cafeteria reserved for medical doctors in our hospital. We were talking about the current political situation, which was then very tense. One of us present there, Dr. Merkel, pronounced: "My dear gentlemen, we are living in historical times, and this is our disaster."

I was surprised at Dr. Merkel's use of the term *disaster*; it was exciting to live in historical times, and there was some danger, but he seemed to be overly alarmed. Indeed, none of the rest of us took the current situation so tragically. It was common to think that Hitler was bluffing and that it was by this bluffing that he had been able, over the past several years, to advance German power so frighteningly without a shot being fired. He had occupied the Rhineland and militarized this area in violation of the Treaty of Versailles, then taken Saarland and Austria, and then, in the 1938 Munich agreement, obtained the Sudetenland (the part of Czechoslovakia that was inhabited by ethnic Germans).

Now, in March 1939, Hitler had just disregarded his pledge at Munich that he would go no farther and marched his armies into Prague, taking all of Czechoslovakia. He was playing on the deep reluctance of the Western Allies to fight another war. However, his violation of the Munich pact made it clear to the Allies that he would not keep any agreement, and they began rearming themselves. It was known that Poland's turn was coming, and the general conviction was that Hitler wanted to continue his bluffing and acquire Polish Pomerania and Gdańsk (Danzig), thereby connecting East and West Prussia. With the Allies no longer believing in

1

appeasement, however, it appeared that Hitler's bluff would be called. Most people felt that he would then not dare to actually start a war, and that if he did, Germany would quickly lose.

German military power was underestimated then. People thought that during the few years that had elapsed since Hitler came to power Germany could not possibly have remilitarized sufficiently to face the powerful French army. France had a long-standing treaty guaranteeing that it would go to war to defend Poland, and there was widespread confidence in the might of the French. A motion picture that presented the power of France and its army was being shown in the Lwów movie theater Europa for several weeks. Even if France alone were not enough to soon defeat Germany, people counted on Great Britain to honor its commitments and join the war. In addition, they kept in mind the United States' role in the war of 1914–1918 and hoped that the United States would again indirectly and then directly help the Allies. Finally, there was the Soviet Union. The Western countries were negotiating with the Soviets to form a united front against Germany, but even if the Soviets didn't agree to this, it was known that Hitler's Germany and Soviet Russia were like fire and water, so that cooperation between them could not come about.

The doctors at our breakfast discussion, therefore, like people in general, were more concerned than before but hardly panicking. Nobody was worried enough to consider emigration, for instance (unlikely in any case, since most doors were closed at this time). Life went on as before. No major events occurred until August.

In August 1939 new events shocked us. The political situation was becoming increasingly tense. Unexpectedly, Soviet Russia and Germany signed a pact, the Molotov-Ribbentrop Pact, on August 23, and war was around the corner. The Polish government ordered a mobilization.

There was still, however, no panicking. Everybody was convinced, as I said, that the war would be a short one, ending with a defeat of the Germans. Mobilization turned our hospital into a military one. Still, we were to continue working there as before until the transformation was completed, at which time we would be replaced by army doctors.

On the morning of September 1, when I came to the hospital, colleagues told me that the radio had already broadcast news of a German invasion of Poland and the bombing of Warsaw. The hospital was immediately put under army control, but many civilian doctors, including myself, were kept on for the time being. At around noon of the same day, when I was going back home from the hospital, passing through the center of town, I saw airplanes appear in the sky. People were sure that these were Polish aircraft doing exercises, and stared at them. Suddenly bombs started to fall, one after another. This was terrifying and surprising, not least because Lwów was far from the Polish-German border and thus nobody expected that the Germans could get there that fast, even with airplanes. Later, we found out that these planes had attacked from German-occupied Czechoslovakia, from airfields relatively close to Lwów. From that day on, German planes reached Lwów more and more often, causing destruction of houses and many civilian casualties.

My wife, Frania (short for Franciszka), and I had been married just ten months when the war broke out, and we were living with her family at the time, trying to save enough money to buy an apartment with an office for my medical practice. Her family consisted of her parents (Maurycy and Amalia Leibel) and her two brothers (Leopold and Alexander, nicknamed Zyśko). The apartment we all shared was on Panieńska Street, in a middle-class residential area in the northern part of Lwów, not far from the suburbs. Our apartment was also unfortunately quite near to the Podzamcze railway station; German planes, trying to destroy railway stations, visited us ever more frequently, which made the inhabitants of our neighborhood stay in the cellars most of the time.

Frania and I on our wedding day in November 1938.

By listening to the foreign radio stations we learned that the Polish army was suffering defeat after defeat and that the German army was rapidly progressing eastward, approaching Warsaw (about 360 kilometers from Lwów). In a short period of time the first German units appeared in the suburbs of Lwów.

During the daytime, and even more so in the night, shooting was heard. This was the sound of fighting between the advance troops of the German army and the Polish defenders. On September 17 we learned from the radio that Soviet Russia had decided, in spite of its existing nonaggression treaty with Poland, to invade Poland's eastern territory in order to, as the officials proclaimed, defend their brothers, the Ukrainians and Belorussians.

The Russian army quickly advanced westward, and in short order Lwów was surrounded on its one side by German troops and on the other by the Soviets. Lwów was the main center of communication in southeastern Poland, and the main road from western Poland to the Soviet Union passed through it, so the city was of considerable military value. After lengthy deliberations, the municipal authorities of Lwów, headed by the mayor, a man named Ostrowski, made up their minds and surrendered to the Soviet army. This decision, though, had no effect on the outcome. At the same time it became known that the Molotov-Ribbentrop Pact that Russia and Germany had made in August contained a secret clause. According to this clause Poland was to be partitioned between them, with the western part taken by Germany and the eastern one to be incorporated into the Soviet Union. The border agreed to in August 1939, which took effect when Poland was conquered in September, was somewhat west of the current eastern border of Poland (that is, the Soviet Union, after World War II, annexed most of the part of Poland that it had been given in its pact with the Germans). Lwów was included in the eastern part. We became citizens of the Soviet Union.

CHAPTER 2

INTERREGNUM

Life under the Soviet occupation, from September 1939 to the beginning of July 1941, was very unusual and interesting, although not comfortable at all. It is very hard to explain to people used to a democratic society; to portray it properly would almost require a book in itself. However, since the main topic of this book is the Holocaust, I shall give only a brief glimpse of what life was like for us during the Soviet period, using a few telling incidents.

The Soviet occupation brought us a complete revolution, imposed in an instant by a foreign power, a revolution in political, economic, and cultural terms. The changes were dramatic for society at large and for the life of every individual. In the (albeit imperfect) democratic society of Poland we had had freedom of speech, press, and religion; the right to strike; and the right to move about freely. Now we lived in an absolute Communist dictatorship marked with terror and complete state control of each individual's life. No private enterprise was permitted. All institutions and factories, and all rental properties, became nationalized. Thus, for instance, my parents' small family business now belonged to the state and they had to seek new employment.

At all times, everybody had to carry a "passport," a document that did not entitle one to travel but served as an identification paper. Whoever was caught without a passport by a policeman was immediately arrested as a suspected foreign spy. Every worker also had a worker's book, listing his employment. He was not allowed to leave his job without his manager's permission. To do so was like deserting the army, and it was punishable by prison. Nor could he go to another city and start over, for he would be in trouble when he tried to get another job and his discharge did not appear in his book. What's more, if his worker's book wasn't in order he couldn't get any housing.

When the Russians arrived in Poland they were amazed at the level of life they saw, and they bought everything they could; stores throughout Lwów were emptied within a few weeks. Some time later, at work, I overheard Russian patients talking with each other, unaware of my presence. They were sharing their surprise at what they had seen in Poland, and their realization that they had been lied to by their government all these years. They had been led to believe, by Soviet propaganda, that the masses of Poles were impoverished and oppressed by the bourgeois; they had even been told that the farmers in Poland had to plow their fields with their bare hands while a boss urged them on with a whip!

Early in the Soviet occupation, we all got a sample of the nature of Soviet propaganda. The store windows on Lwów's main streets displayed lovely posters of the workers' paradise in Donbas, a Soviet mining and industrial region. Photographs showed beautiful living quarters and excellent working conditions. Many workers, eager for jobs, stood in line from dawn to apply for work in Donbas. After a few weeks, people started coming back, some so anxious to leave they had traveled the great distance on foot! They were also risking getting into trouble, but this was early on, and the Soviets had not yet instituted the worker's book in Lwów, so it was possible to avoid punishment for leaving the job.

It took me some time to realize the extent to which our freedom had disappeared. One day I was in a movie theater seeing a historical film about the Russian revolution. When Stalin's image appeared, everyone applauded immediately. I didn't. My friend next to me gave me a sudden jab in the ribs, saying, "Applaud! Are you crazy, do you want to go to Siberia?" Eventually I came to see that one was always being watched, always in danger of being denounced to the authorities.

In the first few months of Soviet rule, the situation was very chaotic. Because the state was the only employer, there was great competition for jobs and good ones were often hard to get. After some time I found a very desirable position: I worked from October to May as a doctor in the University Hospital of Lwów, and the other half of the year as an assistant to Professor Węgierko in the spa clinic in Morszyn Zdrój, a spa resort seventy kilometers south of Lwów. Here we were treating patients as well as conducting medical research. Professor Węgierko had been one of the leading medical researchers in Warsaw, which he fled when the Germans came. He was internationally known, the top diabetes specialist in Poland.

The staff of the department of internal medicine of the State Hospital in Lwów, affiliated with Jan Kazimierz University, during the winter of 1940–41. I am standing fourth from the left; my best friend, Norbert Sztekl, is standing eighth from the right.

I was very happy to be working for him. It was good, in these politically gloomy conditions, to have real satisfaction in my career.

In my personal life there was also good fortune, for on June 2, 1940, my daughter, Sylvia, was born. Frania and Sylvia were with me in Morszyn when I worked there, and during the winter season the three of us lived in Lwów, in the apartment at Panieńska Street that we shared with my wife's family.

Doctors' salaries were at that time very low: about three hundred rubles monthly for seven hours a day, six days a week. On this amount an individual could live modestly, but not a family of three. Therefore, many doctors took additional jobs. Professor Węgierko, who liked my work very much, gave me two extra jobs so that I could support my family.

My work in Morszyn was very interesting, not only from a medical point of view but also because my patients there came almost exclusively from the Soviet Union, from all regions and from all levels of Soviet society. Many of them, developing confidence in me, secretly described life in the Soviet Union. What I heard from them was sad and often frightening. I heard of the terror when many thousands of citizens disappeared forever. The secret police, when they wanted to arrest a suspect, would let him go

With Frania and Sylvia in early 1941.

about his normal business for a while, keeping him under surveillance. When they did arrest him, they also took anyone to whom he had spoken. It was therefore dangerous to even greet someone on the street, for if it turned out that he was being watched, you might well disappear along with him. The Soviets' approach was that if only one in a hundred were guilty, they would rather arrest all hundred than risk letting that one go free.

I did not have to rely on other people's word to know to what extremes the Soviet authorities would go. In Morszyn, also, events occurred that filled one with fear. One day a cleaning woman stole a small jar of butter in our sanatorium there. For this she was sentenced to two years in prison. At a meeting of the Workers' Committee, a Dr. Fajwlewicz brought up this incident, saying that it seemed an injustice to him that she should get two years for stealing, out of hunger, this small amount. He was told, "Doctor, this is Soviet law," to which he replied, "This is a Draconian law!" A week later, at a general workers' assembly, the leader of the Communist party for our region said, "Dr. Fajwlewicz, I hear that you called Soviet law Draconian. You are an educated man, and you know the meaning of the word *Draconian*. You will pay for this." The next day the doctor disappeared, and none of us heard from him again.

Of the roughly thirty doctors in Morszyn, only two had been Communists in prewar Poland. They had both even served prison time for their beliefs, for the Communist party was outlawed then. One was Dr.

Fajwlewicz. The other, while we were all registering for military service, made a casual remark in the presence of a Soviet officer, a Party member. Seeing a portrait of Kalinin (then president of the Soviet Union), he noted that his beard made him look like Trotsky, Stalin's archenemy. The next day this doctor disappeared. Perhaps these two doctors thought that they were safe because they had suffered for the cause, or perhaps their belief in communism blinded them to its ruthless reality.

The threat of punishment for even the smallest political incorrectness was so real that it was a tool to force compliance in even trivial matters. During my time in Morszyn I was invited to a dinner as the guest of honor by the chief director of one of the sanatoriums there, who liked me and my work. Just before dinner he poured for each of us a huge glass of vodka, about the size of half a soda can. I excused myself, saying that I could not possibly drink this vodka—for medical reasons. He felt insulted, and said, "What do you mean, you can't drink it?" I explained that I had a kidney condition, that I wasn't allowed to drink vodka. He replied, "I will show you that you *will* drink."

He got up and loudly announced, "Comrades, I propose a toast to Comrade Stalin's health." Then he turned to me, smiling, and said, "Now I would like to see if you dare not to drink." I was desperate. I had to either follow custom and down the entire glass at once or risk being sent to Siberia as a traitor. Just then, not for the first time in my life, my lucky star intervened. The director's chief bookkeeper came in with something needing his attention, whispering in his ear. As his attention was distracted, I acted quickly. Sitting across the table from me were two registered nurses who drank like fish. They had already emptied their glasses, so I switched my glass with one of theirs. When the director turned to me, I had an empty glass in my hand. Incidentally, the nurse who took my vodka ended up so drunk she had to be carried out in a stretcher, while her companion merely got drunk enough to become embarrassing and had to be taken home early.

For Jews, there was one positive aspect to Soviet life: open anti-Semitism was outlawed, in contrast to the conditions in prewar Poland, where it had been open and legal. A brief description of the situation for Jews in Poland prior to 1939 will be helpful here as a backdrop for what came later. There had been no official government anti-Semitism in Poland, and Jews had the same legal rights as Poles, participating fully in the political and economic life of the country. Every Polish government categorically denied that it supported anti-Semitism in any way. However, it did exist in the private sector and was very common—in the form of quotas and discrimination, and sometimes worse. The Catholic Church and the universities (which were hotbeds of Polish nationalism) were the centers of anti-Semitism in Poland. The government also practiced anti-Semitism in hiring, even when it denied this.

All medical schools in Poland had very tight quotas for Jews, and these quotas diminished each year. The Lwów medical school, an excellent and prestigious faculty of Lwów's Jan Kazimierz University, was particularly tough in this way. It allowed only eleven Jews in 1930, the year I applied. (Six hundred Jews applied for those eleven openings. By 1936 or 1937 the quota had shrunk steadily to zero—Jews were simply not admitted anymore.) For a Jew to get in required exceptional talent, but this was not enough. Some influential backer was also required. Many friends of mine considered it hopeless and went abroad to medical school, although that meant problems later with being allowed to practice medicine in Poland. It was a major event for me when I was accepted to the Lwów medical school.

To become a university professor in prewar Poland, a Jewish candidate had to convert to Catholicism; in the late 1930s even this was no longer sufficient. By an unwritten law, Jews rarely could get a government job or become a judge or a higher army officer. Besides such restrictions, there was also an economic boycott of Jewish businesses launched in the mid-1930s by the extreme Polish nationalists and condoned by the government. Many small Jewish businesses were hard hit by this. My parents had a delicatessen and luncheonette that had done fairly well, but after the boycott they eventually had to close it. My aunt Andzia, my mother's sister, helped my parents start another business, but this also struggled because of the boycott.

Until the death of Marshal Piłsudski in 1935, anti-Semitism was rarely violent. He was a national hero who had a major role in creating the state of Poland, and he took power in a coup in 1925, setting up a "guided democracy" with himself as strongman. He curbed the influence of the nationalists. After his death anti-Semitism grew more and more violent, especially in the universities, and the economic boycott started. The increasingly militant anti-Semitism in the late 1930s was also influenced largely by the actions and propaganda of neighboring Nazi Germany.

At the university in Lwów, the extreme nationalists terrorized Jews, for they felt Jews had no right to be there. Gangs of these students would attack Jews with impunity. Once, as I was waiting in front of a clinic to take an oral exam, I saw such a group approaching. Just then the professor appeared, so I thought I was safe. Nonetheless, in full view of this professor, one of the gang hit me on the head with a stick. It might have been

My alma mater in Lwów, Jan Kazimierz University, in a photograph taken before World War II. *Courtesy of the Josef Piłsudski Institute of America*

worse, but the professor's outraged shouts sent them running away. When I graduated, I was supposed to go to the dean's office to pick up my diploma and take the Hippocratic oath. But I was terrified, because anti-Semitic students were blocking the entrance, determined to keep Jews from getting their diplomas. They were armed with canes that had razor blades stuck in them. I tried every day for two weeks to get in, watching from a distance for a moment when it might be safe, finally finding it unguarded. I knew their threats were not just bluff. Many Jews had been badly beaten by them before; two had even died at their hands. However, it must be said that even at its worst, Polish anti-Semitism never compared to what the Jews later experienced at the hands of the Germans and Ukrainians. By that comparison, life in prewar Poland seemed a paradise. What's more, it was still better to be a Jew in democratic Poland than to live under the Soviets in equal fear with everyone else.

CHAPTER 3

JUNE 1941

Under the Soviet occupation, although it was not officially illegal for anybody owning a radio to listen to foreign stations, it was something one did discreetly, not wanting it to come to the attention of the authorities. Listening to London radio, we learned that relations between the Soviet Union and Germany were getting tense, that the Germans were preparing for an attack on the Soviet Union.

At that time it was the summer season, so Frania, Sylvia, and I were living in Morszyn. The main town in the county, thirteen kilometers from us, was Stryj, which is seventy kilometers south of Lwów. On Saturday, June 21, at ten P.M., we were listening to the Moscow radio news. TASS, the official Soviet press agency, broadcast a communiqué saying that the imperialist circles in England and in America were disseminating false information that German troops were concentrating on the Soviet border and that a German invasion of the Soviet Union was expected any day. TASS officially informed us that all these rumors absolutely did not reflect truth, that relations between Germany and the Soviet Union were still friendly. This was at ten P.M. A few hours later, at four in the morning of June 22, we were awakened by the explosions of falling bombs. I ran out onto the balcony, looked in the direction of the town of Stryj, and saw the bombing of its airfield. As I learned later, all Soviet airplanes on the airfield had been destroyed. So, Germany attacked the Soviet Union by surprise and we had a new war.

I had actually had some definite indications before this that the newfound brotherhood of Germany and the Soviet Union was not as firm as propaganda would have it. I had been to Lwów, just by myself for a day to visit my parents, brother, and sisters. This was on Friday, only a day and a half before the German invasion. On the way there I saw that my train was full of Soviet soldiers moving westward, toward the border. At that time I suspected that something was up, that the Russians might be preparing to attack or to guard against a German aggression. Coincidentally, I had seen similar Russian troop movements in 1940, on trains and roads going toward Romania, just before the Soviet army in fact crossed that border and forced Romania to cede the provinces of Bukovina and Bessarabia. Therefore, I had reason to doubt the official statements of solidarity between Germany and the Soviet Union, and I was not very surprised when war broke out between them, though it was still an awful shock and filled us with fear.

The Soviet authorities turned off electric power at once. Our radio sets were entirely useless and we did not have any idea what was going on at the fronts. Soviet functionaries, when asked, were telling us various stories: that the Soviet forces were fighting well; that they were counterattacking and were now marching westward; that they had taken Kraków; and so on. We saw, though, that they were preparing themselves for evacuation. At the same time the Ukrainians started guerrilla warfare and frequently, especially during the night, were shooting at Russian positions.

In Morszyn during the summer of 1940: Me, Sylvia, Frania, Uncle Nahum, Amalia (Frania's mother), and Norbert.

The Germans had promised them a free Ukrainian state and had been inciting them, first against Poland and then against the Soviets. The Russians, during these attacks, were often taken by panic, shooting wildly. Even greater panic, though, reigned among the Jewish population, for we were fully aware that when the Germans entered—which was almost certain—we would not be in for anything good, neither from the Germans nor from their friends the Ukrainians.

On the third or fourth day the Russians started to evacuate their offices and to send their people eastward. Out of the local population only medical doctors were to be evacuated, but without their families. There were thirty Jewish doctors in Morszyn. My closest friend, Dr. Norbert Sztekl (see photos, pages 7 and 13), came running to me amid a great panic and asked me to join the other evacuees. I had known Norbert since I was ten. We grew up in the same neighborhood. He hadn't made it into Lwów's medical school, so he studied medicine abroad and then was put on a long waiting list to take exams that would allow him to practice in Poland. When the Russians came, they treated all degrees equally, so Norbert was now working as an internist with me. He was a very good doctor. He had, just like me, a wife in Morszyn, with a daughter over a year old, and the rest of his family in Lwów.

Norbert told me that trucks were waiting to take medical doctors from Morszyn to Stryj, from where transports would go to the east, to Russia. I said I would not go. Norbert implored me and argued that we had to save ourselves, that we would not help our families anyway, that we must be saved and go to Russia. I refused. I said I would not abandon my family. "Whatever happens to them," I said, "shall also happen to me." Ceding to pressure exerted by Norbert and to the persuasion of my wife and friends, I decided, though, to go with the transport—but only as far as Stryj. There I would jump out, not going to Russia, and instead would wait through the probable first Ukrainian pogrom* to occur just after the German troops came, and then return to my family.

Norbert and I were going with the trucks to Stryj. All this time he kept imploring me to go with him to Russia. He explained to me over and over again that if we stayed we would anyway be unable to help our families, that the Germans would not attack women and children, while we, by fleeing to Russia, would avoid torture, torment, and eventual death.

Nobody at that time expected the Germans to commit genocide. Certainly we feared persecution, but the beatings and destruction of property that we knew had taken place in Germany gave little hint of the systematic murder that was to come. We feared a pogrom for the men, but still thought the women and children would be relatively safe. Several of the doctors in our group at Morszyn had fled from the German-occupied part of Poland in 1939. For the most part, they now regretted this, for life under the Soviets was worse than they had expected, and everything they heard from friends and family in western Poland indicated that it was no worse under German rule. All of them now chose to stay in Poland, and were happy that the German invasion gave them a chance to return to their homes.

Norbert had another reason for urging that we go to Russia: he was much under the influence of his wife, Giza, and always took her advice. It was she who convinced him that the best solution was to save himself in this way. Giza, energetic and intelligent, whose advice we all respected, also persuaded Norbert that above all he was to keep close to me and do everything I did. For she believed that I had a lucky star. And that is why Norbert insisted so much on our going away together. I agreed with his analysis, but he still did not convince me; I simply could not leave my family. I was sure I could help them in some way, when need would arise, and did not want to leave them with no income. When we reached the railway station in Stryj I immediately took my suitcase, hastily, and went toward town. Reluctantly, but complying with Giza's instructions to always follow my steps, Norbert went with me to town. It was already past eight in the evening. Martial law was in effect, imposed when Germany attacked. At this hour no one could be out in the streets. Patrols of Soviet soldiers stopped us, but I showed our documents and explained that we were medical doctors about to be transported to Russia and that we were only stopping to say good-bye to our families.

They let us go and thus we reached 3 May Street, number 12, where my wife's uncle, the dentist Grossman, lived. We knew we could stay with him, although we had had no way of contacting him beforehand. We thought we would be safer with him here in Stryj, for Jews were more numerous in this larger town, less isolated and exposed to pogroms. It was a three-story building. At the ground floor there was Grossman's dental office; at the second floor the owner of the house, a lawyer, lived with his paralyzed mother; and the third floor was occupied by Grossman. We got there, and after supper we went to sleep on mattresses he put down on the floor. We could not sleep, though, for there was a hell of a lot of shooting going on. It went on and on. It was common knowledge that the Ukrainian fighting groups were helping the Germans by waging guerrilla war against the Russians at night, sniping at Russian positions. The Russians, seized by panic, were shooting not only where Ukrainians really were but in any direction where they thought Ukrainians might be and could shoot at them. Suddenly, I saw sharp light through the closed windows of the apartment. The room got all illuminated, and seconds later there was devilish shooting and the noise of breaking window glass. Russians were aiming at our apartment. Crawling, we got out and ran down the stairs while Russians were still shooting without a break from various kinds of guns in the direction of our house. The owner of the house, carrying his paralyzed mother on his back, also went quickly down to the cellar. There we stayed hidden, waiting for things to come.

The shootout continued for a while longer before everything got calm. At dawn we heard heavy military bootsteps on the stairs leading to the cellar. Soon Russians appeared, a higher officer surrounded by several soldiers. He asked harshly, "Who was shooting at us from here?"

We started to explain that we were not soldiers, that we had no weapons nor any reason to shoot at Russians. We were medical doctors, Jews; when the shootout started we had simply, for obvious reasons, fled to the cellar. The Russian officer looked at us suspiciously. Finally, he decided he would make up his mind later what to do with us. He went out, leaving behind only two soldiers who were to watch us. We were, of course, much afraid, for we knew that the Russians did not make much ado at that time and executed without hesitation not only the guilty ones but also any who were only slightly suspected.

For some time it remained quiet. It was daytime, so the snipers were not around. Suddenly, we heard the drone of airplanes. It was a German air raid on Stryj. It lasted about fifteen minutes and then everything got quiet. We then noticed that the two Soviet soldiers had disappeared, most probably out of fear. This was an opportunity for saving ourselves. We got out quickly and went up to the roof. From there Norbert, Grossman, and I continued over the roofs of neighboring buildings until we came to the center of town. Here we could find other Jews, acquaintances. From them we learned that rumors were already going around saying that Ukrainian guerrillas had been shooting from our house and that the whole house had been destroyed.

After these experiences with the Russians, Norbert and I decided not to stay in Stryj but to return to our wives in Morszyn. With the power still cut off we had no way of communicating with anyone, and could only worry and hope about our families. I thought a lot about the rest of my family, in Lwów, but assumed that it was safer there because it was larger, just as Stryj would generally be safer than Morszyn. We hoped eventually to get back to Lwów.

Without much difficulty we returned to Morszyn and found that our families and friends there were all safe and well. We heard that out of thirty Jewish doctors, half had gone with the transport to Russia; the rest of us remained.

After the war I learned that of the fifteen who had left, fourteen came back to Poland later, when the war ended. Only one of them was killed, in Krasnodar, in military operations. Of the fifteen who stayed I was the only one who survived. I know two who were tortured and murdered by the Germans and the Ukrainian police. My best friend, Norbert, while hiding with his family in his apartment during the August 1942 action, was found by the SS and shot to death on the spot together with his two-year-old child and his in-laws. His wife, Giza, was wounded in the thigh and taken to the hospital. Here she begged the doctors to end her life with an injection. The next day the SS came to the hospital and took her with all the other patients to the gas chambers in Bełzec. Unfortunately, my lucky star was no help for them. Beside my grief at losing them, I have always felt badly that my decision not to go to Russia played some part in their tragedy. But in June 1941 we of course had no way of knowing what consequences would come for those who chose to stay. Yet if I had gone, and escaped the horrors, I could not have lived with the thought that I had deserted my family, saved myself when I could have done something for them.

We still did not have any information in Morszyn as to what was happening on the military fronts. There was mounting evidence, though, that the Russians were about to withdraw. Everything that was of military or economic value was either sent out to the east or—whenever they could not do this—entirely destroyed, as was the case with bridges. Besides that they were purging the prisons. They were shooting and burying in mass graves both those prisoners who had already been sentenced and those who were only suspected.

One day, at the beginning of July, the Russians disappeared. Radios were still not functioning, but rumors reached us that the Germans had marched into Stryj. Simultaneously, Ukrainian fighter squads came out of hiding and started to take over. The Germans were concerned with taking the larger towns and advancing eastward. They could not be bothered with a small resort spa like Morszyn, and in fact no German soldiers appeared there while I was there. They gave most of the countryside and towns to their Ukrainian allies, at least until German civilian authorities could arrive and rule directly.

I later learned that the region around Stryj and southeastward was the last pocket of Russian resistance in Galicia, held long enough to evacuate their people and destroy bridges and other key structures of military value. The Germans had already taken Lwów a few days earlier, on June 28, 1941.

We were expecting with anxiety and fear what the nearest days, or even hours, might bring us. Certainly nothing good. I recalled then the words of Dr. Merkel, pronounced by him two years earlier at a breakfast in the Hospital of Social Insurance: "My dear gentlemen, we are living in historical times and this is our disaster."

A new era was starting, the most tragic, most dreary, and most atrocious one in the history of Jewry and of the world.

CHAPTER 4

GERMAN OCCUPATION

Early July 1941—it was the first day of this new era. Frania and I were sitting with some friends on the balcony of our apartment house. It was a former hotel that had been converted to housing for employees of the spa treatment complex at Morszyn. Frania, Sylvia, and I lived in two rooms across the hall from each other. The others on the balcony were doctors and other employees, and also lived in this house. We were looking with tension and anxiety at what was happening around us. Young Ukrainians, armed with rifles, were going from house to house and taking out men—Jews—doctors and not doctors, no difference. Then they took them away in an unknown direction. When I saw what was going on I ran inside, down the corridor, and hid myself in one of our two rooms and locked the door. Frania sat with the baby on her lap in our other room and when one of the Ukrainians came for me she said I was in the clinic, working. He accepted the information with indifference and said that when I came home I should turn myself in, for they would come for me again anyway. After he left, I waited a few hours; the Ukrainians had not returned, so I felt safe enough to come out to the balcony, at least for then.

Panic had overtaken our place. Virtually all the men had been taken, including my friend Norbert. I don't recall if any beside myself managed to successfully hide. The wives of abducted men, and particularly Giza, Norbert's wife, were in extreme despair. One could hear single shots from far away, but beside that there was dead silence. Tense, we waited for the return of the abducted men. Hour after hour passed. No one was coming back. It was already late evening. Giza was seized by sobbing fits. We waited on the balcony until late in the night. Around midnight the silhouettes of returning men appeared. They came back. There was great joy. Norbert told us later how it had been.

They had been conducted to the place where lay the dead bodies of prisoners murdered by the Soviet police before they withdrew. Corpses were already decaying. The Jews, brought there by Ukrainian vigilantes, were ordered to dig out fresh graves and to bury the murdered prisoners in them. During this work the Ukrainians showered the most vulgar curses on the Jews and threatened that all of them would be made responsible for the crime and should pay with their own lives. The Ukrainians ignored all explanations that the Jews were innocent, even the fact that one of the killed prisoners was circumcised. In Eastern Europe at this time Christian men were circumcised only if there was a medical condition requiring it. Jews, on the other hand, were circumcised at birth according to religious law. This is one reason it was so hard for Jews to escape the Nazi persecution, for any man suspected of being a Jew in hiding was simply ordered to pull down his pants. Being circumcised was considered full proof that he was a Jew.

When, after several hours, the work was finished, Norbert was sure that there would follow a summary execution of the Jews, for the Ukrainians' threats and demeanor strongly suggested this. But, all of a sudden, a man appeared, a teacher, who apparently was a known Ukrainian activist, for the mob manifested their respect toward him. He made a short speech, defending the Jews taken by the vigilantes, explaining that these Jews were innocent and could not be blamed for Soviet crimes and that the freedom of the Ukraine could not be founded upon the blood of innocent people. He persuaded them to let the Jews go back home.

The next day, Norbert and I, together with our wives, were deliberating what to do. After the events of the previous day, which had ended luckily, we knew that there would be another time, another action, that could end otherwise, that we were in danger during day and night, and that we had nowhere to hide. In a big city one could disappear in the crowd and defend oneself against lone attackers, but not there, not in Morszyn. At this time Jews were not yet being rounded up by the Germans; there weren't even ghettos yet in our area. However, when the Germans took over any area, the Jews there were no longer under any protection of law. Anybody could rob or beat or even kill a Jew with no legal consequences or police intervention. In the few days until we left Morszyn the

Ukrainian vigilantes didn't return, but that could have changed at any time. We decided to move to town—that is, to Stryj—and from there, if it only turned out to be possible, to go back to the rest of our families and to our apartments in Lwów.

Deciding was easy, but carrying out the decision was very difficult. Means of transport were scarce and all public transport was forbidden to Jews. We decided that Norbert and I would go by foot to Stryj, find a way to stay there, and afterward return for our families. We put on the Red Cross arm bands, although we were told that the Germans did not allow Jews to carry them. We set out frightened as hell, for everywhere—on the roads and in the villages—Ukrainian squads roamed. On our way we met two Ukrainians, educated men, going in the same direction. They knew us as medical doctors and were kind to us, so that we talked to each other during the way. The two belonged to the Ukrainian National Democratic Organization (UNDO), the main Ukrainian political party in Poland, whose aim was the creation of a Ukrainian state in eastern Galicia. They saved our lives when, during our march over the road to Stryj, there suddenly appeared before us a Ukrainian mobster with a bandit's face and a rifle ready to shoot. His hands were smeared with the blood of his previous victims. He demanded our documents and ordered us to follow him. Luckily, our chance companions, whom he obviously knew, told him to leave us in peace, and, although he did it grudgingly, he obeyed and went away.

Finally, after a long march, we reached the town. In order to get there, however, it was necessary to cross the bridge over the Stryj River. This bridge had been destroyed by the Russians before they withdrew. At the time the bridge was being repaired by Jewish workers under the supervision of German soldiers and Ukrainian police. We felt uneasy, for we were told stories of Germans and Ukrainians often throwing these Jewish workers, or even passersby, into the river, where they drowned. However, we luckily crossed the bridge and went to the town administrator, Engineer Bandera. He was the brother of the very famous Ukrainian leader Stefan Bandera, whose radical nationalist guerrilla group was allied with Germany and murdering Jews. He met us coolly but politely. We told him we were doctors from Lwów, having worked over the summer season in Morszyn, and we asked for an apartment in Stryj until we were able to return to Lwów. We also asked for a permit to move with our families from Morszyn to Stryj.

Engineer Bandera was not anti-Semitic as far as I could tell. He seemed to me a very decent person, and he had respect for doctors. He assigned us an apartment in a house at Potocki Street, where Russian officers had stayed before their evacuation. Having gotten our permits, we went back to our wives, and on the following day we moved to Stryj. It turned out that the house at Potocki Street already hosted several families of Jewish doctors, and that one floor was occupied by a Ukrainian, Ivanov, who became the director of the local jail. He was a good neighbor to us.

Besides doctors from Morszyn who fled to Stryj, there were also numerous doctors from other localities who reached this town to save themselves from Ukrainian pogroms. We learned from them of terrible, bloodcurdling cruelties and murders perpetrated by Ukrainians on the Jewish population. They were beaten and shot at in the streets. Those who had been beaten until they fell continued to be hit and kicked. In some places Jews caught in the streets had heavy stones attached to ropes tied around their necks and were thrown into the water. In other places Jews were hanged on meat hooks in butcher shops.

One of the doctors who fled from Drohobycz, or Borysław, told us how Jews were murdered in these two places and in Schodnica. These three towns are clustered together about thirty kilometers west of Stryj. In some localities, where the Ukrainians had no weapons, Jews were clubbed to death.

My friend, the dentist Rubin, who grew up in Stryj and was working in the summer in Morszyn like me, had been visiting Lwów when war broke out. He survived the pogrom of Jews conducted by the Ukrainians in the first days after the German troops came, then fled to Stryj. He was all pale, trembling with fear; only a few days later was he capable of relating the dreadful scenes he had witnessed in Lwów. The Germans, after entering the city, had given the Ukrainians a free hand in disposing of the Jews.

As I listened to Rubin's stories, the anxiety that I had been experiencing about the safety of my family in Lwów grew immensely. There was at this time no way for us to contact each other, and I knew they must be very worried about me as well. I was still waiting for permission to go to Lwów, public transport was forbidden for all Jews, and both telephones and mail were in military hands, not for use by any private civilians, let alone Jews. It was a terrible frustration to know that my beloved ones might be dead or tormented and to have no possibility of knowing anything about their situation. Indeed, it was months before I could finally see them and know what happened. This agony of uncertainty was especially hard for me, for our family was an extremely close one. Since their fate during these years is a large part of my story, I should take this opportunity to describe them a little.

My father, Simon (Simcha) Drix, died of pneumonia in May 1917, as an Austrian soldier during World War I, in a military hospital in Teschen

My stepfather's father, Zanvel Hausen, surrounded by all his children except his eldest son, Frank, who lived in America. Standing are Ignacy (my stepfather), Fanny, Frieda, and Adolf (also called Abraham); seated are Rosa and Laura. Adolf was the father of my favorite cousin, Milek, with whom I lived in Lwów after the war.

(Cieszyn in Polish) on what later became the Polish-Czech border. I was five years old at the time. My mother, Mina Feuer, remarried five years later. Her new husband, Ignacy Hausen, was a widower with one child, a seven-year-old girl, Gina. My mother at that time had three children, myself and two sisters: Rózia, who was two years older than I, and Ida, four years younger than I. About a year later my younger brother, Jozef (nicknamed Józek), was born. My parents used to joke about having three sets of children, "yours, mine, and ours." We were a tightly knit family, and each loved the others regardless of which "category" they belonged to. Our house was a center for three families; relatives of my father, my stepfather, and my mother would stay with us when they came to Lwów. My stepfather's father, Zanvel, who lived with us, was in many ways closer to me than to his natural grandchildren, my cousins. Although he was not rich, he showered me with gifts when I was a child. He was nearly ninety when the war started, yet always neatly dressed, alert; he liked to walk with his cane to the park and discuss politics with his friends there, as he also did with me.

My stepfather and I loved each other deeply. I will never forget his tears of joy when I was accepted into medical school in Lwów. Józek was almost eleven years younger than I, and my feelings for him were in some

ways fatherly as well as brotherly. When he attended my gymnasium (secondary school) it was I and not my parents who came to the teacher con-
ferences to discuss his progress.

My aunt Andzia, the youngest sister of my mother, was to us children a
second mother. When my mother became a widow with three children,
Andzia came to our home and took care of us while my mother took care
of the business, a delicatessen and luncheonette. We loved Andzia very
much. She was childless, and loved us as if we were her children. When
our family business declined because of the anti-Semitic boycott, she
helped us financially. (She owned a very prosperous retail store on one of
Lwów's main streets.) She also paid for my examination fees for medical
school. When she had a stroke, I postponed my exams for about half a
year so that I could take care of her day and night.

I had two uncles who were very dear to me. Uncle Nahum (see photo,
page 13), brother of my mother, was deeply religious and had a great
knowledge of the Torah and Talmud, as well as Jewish history. In the
absence of my father, he was the one to whom I owe my religious and
Jewish national upbringing. He was very intelligent, good-natured, decent,
and was regarded with high esteem in the synagogue, by neighbors, and by
all people who knew him. He was married but childless, so he embraced
us as his children, especially me and my brother. My other uncle was
Adolf, Aunt Andzia's husband. We were also very fond of one another. We
frequently went to soccer games together.

These were the very closest to me, but there were many others. My
natural father had six brothers and one sister; my stepfather had four sisters and two brothers; my mother had two sisters and a brother. All but
one of these siblings were married, so I had thirty-one aunts and uncles in
all! I also had approximately twenty-five first cousins (counting the family
of my stepfather, who were not blood related but felt as close). Virtually
all of them were in or near Lwów. All these people and others, more distant relatives and friends, were very much on my mind and in my heart as
I listened to Rubin's distressing stories. The pogrom in Lwów that he
described to us lasted from June 30 to July 3. I later learned that it is esti-
mated that 4,000 Jews were killed in those few days, although it is hard to
get reliable numbers. It was not a German action, documented with
German exactness; it was a mob frenzy, semiorganized, with no real civilian authorities who could intervene, control, or document anything. The
terrible pogrom that the Ukrainians carried out in Lwów, and elsewhere in
eastern Galicia, immediately following the German takeover was followed
by others. One particularly notable pogrom, late in July, was called the
"Petlura action," to honor their hero, Semen Petlura (1879–1926), leader

My relatives and their friends enjoying each other's company before the war in Horodenka, a resort near Lwów. My cousin Lusia is sitting on the bannister, held by her first husband, Landes. Her twin sister, Irene, is on the extreme right. My sister Rózia is to Irene's left, and to Rózia's left is Lusia and Irene's mother, Frieda. My sister Ida is on the extreme left. The sign is for Lusia's father's photography studio.

of the Ukrainian nationalist movement during and after World War I. He briefly succeeded in making a virtual Ukrainian state in Galicia until it was annihilated by the Red Army and the Polish army. His forces were responsible for numerous pogroms of Jews. Petlura was killed in 1926 in Paris by a Jew named Schwarzbart, who took vengeance for the killing of his family in the Ukraine.

On the basis of stories told by many witnesses, I became convinced that the pogroms organized and carried out by the Ukrainians in 1941 were the most extreme in the whole history of pogroms of Jews, both in terms of the numbers killed and the cruelty of the deeds. One can hear or read only very little of these pogroms, for in the sea of six million Jewish people murdered by the Nazis, these tens of thousands killed by Ukrainians have ceased to count at all. They are forgotten. I hope that in the future historians will reveal this tragedy, fallen now into oblivion, and will assign it a proper place in the history of mankind.

I would like here to allow myself a historicopolitical digression. In the southeastern part of Poland, the region that had for over 140 years been called eastern Galicia, which the Poles called Eastern Małopolska (Little Poland) and which included Lwów as its main city, there lived a Ukrainian majority together with Polish and Jewish minorities. Ukrainians dominated in the countryside, while in both smaller and bigger towns Jews and Poles outnumbered them. As I stated in the introduction, the Ukrainians aspired to the creation of an independent Ukrainian state. But at this time the lands where they lived belonged to three different countries and the Ukrainians in one region had cultural and religious differences from those in others, based on their differing historical experiences. The eastern part of the Ukraine was in the hands of Soviet Russia and was kept under the boot of communism, while the western part, mainly Eastern Małopolska, belonged to Poland. This region has been considered by Poles to be a part of Poland since the Lublin Union of 1569. The Ukrainians hated Russians, hated Poles, and hated also the Jews, for the latter were citizens loyal to the current authorities. The Ukrainians also hated the Hungarians, who ruled another region, the Carpatho-Ukraine.

Personal relations between Ukrainians and Jews were often friendly—Jews have never taken part in any anti-Ukrainian action—and in 1930 Ukrainians from the popular organization UNDO (Ukrainian National Democratic Organization) created, together with the Jewish leader from Warsaw, Icchak Brinbaum, the so-called ethnic minorities block in parliamentary elections. They worked together for full rights for all minorities (this was the high point of Ukrainian-Jewish cooperation).

Still, hatred toward Jews as a people was great. When the Austrian monarchy fell apart in 1918 the Ukrainians rose and seized Lwów. Immediately, fierce fighting broke out between Poles and Ukrainians over the control of eastern Galicia. Various different leaders among the Jewish population in Galicia officially proclaimed that the Jews were neutral with regard to the two sides; in reality, however, individual Jews supported either the Polish or the Ukrainian side, predominantly the Polish. Jews felt a greater cultural affinity with the Poles. They both were urbanites and town dwellers, unlike the more agrarian Ukrainians. Jews attended mostly Polish schools and universities. In Lwów, for instance, there was only one Ukrainian secondary school and no Ukrainian university. Under Austrian rule in Galicia there had been a large degree of autonomy, which was in effect Polish rule. The official languages in Lwów at that time were German and Polish. Poles, like Jews, were by and large more literate and educated than the Ukrainians. Poles and Jews both looked to the West, considering themselves part of Western culture. For all these reasons, more Jews supported the Polish side in 1918. In consequence of this, the

Ukrainians, then led by Petlura, organized pogroms of Jews in many localities, accusing them of a pro-Polish attitude. And in Lwów—I remember this, though I was six years old then—the Poles, just after having regained the city from the Ukrainians on January 22, 1919, set fire to a synagogue with Jews inside and shot those who fled the flames with Torahs in their hands. This was to be the vengeance for the alleged participation of some Jews in fighting on the Ukrainian side. In short, both Poles and Ukrainians hated the Jews and blamed them for supporting the other side. Anti-Semitism among the Poles, however, was not nearly as widespread and virulent as among the Ukrainians.

So now, in 1941, when the Germans marched into southeastern Poland—that is, according to the Ukrainians, into western Ukraine—the Ukrainians had accounts to settle with the Poles, whom they hated. But they were afraid to touch the Poles, who were armed, numerous, and had a strong undergound army that could avenge an attack. Instead, they started full swing to torment the Jews, who had no weapons and a long history of nonviolence. This was easy. They could, without any risk, be "national heroes" for the Ukrainian cause by attacking defenseless Jews, having the complete support of the German invaders.

Already during the first days of our stay in Stryj we heard every morning the Ukrainian militia marching under our windows and singing patriotic Ukrainian songs, and especially one song, in which the words recurred: "Death, death, death to the Lachs, death to Muscovite-Jewish Communists" (Lach was a derogatory term for "Pole," used by Ukrainians). Even after the horrors of the several pogroms they had carried out in the first month of the German occupation, the Ukrainians were still not satisfied that they had sufficiently settled their accounts with the Jews. For the sake of truth I should add that not all Ukrainians were such Jew-killers. There were also, although few in numbers, those who helped Jews in escaping the German holocaust machine, often putting their own lives at stake. I know this from others as well as from the experience of my own family.

Life was hard for us in Stryj during our stay there, July to October 1941. Food rations for Jews were less than meager, which constituted a special problem for my family and Norbert's—each having a small child. We were waiting for permission to go back to Lwów. Frania, Sylvia, and I were living in the two-room apartment that Mayor Bandera had given us. Norbert and his family were in the same building. Getting a job was out of the question for a Jewish doctor. Since, however, one had to work somewhere,

Norbert and I registered as doctors in the Jewish hospital. This, however, was just a formality, for there were then more Jewish doctors in the hospital than Jewish patients.

Stryj had a Jewish hospital from before the war, supported by its Jewish community, as was common in prewar Poland. Such hospitals were non-profit and charitable. Non-Jews could also be treated there. At that time Jewish doctors could work in any hospital, although there were some restrictions. Now, under German rule, this was impossible, and the Jewish hospital was the only option; however, all the paid positions there were filled, so I worked without pay. As a refugee I also had no chance to set up a private practice with all the needed equipment.

All institutions, not just the hospitals, were now segregated, virtually completely. For instance, there were two tax payment offices, one for Jews and one for non-Jews.

In the meantime, as elsewhere in eastern Galicia, the administration of our county, which had been in the hands of the German army and the Ukrainians, was taken over by the German civil authority under the directorship of a *Kreishauptmann*, a regional headman. Our efforts to obtain from him permits to return to Lwów were as yet to no avail.

We did not have any idea what was going on at the fronts and generally in the world. Newspapers were under state control and printed only propaganda. Immediately after the German troops marched in, the German authorities issued, as one of the first, the order for all Jews to give up their radio sets to German administrative offices. Jews were allowed neither to have a radio nor to listen to one. There was a death penalty for such an offense. Non-Jews could, at that time, have radio sets, but were not allowed to listen to foreign radio stations, especially anything broadcast from London. Still, every day news was coming from someone who heard it from somebody else who listened secretly to London. Bad news saying that the Germans were winning on all fronts was, alas, true. Good news was a fantasy.

On September 1, 1941, in order to commemorate the second anniversary of the beginning of the war, the Germans undertook a so-called action in Stryj. From early morning on, Ukrainian militiamen, accompanied by armed Germans, went from house to house where Jews lived and arrested the men. There was tremendous panic. We hadn't been expecting anything, but when we awoke we heard the sound of boots in the street, and watched what was happening from our windows. When I saw Ukrainian militiamen approaching our house, I started furiously seeking some hiding place, but I could not find one. Finally, I hid in a chest in which dirty clothes were kept. I had, though, to leave it from time to time because of the lack of air. This action lasted the whole day. Several hundred Jews were arrested and put into Stryj's prison. Ukrainian militiamen did not enter our house, either because they had yet some respect for the doctors or because of the influence of our neighbor Ivanov, who was the prison director.

That night we again heard boots in the street, and we feared that the day's action was resuming. Sylvia had come down with whooping cough some days before, and was now having coughing fits. We were terrified that her coughing would draw attention to us and that the Ukrainian police might remember that they had missed this house and would check our apartment. Luckily, nothing came of it.

The whole Jewish community trembled at the thought of the fate of the arrested. Soon rumors spread that the Germans required a contribution in money, gold, silver, or jewelry for letting the arrested out. Members of the Jewish Committee, the forerunner of the *Judenrat* (Jewish Council), were going from house to house asking for such donations to save the prisoners. Since we had nothing else of value with us in Stryj, Frania gave away her wedding ring. No matter how much was collected, though, it was always too little. Contributions had been collected over several days. At that time a few persons were released from prison for a large sum of money. Others stayed inside without any contact with their families.

After several weeks the news from eyewitnesses, non-Jews, came that the prisoners had been taken out of town in trucks during the night and murdered there. Since then, rumors circulated all the time that a new action would soon occur. Our situation became unbearably dangerous. We multiplied our efforts to get the permits to return to Lwów through the intermediary of Hutterer, the chairman of the *Judenrat* in Stryj. We got the permit and the appropriate pass only at the beginning of October. Public transport being forbidden for Jews, we hired a Pole to transport us in his truck. Finally, Norbert and I, with our wives and children, could go to Lwów to our families and our apartments.

CHAPTER 5

Lwów

When we met our families the joy was immense. I was relieved to find that all of my beloved family had survived these frightening few months. Frania, Sylvia, and I moved back into the apartment on Panieńska Street that we shared with her parents and two brothers. My sister Rózia and her husband lived across the street from us. My other sisters, Ida and Gina, and my brother Józek lived with my parents and grandfather in a different part of the city. When I got together with all of them, as well as my aunts, uncles, and other relatives, we told each other what we had gone through. I heard anew things I had learned before in Stryj, from my friend the dentist Rubin, of the terrible anti-Jewish actions organized in Lwów by the Ukrainians under the protection and guidance of the Germans; of cruel mass murders in the streets; of Jewish men and women dragged out of their houses and then driven to prisons and army barracks, where they were forced to do various humiliating things—cleaning lavatories, floor scrubbing, and so on, with the accompaniment of beatings and torture. Most of them were murdered during work or after having finished it. Only very few of these people were saved.

I heard that thousands of Jews were rounded up on the streets and taken to Pełczyńska Street, to a large courtyard in front of the old municipal power station building, occupied at that time by the Gestapo. My father-in-law and my uncle Adolf were among those taken there. All these people were kept there for two days and two nights, beaten and tortured, and then taken by groups in trucks to be executed. After many groups had been taken away, those left sitting in the courtyard were suddenly dismissed, for no apparent reason. My father-in-law and my uncle both had the great luck to be among this small remnant that was left alive. My joy at their survival, however, was tempered by the pain of knowing what an ordeal they had suffered.

All these events had occurred in the massive pogrom of June 30 to July 3, but other attacks followed. We were told, for instance, that the Gestapo had arrested many prominent community members in August—social activists, industrialists, businessmen, lawyers, doctors, and engineers. Tremendous contributions from the Jewish community were asked for the release of these hostages. Enormous amounts of money, gold, and silver were collected. These were given to the Germans, but the hostages were not freed. They were murdered.

The stories of the terrible events that had taken place during our absence were endless. It was now October 1941, and the harassments in Lwów were still happening. Thus, it turned out that we had escaped from a small hell in Stryj in order to get to a greater one in Lwów. Every day there were random roundups of Jews in the streets of our town, mainly for various forced labor purposes. There was no apparent pattern to them. Since Jews were officially outside the law, they were subject to arrest at any time for no reason. Most exposed, of course, were those living in mostly non-Jewish areas; these roundups also were used to aid in concentrating and isolating the Jews.

Soon after we had returned to Lwów the order was issued that every Jew or Jewess, under threat of the death penalty, would have to wear a white armband with a blue star of David. This greatly facilitated the task of the Germans and their eager Ukrainian assistants in organizing street roundups. Doctors received, from the Chamber of Physicians, armbands that were also white with the star of David, but with the additional inscription in red letters "Arzt," that is, "Medical doctor." Besides that, the Chamber of Physicians also issued cards, with a photograph and a German official stamp, stating that we were indispensable for maintaining the health and well-being of the population and that we should not be coerced into any forced labor.

Just as everything else of this sort, these cards had little significance for the Germans, which I found out in a few days' time. One day, I was stopped in Żółkiewska Street, two blocks from my house, by a German soldier. "Come here, Jew!" This was addressed to me and to two other Jewish passersby. He ignored my armband and my card, and uttering numerous invectives forced us to push his motorcycle, which finally started, and then he went away.

My sister Gina also had an experience involving an armband. Gina had worked in a laundry since before the war. Her employer, Mr. Faliński, half

Polish and half Ukrainian, was very much in love with her. She liked him also. He was doing all he could to protect her now, and was having false Aryan papers made up for her. He was also very helpful, not only to others in our family but to other Jews as well.

One day Gina, who was expecting to receive these papers any day, was walking on the street without her armband. (If she wore an armband she could be noticed by someone who would later see her pretending to be an Aryan.) A Ukrainian policeman stopped her, demanding her identification papers. Because she had not received these yet, he arrested her. She knew she would then be found out as a Jew—and without her armband, that meant death.

Suddenly, a high officer in the Ukrainian police approached them. Gina recognized him as Włodek Ślipko. He had been a childhood friend and playmate of mine, and I had liked him very much. He had always shown true sportsmanship. As children the difference between us, Ukrainian and Jew, had not mattered, but as we grew older we naturally drifted apart and hadn't had any contact with each other in years, even though we lived near each other. His family was extremely nationalistic.

"You may go," he told the policeman who had arrested Gina. "I will take care of her." The policeman saluted respectfully and left. Ślipko went with Gina half a block and quietly told her, "Disappear."

Further changes happened around this time. Soon after they took Lwów, in July, the Germans had designated the most beautiful quarter of our town, with modern houses and villas, as the German quarter. This was not officially proclaimed; they simply took the apartments they wanted and booted out the inhabitants, whether they were Jews, Poles, or Ukrainians. Non-Jews, however, were given time to take their belongings to new quarters, and weren't attacked; Jews were forbidden to take anything from their apartments and many of them were beaten or killed. Now, in November of 1941, the Germans divided the city into Aryan and Jewish sections. The Jewish quarter—the ghetto—was in the poorest and most neglected part of town. Jews from the so-called Aryan parts had to move into the ghetto in a month, while Poles and Ukrainians had to move out of this Jewish quarter and take formerly Jewish apartments in the Aryan parts.

Kleparów and Zamarstynów were the two districts of the city that became the ghetto. They were in the north and northwest parts of Lwów, on the periphery. Kleparów was especially dilapidated, with little or no city sewage, water, or electric service. Houses there were mostly shacks, and crime was high. Zamarstynów was better; it had some poor areas but my apartment on Panieńska Street was in Zamarstynów, in a nice middle-class residential neighborhood with many shops, near the edge of what was now the ghetto. What particularly made these two districts suitable for becoming the ghetto was the fact that elevated railroad tracks divided them from the rest of the city, easily demarcating the ghetto boundary. The Germans designated four streets to serve as official entrances and exits, through underpasses. There were, of course, smaller streets that one could try to use, but at great risk if caught doing so. The ghetto was therefore easily isolated and traffic in and out was easily controlled. For a long time the ghetto was open; Jews could walk out to the Aryan section (at some increased risk of police harassment) and non-Jews could come in—to sell goods, for instance. (Later, after August 1942, the ghetto was closed and also reduced, with the nicer section removed.)

When the ghetto was created the streets were crowded with cars, carts, barrows, and other means of transport with which people were carrying their bundles, everything they could bring from their places to the ghetto. It was simply a migration of nations. In 1939 the population of Lwów had been about 400,000, of which 160,000 were Jews. Both populations grew in 1939 with an influx of people, mostly from western Poland, fleeing the Germans. Since then, for various reasons, some Jews had come and others had left Lwów. By November 1941 there were 150,000 or more, about two thirds of them outside what was now declared to be the Jewish quarter. The large number of Jews now moving into the ghetto were allowed to take with them what they could manage to, but the Germans randomly stopped people at the entrances to the ghetto, checked their belongings, and often took things.

The main, most used, entrance to the ghetto was the one at Zamarstymowska Street, under the railway viaduct, over which trains were passing to and from the Podzamcze railway station. The viaduct formed a kind of broad gate, which we called "Under the Bridge." The Germans posted their guards there. German policemen and the Gestapo were monitoring the traffic of people and goods going to and from the ghetto. They stopped people to check identification papers and make personal searches. Here the extreme harassments and unimaginable barbarities took place. The Germans would stop passing Jews not only when they suspected some "illegal" activity, but also simply capriciously. Sometimes they would stop somebody who did not bow adequately, taking his hat off. In other cases it was just the opposite: a man would be stopped just because he bowed or removed his hat. People who were stopped usually were not seen again. In the yard of the police guard building that adjoined the gate terrible scenes took place. Inhabitants of neighboring buildings observed them from their windows. The apprehended persons were beaten with sticks by one Jew and one Jewess, who were forced by the Germans to do it, and who, out of fear for their lives, behaved as if they had gone mad. The apprehended persons had to dance, beaten until they fell down; some of the unfortunate ones had a star of David branded on their foreheads with a hot iron, and were beaten to the very end. Those who survived the beatings generally would be taken away for execution. "Under the Bridge" became the terror of the Jewish population of Lwów. Such scenes took place regularly over several weeks. Nobody knows how many people fell victim to this procedure.

One day I met a colleague of mine, Dr. Schindler, who was working in the hospital in the ghetto at Kuszewicza Street. The hospital was located quite near this hell of "Under the Bridge." He told me, still trembling nervously, that several hours earlier he had been taken from the hospital to this famous yard to examine some Jew. A wasted man was lying on a horse cart, his body covered with boils. After the examination Dr. Schindler was conducted to an SS officer.

"Have you examined him?" the SS officer asked Dr. Schindler. "What have you found out?"

"This man has furunculosis [boils], besides that no other illnesses," answered Dr. Schindler.

"Is this an infectious disease?" asked the SS officer.

"Yes, but not a contagious disease," answered Dr. Schindler, trying to save the poor victim. A contagious disease spreads by contact with people who have it. An infectious disease is caused by bacteria or a virus, but may or may not be contagious. Furunculosis is a skin disease caused by a bacteria, but would not spread even by skin contact except if there was an open cut at the point of contact.

Furious, the SS officer shouted at Dr. Schindler, "I asked you whether this was an infectious disease, yes or no!"

"Yes, but—" Dr. Schindler tried to explain.

The SS officer interrupted him and gave the order to his SS man. "Finish the man."

The SS man then asked the officer, "And what should we do with the physician?"

A minute of silence. Cold sweat covered the forehead of Dr. Schindler. The officer paused, and finally waved his hand. "Get lost!"

Dr. Schindler hastily ran from the building, trembling for several hours from fear and nervous tension after his return to the hospital.

It is hard to describe life in the Lwów ghetto. Some 150,000 Jewish people were crowded into a limited quarter that was roughly one seventh

of the area of Lwów. The housing office of the *Judenrat* was taking care of
the housing situation in the ghetto. They tried to get more and more
incoming families, forced out of the Aryan quarter, to any flat that was at
their disposal. There were several families in each apartment. My own
apartment was fairly typical. Composed of two large rooms, a large ante-
room and a kitchen, it had already been crowded before the war, when we
shared it with my in-laws. It was in the ghetto, so we didn't have to move,
but other members of my family lived in areas that were now Aryan.
When they had to move, we took them in. My parents, my grandfather,
my two sisters Gina and Ida, and my brother, Józek, all came from their
apartment, and my aunt Andzia and Uncle Adolf from theirs. A Russian
woman also joined us; her husband, who had left Lwów with the Russian
army, was a friend of my father-in-law. My other sister, Rózia, and her husband stayed in their apartment across the street; they took in his seriously
ill mother. My uncle Nahum and Aunt Rachel had lived only a few blocks
from us, but their apartment was now just outside the ghetto, and they
moved in with some friends in a farther part of the ghetto. In total, therefore, there were now fifteen adults plus our one-year-old child living
together in my apartment. In many houses the crowding was even worse.
My family brought what they could with them, limited by the difficulty of
transporting things and by the cramped space they were moving into.
Large items, like furniture, had to be left behind.

There was very little food. Rations for Jews were at a starvation level.
We were giving away, piece by piece, what we still had at home in
exchange for potatoes, flour, vegetables, and other foodstuffs to supple-
ment the inadequate rations. This was a great opportunity for peasants
from the nearby villages. For their potatoes or flour they obtained valuable
objects, such as furniture, pianos, and the like. I remember well how I
gave a new, luxurious couch with a glass bookcase attached to the back
for a not-too-great sack of potatoes. The farmers brought their goods
secretly to the yet-open ghetto, probably bypassing the official entrances.
According to the orders of German authorities it was illegal to give or sell
food products to Jews, but this was not being strictly enforced at the time.
The farmers were evading the ban not for humanitarian reasons but
because they got such good deals in these exchanges.

Slowly, but unavoidably, everything that we had withered away. From
the beginning of 1942 it got markedly and progressively worse. There was
nothing anymore with which to buy food. Hunger was increasingly acute.
There were days when we had neither lunch nor dinner, not even a most
modest meal. We tried to at least spare our child from hunger. Our better-

situated neighbors often invited my now one-and-a-half-year-old pretty daughter, whom they adored, and gave her something to eat, which of course pleased us very much.

Hunger and diseases, and especially contagious diseases such as typhoid fever (abdominal typhus) and spotted fever (typhus), were spreading quickly, taking numerous victims in the ghetto. Burying the dead became a greater and greater problem. Jewish doctors could no longer be directly connected with the general Chamber of Physicians of Lwów. A special Jewish section was formed in the ghetto, affiliated with the so-called *Sanitätsamt* (Health Center), which took care of the health of the people inhabiting the ghetto. I worked there as the "block doctor." I was assigned several apartment buildings, which I was to visit and monitor regularly, and I was to report on the health status of the population and especially on contagious diseases. Persons suffering from contagious diseases were sent to the ghetto hospital for infectious diseases at Zamarstymowska Street. Especially frequent were cases of typhus.

Beside this particular hospital for infectious diseases there were two general hospitals for the Jewish population. These had been hastily organized in school buildings in the main Jewish section of the city in October 1941, when the prewar Jewish hospital was made a municipal hospital and all existing hospitals were closed to Jews. One of these recently organized hospitals was in the Czacki School at Alembeków Street (Dr. Oscar Schmalzbach, a colleague from my university, was the director there). It now lay outside the ghetto, but Jews could still go there for a while. The second one was located in the ghetto, in the building of the state high school at Kuszewicza Street (with Dr. Kurzrock as director). There was an excess of Jewish medical doctors crowded into the ghetto. According to the *Sanitätsamt* registration there were 520 of us. After liberation, in the fall of 1944, only seventeen were alive.

The hospital located at the Czacki School was liquidated after a few months, in the spring of 1942. Thus, there was only one general hospital left in the ghetto, at Kuszewicza Street, and the hospital for contagious diseases in Zamarstynów.

As we were to find out eventually, the hardships of ghetto life were not an end for the Germans but only a step in their plan for extermination of the Jews, a plan they had elaborated in minute detail, with perverse psychological cleverness and truly German accuracy. First of all, Jews were driven from various localities and concentrated in ghettos, entirely separated from the non-Jewish population, closed in ghettos not only physically but also politically and morally. An incessant slanderous campaign was conducted against the Jews. They were guilty of everything that was wrong in the world. And especially of what was wrong in a given locality. Hatred toward Jews was implanted with all means available. The purpose was to have nobody pitying them, let alone wishing to help them in whatever way. There was a death penalty for hiding Jews or for helping to hide them. On the other hand, for denouncing a Jew in hiding, the German authorities were giving the reward of some five thousand złotys (the Polish unit of currency; this sum would be roughly two hundred dollars in today's purchasing power) and vodka. This was taken advantage of by the Polish and Ukrainian scum who blackmailed Jews. Besides that, they were beating Jews just for fun. Many of them were coming to the ghetto simply to indulge in this "sport."

One day I was stopped in Zamarstymowska Street, the main street of the ghetto, by a young, well-clad Ukrainian. It was not very unusual to see a non-Jew in the ghetto. He bowed politely and asked whether I did not know where there was a glazier's workshop nearby. I answered politely that I did not know, but that I would try to recollect. I turned to look down the street in order to recall where, possibly, such a workshop could be found. Suddenly, this Ukrainian hit me with a powerful blow to my right cheek and ear, so that, stunned, I fell to the ground. Then this Ukrainian started to revile me, calling me a lousy Jew, and tried to kick me. I jumped up quickly and avoided his kick. He went calmly on, and nobody among the passing people tried to catch him or to help me. They just passed by as if nothing had happened.

A few days later I learned that this Ukrainian was practicing such "sport" every day in various streets of our ghetto. Attacks on Jews and robberies of Jewish houses were the order of the day. Jews were outlaws; one could do to them as one pleased, without any risk of penalty.

There had been, at Zamarstymowska Street, a school bearing the name of King Jan Sobieski, a famous Polish king who had saved Vienna from the Ottoman Turks in the seventeenth century. Here the Germans were temporarily housing young Ukrainians who, of their own free will, were flowing in to work in Germany as a repayment to their saviors. They would often go out into the streets and beat Jewish passersby, amid the laughter and applause of their comrades. One day, Frania came home in tears after one of these youths had kicked her in the back to the amusement of his friends. I sometimes also saw German soldiers entering the Jewish quarter and amusing themselves by beating Jews in the street just because they had not bowed properly or had not stepped out of their way quickly enough.

Later on, a new manner of tormenting and blackmailing Jews developed. Ukrainians and Poles working in Kripo (that is, the criminal police) paid Jewish informers to tell them which Jews in the ghetto were wealthier. Then these policemen would come to such people and, without giving any cause, arrest them and keep them in their interrogation prison. Their assistants would then appear before the despairing families to say that such-and-such an amount of money, in dollars, would get the victim out of prison. Wealthier Jews had been able to take money and small items such as jewelry with them into the ghetto. A few had also left their valuables with trusted Polish or Ukrainian friends, who brought them some of it as it was needed. After an adequately large sum in dollars had been paid, the blackmailed Jew would come happily back home. This kind of "sport" was also spreading in the ghetto.

Besides that, the German authorities were ordering from time to time that a contribution be paid by the Jewish population. When, during the winter of 1941–42, the German offensive stopped just before reaching Moscow and the German army was caught unprepared for winter, the Germans ordered all Jews to give up their fur coats under penalty of death. This action, in which the Germans were assisted by Jewish clerks from the *Judenrat*, was performed quite accurately.

In December 1941 trucks drove up to various houses in the Jewish quarter and the German police, aided by the Ukrainian militia, took away older people for resettlement, as they said. This action lasted a few weeks. At the beginning nobody could understand this. Why, what for, and where to, would the Germans, a civilized people, be resettling just these older people? After several weeks the dreadful truth was uncovered. Those people were brought beyond the ancient Łyczaków tollgate, on the eastern edge of Lwów by the city limits, and all murdered. It turned out, then, that the Germans, a cultivated and civilized people, were dealing with the "problem" of the aged by murdering them. This was the very first shock, the first indication of the awful extent of the Germans' plans for the Jews. Until then, although we knew from our own experience and, earlier on, from the press and radio, what the Germans were capable of with regard to their opponents, those they disliked, and anyone who might threaten them, the systematic mass killing of men, women, and the elderly was yet unknown. It was simply hard to believe. The future was to demonstrate that the bestiality of these people, from a nation once admired for its high culture, was beyond any limit.

When the old people were taken I was truly perplexed and believed this was really a resettlement. When I heard rumors of what had happened to them, I simply couldn't believe it. I had not known or even heard rumors before this that the Germans were committing mass murders of people who could not possibly be a threat. When they had only western Poland, people who had fled to the east regretted it after getting letters from friends and family describing their lives under German rule. There were incidents and harassment, but nothing like mass murder. Since then worse things had happened, but this was the first sign that the Germans intended to wipe out an entire population.

At more or less the same time the Germans created a special *Arbeitsamt* (employment office) for Jews, headed by a German, Weber. All men and all unmarried women were obliged to work. They had to be registered in firms working for German needs. Those who worked obtained an *Arbeitskarte* (work card). The other ones, who did not have such a card, were being arrested during the street roundups. Some disappeared without a trace and others were taken, as we later learned, to Janowska camp on the periphery of Lwów.

We only gradually became aware of Janowska camp, and only slowly found out how bad it was—and even then not nearly how bad it really was. In addition, the camp itself was changing at this time, starting as a mere workplace, then being closed (in early October 1941) so that the inmates could not leave, and then increasingly changing from a place of forced labor to one of torment and systematic killing. It also grew rapidly from about 350 inmates to a very large population. Even as we heard of terrible events there from time to time (through relatives of inmates), we thought these must be occasional outrages. Not until I arrived there myself did I realize that outrage was the daily reality.

Of course, everybody tried to get an *Arbeitskarte* at any price. People were paying firms or their managers large sums of money for a card. It was simply a "card for life"—a poor life, in fact, but at least life in so-called freedom. People worked for pennies or, even more frequently, for nothing, only to have the card. Wives of registered men obtained this card as well, which protected them from roundups.

Wealthier Jews obtained an *Arbeitskarte* (or a *Meldekarte*, a registration card, which was either another name for the same thing or covered wives of eligible employees rather than the workers themselves) by investing large sums of money to create enterprises that worked for the Germans, especially for the military. They were also sought by the Germans if they had experience running enterprises. Major firms, such as *Rohstofferfassung* or *Städtische Werkstätte*, were established in this way. These companies produced all sorts of materials needed for Germany, primarily for the army but also for industry—for example, textiles, uniforms, boots, cardboard, bookbinding, underwear, and extraction of raw materials for reuse. To get a job in these workshops one had to buy one's way in with quite a lot of money, unless one was a really good specialist whom they badly needed. Doctors were of no use to the Germans; they sought technicians, machine operators, electricians, auto mechanics and mechanics in general, and other craftsmen of this sort.

Fortunately, I and most of my family had working cards of one sort or another at this time, and we were safe for a while. We were afraid for the others, but so far they had been left alone. Jews who did not have a *Meldekarte* were often hunted for through street roundups. These random roundups caused panic among people living in the ghetto. The Jews caught were most often driven to the Janowska camp. The commanders of that camp, SS officers Gebauer, Rokita, and Willhaus, whenever they appeared in the city, would catch new victims from among the people in the street. By February 1942, terrible rumors had come to us from there that told of torture, hunger, and killings. Janowska camp had by then become a terror for the Jews of Lwów and all of eastern Galicia.

CHAPTER 6

"ACTIONS"

In the middle of March 1942, during the Passover holiday, the German authorities proclaimed that, due to the overpopulation of the ghetto, the unemployed, the sick, and "asocial elements" would be resettled to other localities, and that they could take with them no more than twenty-five kilograms of luggage and food for the way. The resettlement action started immediately, directed by German police assisted by Ukrainian and Jewish police. They were going from house to house, from apartment to apartment, and dragging out people who did not have the *Arbeitskarte* or *Meldekarte*. These people were brought to the school building, previously the King Jan Sobieski School, located at Zamarstymowska Street. There the abducted people were segregated. Individuals on whose behalf German firms intervened, whether they were needed specialists, personal favorites, or had money to bribe with, were set free. The rest were transported to the Kleparów railway station, in the northwest of Lwów, on the outskirts, just past Janowska camp, and then by train farther on in an unknown direction. People saw these things and the news spread to us by word of mouth. This action lasted more than two weeks.

An action, unlike a random roundup or the spontaneous violence of a pogrom, was a systematic, house-to-house search by the SS with the assistance of the Ukrainian police and sometimes the Jewish police as well. Those without proper cards, and eventually even many with such cards, were taken away for resettlement, and we only later came to understand what that meant. This one, in March 1942, was the first of the major actions, the first time I had heard that word used in this way. In this action fifteen thousand Jews were taken. The actions were only for Jews, no other groups.

During this action a German SS man and a Ukrainian policeman came to our apartment on Panieńska Street, during the systematic searches, to check our papers. Many of my family were out at the time, either at work or hiding because they had no valid card. Our apartment had two separate sections, each with its own entrance. I was in one part, with Frania and Sylvia; my mother, Andzia, and my grandfather, Zanvel, were in the other. We all had valid cards except Zanvel, but he was over ninety and too weak from hunger to be moved anywhere, so he lay in bed, covered completely by a featherbed quilt. The German came into the room where I was and told the Ukrainian to check the people in the other room. The German looked at our cards, nodded, and walked out. Here he met the Ukrainian, who said that all was in order in the other room. I was delighted, and when they left, I went to ask my mother how Zanvel had escaped detection. She said that a miracle had occurred. The Ukrainian policeman had gone straight to the bed, pulled back the cover, and saw Zanvel lying there, pale and still, but dignified with his long white beard. The policeman looked for a moment, then quickly covered Zanvel up again and walked out. This man's compassion was extremely unusual for a Ukrainian policeman; they were generally even worse than SS men. Zanvel died a natural death by starvation a few weeks later. He died in my mother's arms.

Thousands of people were deported from Lwów during the March action. Nobody knew where they were deported to. Different rumors were abroad in the ghetto as to their fate. Fear and depression reigned in the ghetto. There were some who had allegedly somehow, from somewhere, received letters from their deported relatives saying that they were in labor camps and were very satisfied. With time, however, there were more and more rumors that all the deported people had been murdered. Some told us of gas chambers in Bełzec, but nobody wanted to believe it. This news, apparently, came through Polish railway employees. These men knew that they were not allowed to go near Bełzec, but were replaced near it by German SS. They saw signs forbidding any approach to the place, and smelled a suspicious stench. They deduced what must be happening and quietly told their friends and families. Eventually, these stories reached Lwów and its Jewish population. Skeptics maintained that the labor force was very important for the army during the war, and because these thousands of people were fit for work, they wouldn't have been killed.

Bełzec was first built as a labor camp in 1940 (it was in the western, German-held portion of Poland, close to the border of the then-Soviet zone). It was transformed into an extermination camp in spring 1942. These rumors after the March action were therefore the first time we had heard of gas chambers, and most of us didn't believe them. We had heard of Bełzec before, but it had held no particular significance until now, for there were many work camps.

After this March action, the Germans ordered a new registration of working Jews, and those who worked in German establishments or for Germans obtained new, brick-colored *Arbeitskarten* and *Meldekarten*. The situation became more and more hopeless in the ghetto. Hunger and diseases, especially typhus; the roundups; Janowska camp; and war, dragging on, with daily German reports of victories on all fronts; the helplessness of the Allies and their indifference to the tragic fate of the Jews in Poland—all this made us gloomy and despairing. News of German actions, liquidations, in various towns and townships reached Lwów again and again. The Germans had established the so-called *SS-Einsatzkommando* (special action commandos). Eventually, we came to realize that these special units' purpose was to direct and carry out, with the local SS, the extermination of the Jews; we then referred to them as *Vernichtungskommando* (extermination commandos). These units were carrying out actions in Kraków, Tarnów, Rzeszów, and other towns eastward, coming toward us. Thus, we could expect at any day or week an action in Lwów.

The poison potassium cyanide became the most demanded and expensive chemical product in the ghetto. Jews were buying it in order to be able to commit suicide when caught by the Germans. A portion of cyanide had been very cheap before the war, when it was used to kill rats. Now, when it was for use by people, it was extremely expensive, and in addition getting it required having adequate connections. Some people, cheated by hucksters, bought what they thought was cyanide only to find, when they needed it, that it was some phony substitute.

On June 2, 1942, the second birthday of my daughter Sylvia, I wanted to bring her some joy. She had said several times that she would like to have a doll with blue eyes and light blond hair. I set out to the Aryan quarter and there, in a toy shop in Sixtus Street, I bought her a very small and very cheap doll (for I did not have more money) that had blue eyes and light blond hair. When I handed the doll to my daughter, her wonderful black eyes and sweet face radiated with joy. This was her last birthday.

In the middle of June 1942, suddenly, there was a new action in the ghetto. This one lasted only two days. Several thousand men, women, children, and old people were transported through the Janowska camp to Bełzec to die in gas chambers. The Russian woman living with us was taken during this action. I never heard for sure what happened to her. After this action the situation slowly returned to a degree of calm and normalcy, for the Germans were carrying out their extermination of the Jews according to careful plans, taking into account politics, economics, and psychology. The Nazi government knew very well that to murder three and a half million Jews living in Poland, dispersed throughout the whole country, would not be easy, that they might encounter strong resistance from a million people of fighting age conscious of the fact that they were going to be completely liquidated. This could cost many German casualties, which would be very bad for the war, now being conducted on two fronts—with the Allies in the west and Russia in the east. Thus, they first separated the Jews from the Aryan population by forming ghettos in the cities and smaller towns while simultaneously waging a biting propaganda campaign against the Jews. Then they started liquidating small ghettos, concentrating the rest in large ghettos and camps. Next they liquidated the ghettos and small camps, in this period killing hundreds of thousands in gas chambers until a relative handful was left whose potential resistance could more easily be overcome by the powerful German army and police. Before that, though, in order to pacify the Jewish population, they proclaimed after every action that this particular one was the last and that the remaining Jews would stay alive, provided they worked for the Reich.

Jews were easily lulled into believing such proclamations—for several reasons. First of all, mass extermination in the twentieth century by an advanced nation was inconceivable. In addition, it made no sense for the Germans to lose a labor force badly needed during war. Also, the repeated assurances that no further actions would occur came from, among others, high officers of the German army whose word and honor were highly valued. For Jews especially, survival in the Diaspora had always depended on loyalty to and respect for local authorities. In addition, hope was always urging belief that one would now be allowed to live; it was terrifying to consider that all were destined for slaughter. A further and significant factor aiding such belief was the often elaborate effort at deception the Germans used to disguise their intentions. This included having Jews destined for the gas chambers pack their suitcases and catalog their belongings so they could be returned to them later, as well as having occasional letters sent back from someone who had been taken, to keep up the myth that such people had merely been resettled. Indeed, the Germans, even in the death camps, never talked of the extermination in the gas chambers but always called it "resettlement."

Mass murders in gas chambers were kept conscientiously secret, not only from Jews but also from the local population. Unclear rumors at the time said only something of Bełzec, but very few Jews wanted to believe this. When it was already known, although not in all details, that the transports went to Bełzec and not anywhere else, and that extermination was carried out there, it was too late. The Jewish population was decimated, and it was practically hopeless to try to organize armed resistance against the Germans. The resistance of individuals or of small groups would not be an important problem for the Germans.

In sum, the diabolically clever plan that the Germans followed had the effect of producing a psychological paralysis. Even to the end, people somehow believed that they would not be killed, or were broken to the point where they no longer cared to live, and this prevented any sort of effective action that, if it did not save them, would at least have cost the Germans some losses. One prime example of this was a man named Gross, a heavyweight vice-champion before the war, strong enough to have killed a man with a blow during one boxing match. He was also a tough personality, part of a very feared group of young men. When he was taken for execution by the camp commander in Janowska, he could easily have taken the commander's life, and maybe others' as well, before being shot. Instead, he pleaded for his life on his knees and made no effort to resist the death that came to him.

CHAPTER 7

THE NOOSE TIGHTENS

In the middle of July of 1942 the SS ordered a roll call of the Jewish police in the ghetto. A significant number of them were taken out of their rows and sent as prisoners to the Janowska concentration camp. The Jewish police had been formed in October 1941, just after the ghetto was created. Its members were under the control of the *Judenrat* and their duty was to keep order in the ghetto. They were unarmed, carrying only a nightstick. In several actions the Germans used them to assist, together with the Ukrainian police, in the searching of homes. In the beginning, many idealistic Zionist youth volunteered, hoping to help somehow and to be a trained fighting group in the future, when the Germans might be retreating. As they saw what they had to do in helping the Germans, they became disillusioned and ashamed. Some of these people were taken to Janowska at this time. Eventually the police consisted more and more of low characters who used their position to extract personal gain at the expense of their people.

Our situation was becoming desperate. Fears of a new, more terrible action haunted us all, but there was no way out. There was greater and greater hunger. There were days when we had nothing to eat. I thought of ways to improve our situation at least with regard to our child's nourishment. Then I recalled that a classmate of mine from medical school, a Ukrainian, Dr. Stefan Bryk, with whom I had quite friendly relations, was an important official among the province authorities. He was, namely, the chief of the Personnel Division in the Health Care Department for the District of Galicia. I decided to go and ask him (I was convinced that this was entirely within his capacities) to send me to a provincial town or a village as a doctor to fight contagious diseases such as typhoid fever or the like. Being out in the countryside, having peasants as patients, I would obtain as my fees food products, and I would be able to nourish my family and myself. Perhaps we could also avoid the holocaust by hiding at somebody's place.

I learned that Dr. Bryk also had a private medical office for Germans in the elegant quarter at Piekarska Street. During his studies Dr. Bryk had not been trying to conceal—on the contrary, he let everybody know— that he was a fanatical Ukrainian patriot. He hated Poles and had great sympathy for Hitler's Germany. During summer vacations he regularly visited Berlin, which, as we all knew, was the location of the headquarters of the Ukrainian nationalists, from which instructions were issued for the underground Ukrainian organizations in Poland. In the last year of his studies, after having come back from Berlin, Bryk was wearing a Nazi badge with a swastika on his jacket lapel. (Later, during the Nazi occupation, I learned that this was the badge of the members of Hitler's party.) At this time Poland and Germany were still on good terms; when, in a few years, relations between them cooled down and even became tense, this Hitlerian badge disappeared from Dr. Bryk's lapel. One day, in 1939, when we were together on duty in the Hospital of Social Insurance in Lwów, Dr. Bryk told me in a friendly talk on a balcony of the hospital, "I hate Poles and I assure you that we Ukrainians, no matter whether a brown *Gauleiter* [that is, a Nazi provincial chief] or a red commissar comes, we shall settle our accounts with the Poles."

When the Red Army took Lwów in September 1939, the Russians convened a general meeting of the city's medical doctors in the Chamber of Physicians. Before the meeting opened, a group of some dozen doctors entered the overcrowded room, each of them wearing a red ribbon on his lapel. Marching through the center of the room, they took seats in the front row. Dr. Bryk was in that group. A few weeks afterward, however, colleagues told me that Dr. Bryk felt he was being hounded. Apparently, the Russians had learned something of him, but he escaped in time to the west, to the Germans. When the Germans marched into Lwów in June 1941, Dr. Bryk was, we were told, with the first German units, and soon was nominated chief of the Personnel Division of the Health Care Department for all of District Galicia.

Now, at the end of July 1942, in my desperate situation, I decided to ask him for aid. I hoped he would help me. One day, wearing my armband with the star of David and the *"Arzt"* inscription, I went out of the Jewish quarter into the Aryan part of town. I saw, on a beauti-ful building at Piekarska Street, a plate reading: "DR. STEFAN BRYK, DEUTSCHER ARZT" (German doctor). I walked up to the second floor, where his apartment and consulting room were. I opened the door to the waiting room and quickly closed it again. There were plenty of Germans in military outfits in there. I was afraid that my intrusion might entail an unpleasant situation both for me, with my armband showing the star of David, and perhaps also for him. I rang the bell to the private apartment. A maid opened the door and told me that Dr. Bryk had not yet come back from his office. I decided to go downstairs and, in order not to put him in an awkward position, to talk with him in the street. I stood on the opposite side of the street so as to observe when he came back. I waited some time. Suddenly a luxury car with a chauffeur stopped in front of the house. Dr. Bryk, together with a dog, a big German shepherd, got out of the car and, before I could realize what was happening, disappeared inside the house. I was both disappointed and angry with myself that I had not found the right moment. Then I decided to go back to the ghetto and try again the next week. It was, however, too late; before that week had gone by, events had taken a dramatic turn and I had no further opportunity to see Dr. Bryk.

I should add here that when, in New York in 1960, I visited the former senior assistant of the University Clinic of Internal Diseases in Lwów, a Ukrainian, Dr. Onyszkiewicz, I learned from him that Dr. Bryk, previously a Ukrainian patriot, did not admit to being Ukrainian during the German occupation. He maintained that he was German and was even sending Ukrainian medical doctors to concentration camps. He was said to have succeeded in withdrawing with other SS officers in 1945 before the advancing Russian troops and settled in Argentina or elsewhere in South America. Dr. Bryk's chameleonlike nature was extraordinary; he was an extreme example, but representative of the opportunism that war conditions brought out in some people.

A wave of anxiety and nervousness in the ghetto was increasing every day. An approaching storm was felt in the air. There was a new order: all the *Meldekarten* had to be stamped again by the SS. Gestapo officials appeared in various workplaces where, on this day, all the employees were convened. The Gestapo stamped the old *Meldekarten* presented to them, but some were not stamped and were taken away. On the following day the police came to those people whose cards had not been stamped and took them to Janowska camp.

In some workplaces the Gestapo did not even bother to look at the employees. They stamped some of the *Meldekarten* randomly, putting aside the rest. Tension in the ghetto increased every day. People talked of nothing but stamping. Those who got their cards stamped by the SS were envied. Those who did not were in extreme despair. They were searching for any opportunity to get out of this dangerous situation.

The very name Janowska camp (or Janów, for short) had by this time become terrifying for Jews. When my uncle Nahum did not get his card stamped, he told me that his despair at the prospect of being sent to Janowska was so great that he was seriously considering suicide. This was remarkable, because he was a deeply religious man, and suicide is prohibited by Jewish law.

By then, we knew Janowska was a slaughterhouse. Horrible news of bloodcurdling torture and torments reached us. Those who got there did not come back. The murdered ones, and those who died of hunger, emaciated and tortured, were replaced by others brought from various actions in Lwów or in provincial localities. Besides that, the Gestapo were sending people to the camp for any petty offense that might occur. This equaled a death sentence. Like a voracious beast this slaughterhouse incessantly devoured enormous numbers of victims every day. It was, in fact, a death mill, working without a break, day and night.

Terrifying rumors of incredible things occurring in the camp at Janowska Street also circulated in the rest of the city, among the Christian population. Sometimes, when the ghostly figures of Janowska camp prisoners appeared in the streets, either employed in street cleaning or being conducted to the bathhouse, crowds of people looked upon them with curiosity and compassion, looked at those condemned in rags, in torn shoes, with a wide red lacquer stripe down the backs of their coats. Hands and legs, which barely moved, looked as if they belonged to skeletons. Their heads were shaved, and out of the hollow-cheeked faces the suffering, begging eyes looked only forward. This was the prospect awaiting those who, for some unknown reason, had not gotten their *Meldekarte* stamped, had not found mercy in the eyes of the gentlemen from the Gestapo.

On the afternoon of Sunday, August 9, I was observing the crowd of employees going back home from the German firm of Schwarz at St. Martin's Street. They looked, to a degree, like pupils who had gotten their final report cards at the end of the school year. Those who had gotten their stamp were overjoyed; they had the certificate promoting them to the next grade. A right to live. As it seemed then, the ultimate one. The others, who had not been granted this mercy, were in despair; they had not passed their exams and therefore had to repeat the grade. But no! They had lost their right to live. They were broken down. Some women cried aloud, tears pouring down their faces.

As for me, I was at that time one of those who did not know yet whether they had passed the exam or not. Doctors' *Meldekarten* were to be left in the Jewish Chamber of Physicians to be extended. We were then supposed to come for the answer on Tuesday, August 11, or Wednesday, August 12. There were, however, persistent rumors that an action would begin on Monday, August 10. I asked Dr. Graf, the head of the Jewish Sanitätsamt, about it when I met him on the evening of August 9.

"Don't worry, my friend," he assured me. "There cannot be any action tomorrow if we are to obtain our reponses from the Chamber of Physicians on Tuesday or on Wednesday. Besides, I can assure you on the basis of reliable information that medical doctors shall be, as they have been until now, respected."

CHAPTER 8

CAPTURE AND ARREST

The very same night, at around two or three o'clock, I was awakened by the sound of heavy bootsteps coming from the street. One year under Hitlerian rule had sharpened my hearing. I recognized the footsteps of soldiers or policemen circulating under our windows. I could not sleep again. Was this it? At dawn I jumped to the window. Yes. At the crossing of Panieńska and St. Martin's streets, distant by just a dozen footsteps from our house, there were patrols of Ukrainian militia and German police in helmets and fully armed. The action had started. I alerted all members of our household. "Action! Action!" Everybody jumped out of their beds. Like lightning the news reached all inhabitants of our apartment building. We were seized by deadly fear. Anxiety, terror, chaotic running from place to place, children crying—hell on the earth. Where to hide? Where to go? Despair and helplessness overtook us all. At our place 90 percent of the people did not yet have their stamps, had not yet received an answer. Hence, a deceit! The action started before card control was terminated. What would this mean? I did not worry about my older sister Rózia (Rose), who lived across the street, for she had a certificate that her husband was employed as a laborer for the Gestapo, and thus had the desired stamp. As I later found out, she quickly ran to Mr. Faliński, Gina's employer and friend, who was the director of the *Vereinigte Wäschereien* establishment, near the boundary between the Aryan quarter and the ghetto. Our father and brother also worked there. Their

Meldekarten were with him. She thought that perhaps he had already got the cards, stamped, from the SS.

In my apartment, all the others ran in various directions, searching for places to hide. I thought it more secure for me to go out and pretend that I was going to a sick patient as a doctor. My wife and child were to stay home. She had a document, stamped by the Chamber of Physicians, stating that she was managing the household of a doctor husband. The German authorities had until then respected this document.

I took my physician's bag with instruments and went out. Where to go? I decided to get through to the Aryan quarter and there, wandering, to wait for the first dangerous period to end. And then we would see. And if they caught me on the way I would say I was going to visit a patient.

When I went out into the street I saw that Panieńska was closed off by the police where it crossed St. Martin's Street. At the same time, on the opposite side of our street, Ukrainian and German police were searching apartment after apartment and leading out people. I went in the other direction. But from this side, as well, police troops in complete fighting equipment were advancing toward us. I went into the side street, Wilczków, in order to reach Tkacka Street, parallel to Panieńska, looking for a way out there, but this street was also closed on both sides by the police. I went through another side street and reached Królewska Street. Everywhere it was the same. We were locked in from all sides. Even a mouse could not slip out. Police troops were advancing. The ring around us became even closer. I had to turn back. I was standing helpless at the crossing of Panieńska and Wilczków. Two possibilities were left to me. Either to risk it and try to get through the police cordon (perhaps, as it had been before, they would let a medical doctor through), or to hide in the furniture workshops at Tkacka Street where my father-in-law worked.

At this moment I met Forster, a Jewish policeman who lived in our apartment building. "Doctor, your whole family was taken," he said.

"Impossible, what are you saying?" I shouted. "All of them? This is impossible!"

If, however, that was what had happened, I thought, then I had nothing to live for either. I should go with them. So I went in the direction of our house.

At the corner of Panieńska and Wilczków there stood a villa, inhabited by a Jewish colleague whom I knew from the university and then from work in the hospital, a Dr. Gutentag. He was sharing the villa with a relative, a Dr. Preczep. I thought I could enter the villa and watch from their apartment the people being escorted from their homes by the action. Should I see my family, I would join them.

I came into the apartment. Dr. Gutentag greeted me cordially, but as if with a certain embarrassment. Just then Dr. Preczep came and said, "Please leave here immediately. You expose us to a great danger."

"Doctor," I answered, "I do not expose you to any danger, for if my card is inadequate, they will simply take me. This shall do no harm to you."

"Do get out of here immediately!"

There was nothing I could do, so I left. I crossed the street and on its opposite side I noticed that all the buildings there were sealed. Each door had a notice taped on it, forbidding entry. The notices were in German and bore the eagle and swastika emblem. The action had ended here already. The place was clean of Jews. I went in the direction of my home. I decided to somehow get to the apartment building across the street from us, where Rózia lived and through which the action had passed almost half an hour before. From there I would observe whether the Germans were leading out anyone of my family.

There was a Ukrainian policeman guarding the door to our apartment building. I entered, therefore, the one across the street and surprise! The action was being carried out there for the second time! People were being dragged out of their hideouts. I was noticed.

"Come here!" a Gestapo man shouted to me from the inner courtyard as he saw me in the entrance. He was a blue-eyed blond man with a trimmed mustache. His face expressed sadistic fury. I was the object of his viperous look. He had a pistol in one hand and a whip in the other. "Show me your registration card."

I showed him my card from the Chamber of Physicians, with the German stamp and the notice that, for the sake of the interest of the population, medical doctors should not be taken to any forced labor. He grinned sarcastically. "Stand there." He indicated a double row of people of various ages, taken in this second action, who stood congregated in the courtyard, guarded by an armed Ukrainian. Women and old men dominated in this group. "Do you see these old women?" he said to me, pointing at the silver-haired old women. "When they get sick, then you shall cure them. Ha, ha, ha." He laughed loudly. I was put in the first pair of people. After I had taken my place, I asked the Ukrainian guard, who stood next to me, "Please, if any of my family is taken out from the building across the street, may I be allowed to join them? It will not matter to you anyway whether I am taken in that group or this one."

Before he could even reply, the Gestapo man noticed me talking to the guard and came over at once, pointing his gun at me and shouting, "If you say even one more word, or try to move from your place, you'll get shot at once."

After a dozen minutes the action of cleaning out this house was finished. A procession of victims, led by me, was escorted to the corner of Panieńska and St. Martin's streets, and then to the church, in front of which people taken from neighboring streets were gathered. When their number reached two hundred, the group was conducted to the nearby railway station, Lwów-Podzamcze, near which were the NSKK (National Sozialistisches Kraftfahr-Korps, the Nazi motorized paramilitary organization) barracks. There we were pushed into the stables, where we saw a crowd of people packed like herrings in a barrel. New groups, new victims, were led in from time to time.

I noticed my younger sister Ida led in among the new arrivals. Despite the fear she must have felt, her face showed composure and resolve. I called to her and we moved together, standing close to each other in the thickly packed crowd. I anxiously asked her to tell me what had happened to the rest of the family. It turned out that it was only she who had been taken from our house. Only she from our whole family. They had all hidden away, except my wife and child and our aunt Andzia (Annie), whose husband was employed as a laborer for the *Sicherheitspolizei* (Security Police, a branch of the Gestapo). Andzia therefore had the appropriate documents and should have been safe; in spite of this, they wanted to take her. Then Ida, who had hidden behind a pile of chests and cases, and had not been found, came out of hiding and asked to be taken in place of her aunt. This aunt was like a second mother to us. She had been helping our parents bring us up. The Germans agreed and took my sister. After long deliberations they left my wife and child, accepting for now the statement from the medical society as still valid.

The crowd in the stable was getting denser and denser. There was a hum like the noise in a beehive. Soft sobbing and whimpering of women. SS men were time and again bursting in, looking proudly at their captives and smiling with satisfaction. One of them invented a game for himself. "Who is guilty of this war?" he yelled. Silence. "Answer, you dogs," he barked, and slapped a Jew standing nearby strongly in the face.

"England," whispered the victim.

"English and American Jews," shouted some people in the crowd, seeing that the beast was not yet satisfied.

"All Jews," shrieked the uniformed sadist, and struck another victim with his fist. "So, who is guilty of this war?"

A choir of separate voices answered, "We Jews."

The reaction of the German was: "This is yet not correct." There was another blow and somebody hit the ground. "So, who is guilty of this war?"

"We Jews," the crowd replied.

"Yes, now it's okay." He smiled with satisfaction and went out. Every quarter of an hour he would come back with some comrade of his to repeat the game. He was very proud of his deed.

What would they do to us? People were anxiously asking various questions. A roaring thunder of machine gun shots seemed to be an answer. We heard it repeatedly, with short breaks between.

A horde of German policemen stormed suddenly into the stable. With whips and guns they pushed the first group out, the first of many. Others waited for their turn. A machine gun rattled in the distance. We thought that an execution was taking place not far away. In expectation of death we all moved closer to each other. Our crowd got even denser. Suddenly, a group of higher-rank officers came in, with one of them apparently of senior rank. They were approached by one of the prisoners, Dr. Roller, a known pediatrician in Lwów, who spoke to the highest-ranking officer. The officer only nodded and said nothing. They went out. After a while a Gestapo man ran in.

"Doctors and medical personnel out!" he shouted.

He ordered us to stand separately, against one wall. Some hope came back to me. So, perhaps I would somehow get out of this situation. I hugged my sister. I would say she was my assistant. After we (the group of medical personnel) had been separated from the others, a mass of people, known and unknown to us, started to try to get to us. This one asked us to notify his wife, that one his brother, another his father, women their husbands, some their directors. My pockets were soon filled with pieces of paper with various addresses.

In a short while the same villain appeared who just a while before had simplified for himself the question of responsibility for the war. He looked at our group and asked, "What is this?"

It was explained to him that this was the order of higher officers, that medical doctors and staff were to be separated. "Back, you damn dogs."

We moved back. Whether orders had changed or this villain was ignoring them, in any case our hopes of getting out of this trap by being doctors were dashed. During this time a new group was led out. Finally, at about noon the last group was also led out, including Ida and myself. A horde of uniformed dogs rushed in.

"*Raus! Raus! Los! Los!* [Out! Out! Go! Go!]"

We were hurried with whips.

They made us stand five in a row and we marched through the yard in front of the NSKK barracks complex. Crowds of soldiers looked at us, pleased to see our plight, laughing and shouting something in our direction. We went out into the street. In front of us stood three streetcar wagons, each attached to a load of lorry railcars. We were loaded onto the lorries. They had high sides and no roofs. "*Schell! Schnell!* [Quickly! Quickly!]" There was already a crowd of people on the lorries. We choked. We were so squeezed that even a pin could not get in. "*Schnell! Schnell!*" Rifle butts and whips went to work. Finally, the lorries were shut. German and Ukrainian policemen were in the streetcars, and many others sat atop the walls of the lorries. Their guns were aimed at us. The streetcars moved on. There was crying, whining, shouting. We started to guess where we were bound to. Is it to the Łyczaków sand quarry? Is it for an execution? Or perhaps to Kleparów station?

We were crammed on these lorries in an impossible way. Women and children cried, wailed. Passersby looked at us with interest. I tried with all my strength to protect my sister from suffocation. We approached Gołuchowski Square, where the streetcar rails crossed, and with trembling hearts we waited to see which way our cars would turn. To the left, in the direction of the Łyczaków sand quarry—that is, to be executed—or straight, in the direction of Kleparów station? We sighed with relief. The streetcar did not turn; we were going to Kleparów station, hence to Bełzec or to Janowska camp.

As I stated earlier, people first heard the rumors of Bełzec's gas chambers after the March action but didn't believe them. It was the same now. Most people still thought that Bełzec was a kind of *Durchgangslager* (transit camp), from which inmates were sent to labor camps. It was only after the August action that people started to guess the truth.

We reached the last stop at Janowska Street. We got out. We were conducted not to the train station, nor to the main gate of Janowska camp, but into the adjoining DAW (*Deutsche Ausrüstungswerke*—German Arms Factories). From there, we were led through a gate in a barbed-wire fence that separated DAW from the Janowska camp. We were now inside Janowska, in a rear portion of the camp, close to the main barrack. We were set in two rows. There were some higher Gestapo officers before us, together with Weber, the chief of the *Arbeitsamt, Abteilung Judeneinsatz* (the section of the labor department that dealt with Jewish forced labor). There were also some functionaries of the German police of various ranks. Every one of us, keeping his *Meldekarte*—if he had one—in his raised hand, had to shout out his age and profession and pass, running, before the lords of death and life. Depending upon age, sex, profession, and—most important—appearance, we were directed either to the left or to the right. Women of any age, looks, health condition, and occupation; the elderly; children; and people physically weaker were at once directed to the left. Those directed to the right were grouped in fives. Those to the left were driven straight down a path to a gate leading to another section of Janowska camp, and from there through the front gate of the camp to the road to Kleparów station. We had quickly guessed that the people who had been directed to the right were candidates for Janów camp, while those to the left were bound for Bełzec. I bid my sister farewell. With tears in my eyes I looked for the last time at her emaciated face. Her cheeks were red, the veins on her neck were swollen. She looked at me and gave me four slices of bread, which our aunt had given her for the journey. I did not want to take them. At last, I ceded to her requests and took one slice. Our turn came. We said good-bye again. "Do not worry about me," she comforted me. "I know how to work. I shall manage."

After a while I found myself in the group on the right side—to stay in the camp. My sister Ida was hurried toward the station. I looked at her as long as I could see her silhouette. A long file of pitiful people were running, often with their last strength, toward the gate of the camp. The Germans were in a hurry. Transport waited. *"Laufen! Laufen! Schnell! Schnell!* [Run! Run! Quickly! Quickly!]" People were forced with whips to run. The swish of the whips was heard constantly. An old man could not catch up. The labor department official Weber, who was in the reviewing group, himself jumped toward him and struck him with his whip so that blood appeared. The blood-covered old man stood up with an effort and trotted after the others.

When the selection was finished we were taken through the same gate that the others had gone through, to the front part of the camp, close to the main entrance. We were ordered to sit down in a semicircle, densely side by side, around a turret that served as a watchtower. As we sat there we saw the camp inmates gathering in groups in the inner section of the camp and looking at us from behind the barbed-wire fences separating us. We were to be their new companions. Looking at them, at their emaciated figures in rags, we knew what we were in for. They apparently saw terror in our eyes, for some tried to comfort us: "Do not be afraid. We shall somehow manage."

CHAPTER 9

PRISONER IN HELL

It was around two P.M., about an hour or more since we first entered Janowska camp. It was still Monday, August 10, 1942, although it seemed like an eternity since it had started with my hearing the boots outside my house at two A.M. We were in the outer square, located between the camp's external gate and what seemed to be the camp proper. A Russian guard, with his gun turned toward us, stood on top of the turret around which we were sitting. He was one of the so-called Askaris, Russian soldiers, ex-POWs, who had changed sides of their own free will to serve the Germans. We were warned that we could not move, under penalty of immediate execution. We were separated both from the rest of the immense first square and from the camp proper by a wall of barbed wire. Askaris and Jewish policemen circulated around us.

"Mister, mister, give *chassy, zykharek* ["watch," in broken Russian-Polish], we shall go together to work," an Askari with a wild, pockmarked face shouted to me.

More and more Askaris, like hyenas, started to circle around us. They explained to us that the Germans would take everything from us anyway, so that it was better to give these things to them. They would be escorting us to work, and could therefore be useful to us. Some of us gave some things, but most did not react. The Askaris would disappear at once when an SS man approached.

At around three o'clock in the afternoon a new group of action victims was led in through the main gate. My heartbeat accelerated, something choked me: in the first rows I noticed my older sister, Rózia, whom I loved more than my other siblings. "Rózia!" I shouted. She noticed me. She looked sadly in my direction, as if saying, "And you, too!" I was in despair. I had hoped that she might escape.

Afterward I learned that she had gone of her own will, to save our parents and brother. She was caught in the morning, and though she had stamped working papers, was put on a truck bound for Janowska. But she managed to jump out of the lorry and flee. She went to her husband's workplace; he worked as a laborer in the Gestapo complex. Although she was secure there, she did not want to stay. She wanted to save our parents and brother, to try again to see if Mr. Faliński had their stamped working papers. So she went back toward the ghetto and fell into the hands of the Germans again.

The new transport was primarily composed of women and children. Standing on the opposite side of the square, the camp commander, SS Untersturmführer Willhaus, appeared with a submachine gun in his hand. Willhaus was tall, in his mid-thirties, with dark brown hair. He was ordinary-looking, clean-shaven, wearing the SS uniform with the human skull emblem on his hat and the "SS" on both sides of his collar. He had a slightly odd, waddling walk and a grim, unsmiling face. He ordered the newcomers to sit down on the ground. When some of the women did not hear because of the significant distance and did not sit down, he at once shot a round from the submachine gun into the crowd, and then again. The wounded, just like the sick, were put to one side, presumably for execution once the able-bodied had gone to the transport to Bełzec. The corpses of those killed during the action, which had also been on the lorries, were dragged by their legs, like cattle in a slaughterhouse, to this spot where the sick and injured lay.

After a while we saw a new show. We learned that this same day, during this action, a previous prisoner of Janowska camp was caught, a man named Landau who had been a brigadier here. A brigadier is in charge of a brigade, a group of fellow prisoners who go from the camp together to a particular work site. He was a rascal of rare quality. He tormented his subordinates and squeezed the last pennies out of them. He was a favorite of the SS men. Finally, when he had gathered some money, he escaped from the camp.

When camp commander Willhaus learned about it, he was furious. He started to search for Landau, but to no avail. And now, during this action, in a cart, among Gypsies, Landau was found. The joy of Willhaus and of his deputy, SS Untersturmführer Rokita, was great. Landau was tied to a pole some fifteen to twenty steps in front of Willhaus's villa. The "villas" in the camp were modest but comfortable one- or two-family houses from before the war. The inmates called them villas because they were so luxurious when compared to the inmates' barracks. They were occupied by German personnel. Both Willhaus and Rokita sat down on the bench in front of the villa and started a game. They began shooting at Landau by turns with their pistols, but in such a way as not to kill him, only to hit the pole above his head. Every few minutes they checked to see whose hit was closer to the head. This lasted for some quarter of an hour. Then, from time to time, one of the SS men would go up to Landau and strike him with all his force with a whip in the face. Landau stood tied like this to the pole for twenty-four hours with a bleeding, bruised, and swollen face. The next day he was liquidated.

Early in the evening, the first groups of those who had been selected for Janów camp were conducted to the *Aufnahmebüro* (admission office), where the final admittance to the camp took place. I and other doctors (there were eight of us) waited until midnight for our turn to come. A Jewish policeman told us that interventions on our behalf had not brought about the desired results. Our only privilege was that we were allowed to stay in our clothes. This was through Deputy Rokita's instructions. The others had their clothes taken away and got some rags. In the *Aufnahmebüro* we had to give away everything we had with us. I gave up my physician's bag, which held my stethoscope and other instruments, as well as my diploma. We were registered. An SS man looked through our pockets. Then we were led to the second floor, where we had to undress completely. There were two SS men there. One was a Hungarian German, Blum; short, freckled, keeping a long whip in his hand. One had the impression that the whip was taller than he was. He warned us once again that we had to give away everything we had, especially money. If he found even one penny on somebody, he told us, he would kill this man like a dog. He shook the whip and pointed at a pistol lying nearby.

When we were already naked, we gave our things to be checked. After a few minutes we got them back and got dressed. Then we were conducted to the barbers standing outdoors in front of the *Aufnahmebüro*. The night was quite cool, the sky was cloudy. The only light in the camp was from the moving searchlights on the turrets, illuminating the whole camp. In this light our hair was cut down to nothing. The barbers worked in the Stakhanov style, doing us quickly, one after another. (Alexei Stakhanov was a miner from the Donetsk coal basin. He was famous for working so rapidly that he repeatedly broke the records for work accomplished. The Stalinist regime made him a national hero and role model.) This was a painful procedure for us, since the barbers were cutting brutally, with their cutting machines not cleaned or especially sharpened. Past midnight we were entirely ready to be admitted to the camp.

A new stage in our life had begun; for most of us—the last one. We were fully aware of this. We would not stand this for more than two, three weeks. Almost all of us were saying this. And that was how things really happened. We knew from rumors in the ghetto that this was the average period of life in the camp at that time.

An autumnlike drizzle started drenching us without pity. We trembled with cold. We waited to be let into the camp as if for salvation. But we had to wait until the morning. We were sitting by twos, backs together, to lose as little warmth as possible. The night went on terribly long. I had not had anything to eat during the whole day, apart from the one slice of bread I had gotten from Ida, but I was not hungry. I wondered how Rózia was doing and was worrying about her.

At dawn, I stood up to look at the other side of the square, where those who came the previous day waited, intended for transport to Bełzec. I looked for Rózia. And she also stood up looking for me. We saw each other. She twice sent me kisses with her hand—a farewell. This was the last time I saw her. I cried with bitter tears. My heart could not stand the sorrow. My Lord! My Lord!

About an hour later we were set in fives and our column of about two hundred people marched into the interior of the camp, where we saw, at the far end, a barrack with a kitchen at one end of it. We proceeded around the kitchen to the grounds behind the building and saw that the camp prisoners were now about to assemble here for the roll call. For these prisoners we seemed to become objects of pity on the one hand, and of interest on the other. Many of them were looking for relatives or acquaintances. We were looked upon as if through the eyes of experts in meat cattle, judging how long we might stand this garden of Eden.

A relatively short time after we had entered the interior of the camp, an SS man came up to us, accompanied by the clerks from the office, and the sorting out of people from our group started. Everyone had to name their profession. Carpenters, mechanics, and some craftsmen, needed at the given moment, were separated and put in brigades that would go to DAW, and the rest—that is, people without skills or with unnecessary skills, including therefore also doctors—were put in a group that was to form another brigade.

It was characteristic, and disadvantageous, for our group that the percentage of intelligentsia among us was high. It was sensational to a certain extent that there were eight doctors in the group. In all the previous actions medical doctors had been spared, so that the first camp doctor had worked there out of his own free will, had been free to come and go, and was now no longer there. A few weeks before the August action two doctors from Gródek Jagielloński, a town about twenty-five kilometers from Lwów, were forced to come to the camp, but they were also in the camp as doctors. They had separate housing, food, and in general were not treated like the inmates, although they could not leave. One of these, Dr. Rapaport, was head doctor in the camp, and the other assisted him. As to our group, it was obvious that we would not work there as medical doctors but as laborers. We were the subject of general pity among the inmates. This particular turn in attitude toward Jewish doctors was, of course, commented on as one sign of the strengthening commitment to exterminate the Jews. We also learned that, unlike doctors, musicians enjoyed special favors in the camp, for the deputy camp commander, Untersturmführer Rokita, was a musician, having played in jazz bands in Polish nightclubs before the war.

When the sorting was finished, we were arranged in a row, while two inmates, with a pail full of lacquer paint, painted a broad red-orange stripe on the backs of our jackets. Then voices were heard: "Roll call! Roll call!" Brigades hastily formed in rows on the grounds behind the kitchen. In front of them, on a platform made of stone pillars and wooden beams, several SS men were standing, headed by Scharführer Kolonko. Beside them stood *Oberjude* ("head Jew") Kampf. Near Kampf stood Rysiek Axer, from the camp office. Axer was the son of a famous Jewish lawyer in Lwów. He was favored by Willhaus, the camp commander, and he used this position to help many camp inmates. The highest authority, Willhaus himself, did not appear.

Clerks from the office were going consecutively through all the brigades, checking the number of inmates in each. Simultaneously, SS men, standing on the platform, started to call up particular camp inmates who were supposedly guilty of something, and the administering of justice began. The prisoner called up had to run full force and stand in front of the authorities; after a short talk of a few seconds he had to pull down his trousers and, exposing his buttocks, lie down on the beams. One of the SS men (sometimes replaced by Kampf) pressed with his boot on the head of the culprit so as to immobilize him. Two SS men with long whips stood on both sides of the punished and the blows were dealt, in turns, from one side and then the other. The SS men counted aloud as they beat him, resting for a few seconds before each blow. Red bruises appeared on the buttocks side by side, and crossing, until blood started to gush. The victim yelled, which led to stronger pressure of the boot on his head, and sometimes a kick. The SS men did not like to have their solemn ceremony interrupted by whimpering.

After some dozen blows, a victim ceased to whimper and his body, shaking after each blow, became numb. Some inmates evacuated their bowels after several blows. After the predefined number of blows had been dealt and counted, when the SS man shouted *"Raus! Los!* [Out! Go!]" the victim had to quickly pull up his trousers and run back to the rows. If the punished inmate did not stand up, due to fainting or exhaustion, he received several kicks in the head and then a *Gnadenschuss* (coup de grâce)—a shot in the back of the head from the SS man's pistol.

I was horrified to see this, but soon found out that it happened during almost every roll call. After justice had been administered, the SS man Kolonko gave certain orders and the brigades started marching out to work. This lasted for quite a long time. Our group did not know yet what we would be doing, and therefore we marched last. When we came to the interior gate of the camp, we were stopped. Rokita and Willhaus together with their whole pack stood before us. Rokita, his gun in hand, started a new selection. We were arranged now in one line. Every one of us had to shout, running, his age and profession. Depending upon age and appearance, for no attention was paid to profession, Rokita waved his pistol to the left or to the right. I was directed to the left. At the beginning I did not know, just like the others, which was better. After a short time I noticed that the healthier individuals went toward my side, so I calmed down. When the selection was finished our group was directed to work at construction of new barracks there in the camp, alongside some other brigades. The other group marched in an unknown direction. It was generally suspected that they were to be killed.

Work in construction was not easy, but was not very hard either. Jewish prisoners worked together with the Aryan ones. There were very few Aryan prisoners in Janowska, and this was the only day that I had any contact with them.

At work I was advised by experienced inmates as to the conditions reigning in the camp. The average life span of an inmate who did not have aid from outside was two to four weeks at most. During this period, if he had not died of a bullet, he would die of hunger or sickness. Inmates with longer experience therefore taught the newcomers that in work as well as in marching one should as much as possible keep to the old Latin principle of *festina lente*—"hasten slowly." Working too eagerly and too quickly one could achieve an early death from exhaustion.

When someone was caught relaxing during work, he was beaten without pity, or even killed. The conclusion therefore was to take the middle way, to steer deftly: one didn't want to exhaust oneself, and hoped to spare one's body, fed with minimal calories; but, of course, one didn't want to be caught idle either. In short, one had to take care not to make the power of the Third Reich grow too much from our efforts, which was not an easy art. Many Jewish prisoners paid with their lives for artless behavior. And tens of thousands of them made acquaintance with the fists, boots, whips, and other things used by the guards in convincing the inmates to work more effectively for the Führer.

When noon came on that first day of work, lunchtime was announced. Camp inmates left their work and formed a line to the kitchen. I was terribly hungry, for, except for the slice of bread given me by my sister Ida, I had not had anything in my mouth for a day and a half. And here was a new tragedy. Everybody was standing in the line before the kitchen window with pots or metal bowls in their hands. Only we, the newcomers, had nothing to eat from. We started to run around the square asking those who had finished eating already to lend us their containers. This was not easy, for not all were ready to lend, and there were some two hundred candidates for borrowing. Time passed. The lunch break lasted only one hour. Despairing, with my hunger increasing greatly, I ran to and fro across the square and begged for a pot. Finally I found a benefactor who promised to lend me his pot when he finished his meal. When the desired moment came I grabbed the pot and ran to the line. The smell reaching me from the kitchen window excited my appetite even more. In a flutter I pushed my way through to the window. A benevolent cook poured me a dipper of soup and waved for the next one to come. I looked into the pot. Pure hot water, smelling like soup, but with nothing floating in it. I did not have a spoon, so I started to drink, since there was nothing to eat in this soup anyway. I burned my tongue and palate with this hot water, in which there wasn't even any salt, for our providers scanted it us. Before I could gulp a few sips, the voice sounded, *"Antreten! Antreten!* [Form ranks! Form ranks!]"—the time for lunch had passed, and we had to go to work again.

The rest of that day we continued to work in the camp. In the evening, at "supper," I managed to get something to eat, a slice of bread. At night we all slept in the large and overcrowded barrack that housed all the inmates. I found a place to sleep near the others in my brigade.

The daily routine in Janowska revolved around the brigades, to which all camp prisoners belonged. These were initially named after their brigade chiefs, called brigadiers, corresponding to "kapo" in other concentration camps. About a month or two after my arrival in the camp, they started to be named for the firms for which these brigades worked. These were German military or municipal firms, or private German institutions in the town and its periphery. These firms paid the SS for this slave labor, as we heard, five złotys a day (under one dollar) per each worker. For some reason our brigade was not named in the usual fashion; when it was formed on the day we arrived it was at first named 102, because that was how many we were.

After we had worked one day in the camp, on Wednesday, our brigade, number 102, was assigned to work for the firm of Hannebeck, leveling the ground in the Skniłów airfield, in the periphery of Lwów. Each day, they chose one part of our group to be taken to the airfield by trucks, while the others went to the sand quarry near Janowska camp, close to the Jewish cemetery. I worked some days at one site, some at the other, but mostly at the sand pit; the first week I was there each day. We worked on small hills where, with pickaxes and shovels, we were removing the upper layer of soil, under which was the sand needed by the Germans for field works in the airfield.

Working in the sand pit was hard, especially for those of us from the intelligentsia, not accustomed to physical labor. The palms of our hands were getting sore and swollen. We had to take very great care not to get caught relaxing, for the Germans from time to time checked to see whether we were working well. When we were caught, they beat us ruthlessly with whips, belts, or rifle butts. One day the deputy commander of the camp, Untersturmführer Rokita, came to check on us. Seeing from a distance a prisoner resting at work, he shot a series from his submachine gun in the direction of the workers, injuring some. One day the German *Schachtmeister* (shift manager) complained to the camp authorities that we were working poorly. The very same day two of our brigadiers were beaten by the SS men, attached to two barriers like animals to be roasted, and left hanging there for several hours.

In digging the sand we had to be cautious as well, for sand would fall down in a flash and could cover the working prisoner. One of our fellow prisoners did get into such a sandfall and died, choked by the sand. I should also add that we were not allowed to leave our work and look for a place to shelter during heavy rains or storms. We had to stay in our place and work drenched in water. There was, obviously, no possibility of changing clothes—wet clothes had to dry on our bodies.

Beside the sufferings from this hard and often dangerous work, we also had to cope with despair at our own situation and fear for those we had left behind. The August action had not ended; it lasted for more than two weeks. We were taken on the very first day, August 10, 1942. The hills on which we worked were not far from Janowska Street, and from our place of work we could see, at a great distance, streetcars with lorries loaded with people being transported toward Janowska camp. We trembled at the thought that some of our dear ones could be in these lorries. When we came back from work to the camp, there were crowds of people every day in the external area—mainly women, children, and older people—waiting to be transported to their last life stage, to Bełzec. With our hearts in our throats we looked, marching next to them, for we could not stop, to see whether there was somebody from our families in this crowd.

Within a few days of my arrival at the camp, I received a letter from my wife, Frania, through the intermediary of a Jewish policeman, Danziger, whom I knew and who worked in the ghetto. The original is now in the archives of Yad Vashem, the Holocaust memorial and museum in Jerusalem. The following is a translation, with added notes in brackets:

> My Dearest,
>
> I am desperate that I cannot send you what I would like to; we live on the generosity of my grandmother—but thank God for that. I am sending you bread, I don't have anything more. When things will calm down I will do anything for you. My hands are tied. I cannot go anywhere; everywhere it is burning. You cannot imagine how great the firestorm is. May God save us, like until now, and you, poor darling, should only endure. I cannot sleep at night from worrying about you. I will repay Mr. Danziger's kindness, now I have nothing to give him. I cannot go to Fanka [her cousin, financially well-off] in this situation . . . [four or five illegible words follow]
>
> I am writing chaotically, because Zyśko [her brother] is at my back telling me that Mr. Danziger is in a hurry to go home. I'm ending my letter, the next letter will be more ample.
>
> > I kiss you,
> > Frania

I was excited to hear from her and relieved that she was still all right. I missed her and Sylvia terribly. I also knew full well that with the action continuing they were still in great danger, and I feared for them. I was very grateful for the bread, and anxiously hoping for the next letter.

On Friday, August 14, the fifth day of my stay in Janowska, I received a new blow. I was in the main interior section of the camp after a day's work, waiting for supper to be served, when I saw someone running up to me. It was my brother, Józek! We embraced each other, my heart filled with love and despair. He told me that he had just been put in our camp. I simply couldn't believe that he, of all my family, should end up here, for Józek belonged to the so-called lucky ones who had obtained a good *Arbeitskarte* with the SS stamp. In addition, he had a typical Aryan appearance—tall, athletic, fair-haired, with green-blue eyes, and was slightly snub-nosed. During the action, when SS men stormed into the

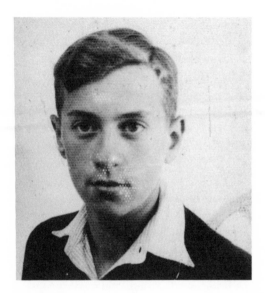

My brother, Jozef.

firm where he worked looking for Jews, Józek, in spite of the fact that he had a good *Arbeitskarte*, had tried to get into a hideout. The SS men and the Ukrainian policemen who accompanied them then found him, took away his good card, and brought him to Janowska camp. Jósek was almost eleven years my junior, not yet nineteen years old, and the terrible events of the August action had made him very nervous, so that he had panicked. Most likely, if he hadn't tried to hide he would have been left alone by the SS.

He told me that, upon arrival in Janowska camp, he had been assigned to the carpenters' workshops in DAW, although he did not know anything of that craft. But there Fabian, the chief of the carpenters' brigade, took care of him out of pity for his youth and nervousness, and gave him relatively light work to do. The disadvantage of this job was that one was constantly within the camp, while people working in most of the out-of-camp brigades could have some contact with friends or family in town and thereby sometimes find help.

Józek then told me that he had some very painful news. Aunt Andzia, who was like a second mother to us, whom we loved very much, and for whom my youngest sister, Ida, had sacrificed herself by offering to go in her place, had been taken by the SS two days later, in spite of the fact that she had a good card showing that her husband worked as a physical worker for the Gestapo. This was a very painful blow for me.

Two days later, on Sunday, August 16, the seventh day of my stay in the camp, came a new blow. I met my father-in-law, Maurycy, among the new-coming prisoners! I was horrified to find him there, and asked for news of the others, especially Frania. He told me that he had hidden together with his wife, his mother, and Frania in a carpenters' workshop at Tkacka Street. On the sixth day of the August action the SS men found them in their hideout. They took him to the camp, but the others—Frania and her mother and grandmother—had been sent to Bełzec.

Blow after blow. Dear Lord! Was there no end to this tragedy of mine? I was disconsolate at the loss of Frania, and my helplessness. I sat down and cried. It was Sunday, so thankfully there was little work for us, so I could be left alone a bit to weep. I also mourned her mother, who was a warm and generous human being, loved by all who knew her. Even when she had been starving in the ghetto, she found something to give to beggars. Everyone in Frania's family had always turned to her for advice and help.

When Maurycy told me what had happened, I immediately asked him about Sylvia. "Don't worry," he replied, "she is in a safe place, with a Polish family." Because he had many Polish friends, and girls did not have to fear being found out by circumcision, I felt relieved that at least Sylvia would be safe. This was a comfort, and gave me a reason to keep living.

Some months later, I heard more about Frania and Sylvia from my cor-dial friend, Dolek Starker. I spoke with him after he was brought to

Frania's mother, Amalia, while living in the Lwów ghetto in 1942.

Janowska camp as a prisoner along with other members of the Jewish ghetto police. Starker told me that, as a policeman, he had been able, on matters of duty, to circulate between the camp and the ghetto, and that in the first days of the August action he had noticed me among the Janowska camp inmates. Having come back to the ghetto, he quickly ran to Frania in order to inform my wife that I was in Janowska camp. Frania, who had not had any news of my fate before, hearing that I was alive and in the camp, was in the first moment so overtaken with joy that she jumped to embrace him, to thank him for the news. Then she quickly realized what torments awaited me in Janowska camp and that almost certain death would follow, so she burst into spasmodic crying. According to the story told by Dolek, my two-year-old daughter, Sylvia, pulled Frania by her dress and said, "Mummy, don't cry, don't cry. Daddy will come back, Daddy will come back."

In the first seven days of the August action, then, I had lost two sisters, my closest aunt, my wife, and her mother and grandmother. In addition, my brother and father-in-law were condemned to the same inferno that I was in. Of my immediate family, the only ones who might still be alive and with some freedom for now were my parents and my sister Gina; my daughter, Sylvia; my uncles Nahum and Adolf; and my aunt Rachel.

Around this same time, I saw my friend Norbert's two brothers, who had also been taken to Janowska camp in this action. They told me that Norbert, Giza, their daughter, and Giza's parents had all been killed in the first days of the August action. The griefs were so many, and so deep, I felt like a man whipped ceaselessly until insensate.

Shortly after I spoke with them, Norbert's brothers disappeared. Whether they were killed or escaped, I don't know.

Day after day dragged on. New transports of people caught in the ghetto were coming constantly. Some of them were assigned to the camp, which swelled more and more. The vast majority, however, were sent to Bełzec. As I later learned, during the two weeks that the August action lasted, about 50,000 Jews were killed, most of them in the gas chambers of Bełzec.

Terrible scenes of murdering, tormenting, and tortures occurred in the camp. Here, one could see SS men beating prisoners with whips until they bled; there, misfortunes hanging from wooden rods by hand and foot, like animals brought home from the hunt. At one of the trees I saw a Pole who, I was told, helped Jews escape from the ghetto. He was tied with ropes to the tree, beaten bloody, his face so swollen from bruises that one could not see his eyes. Every SS man passing by deemed it his duty to strike the face of this poor victim with his whip.

Every day, roll calls shattered our nerves. My brother, Józek, said that if these roll calls were to go on like this, he would go insane. He was a young boy, and it was all the harder for him to stand, these daily tortures and executions. During one such roll call, a young man named Hoch, who had lived in our building at Panieńska Street and who was nearsighted, lost his glasses and tried to find them. This was noticed by the deputy camp commander, Untersturmführer Rokita, who asked what was the matter. The young man told him.

"Oh, don't worry, I will help you," said Rokita. "Run forward," he ordered, and when Hoch started to run, he killed the young man with a shot from his pistol.

On a different occasion I noticed during a roll call a prisoner hanging on the wall of barbed wire that surrounded the assembly area, near the kitchen. It looked as if in an insane, desperate fit, this inmate had tried to climb the barbed-wire wall in order to get outside and was shot, probably by an Askari on duty in the nearby turret. His body was shot many times, and blood was trickling from his mouth and eyes. Presumably to frighten the prisoners of the camp, the Germans ordered the body to hang like this for two days on the wires.

The Germans cruelly avenged any escapes from the camp. Manhunts were organized, and when the escapee was caught in town he was beaten until he was unconscious and finally hanged on the gallows in front of the kitchen during a special assembly, so as to make each inmate know what awaited him should he try to escape. When the man was not found, a group of SS men would enter the ghetto and, knowing where his family lived, take members of his family to the camp to be hung there. And when they could not get his family, then two to five inmates from the brigade of the escapee were hanged or put "behindwire."

Perhaps the most feared place in the whole camp was this famous "behindwire." It was a passageway, about two meters wide, between two parallel barbed-wire fences, leading out toward the Sands, a sandy area north of the camp where executions took place. Every day, when the brigades marched out to work, we had to pass the opening to "behind-wire," where the SS men very carefully checked the laboring cattle (that is, the prisoners) for our appearance. Prisoners who looked sick, or were exhausted and emaciated, as well as "cripples" (those who were injured or lame), were taken out of the rows and sent to "behindwire." Also selected for "behindwire" were those who were to be executed for some sort of offense, or as punishment for the escape of some of their companions from the brigade. Here, isolated by two walls of barbed wire, attentively observed by Askaris from the turret, with their shoes pulled off, they waited. After all the brigades had marched out, they were taken to the Sands, through this very space between wires, to be shot. Sometimes they stayed "behindwire" for hours or even days, lying in cold and hunger, and in winter on snow, freezing, waiting for their execution.

Janowska camp, like a Moloch, devoured an enormous number of the lives of its inmates every day. This, however, was not enough for the SS rulers. In order to accelerate the process of extermination, they organized from time to time during the march out to work the so-called death races. Aryan brigades were excluded from this kind of sport. We were arranged in fives and when we heard the command *"Laufen!* [Run!]" we had to run some forty meters, one group after another. Those who looked weak or did not run quickly enough were taken out of the rows and put "behindwire." SS men, standing aloof, often tripped the runners to increase the number of victims. And thus, brigade after brigade went by. The numbers of those put "behindwire" increased. After a few hours they were conducted in the direction of the Sands, where they were executed. In other cases they were added to those transported to Bełzec.

Once, the group of inmates selected through the death race were kept in camp to clean the ground of the assembly areas. They were called the *Krüppelkommando* (team of cripples). Rokita promised to send them to a nursing rest home. A few days later they were led outside the camp, most probably to the Sands. We heard, from our sand quarry, rifle volleys.

When I had already spent three or four weeks in Janowska camp we were kept in the camp one day, not going to work. Rokita came with a pack of SS men and proclaimed that there would be a check. Everyone had to give up, in a specially prepared container, all money, documents, and similar objects. Whoever failed to do so would be appropriately punished. This was a terrible dilemma. The only way one could survive in this camp was with some money that one either snuck in upon entering or got through contacts with friends or family when at workplaces. With this money one could buy needed food on the way to or from work, or from other inmates. One could also bribe a brigadier, or someone in the office, to get placed in a better work situation. Those prisoners from provincial areas outside Lwów were especially dependent on what they had, for they had no one to give them further help once their money was gone. Their only other recourse to survive would be stealing from their fellow prisoners, which was death if they were caught. Those with contacts in the city could have friends supply them with a little money at a time. Now, giving up one's money could mean starvation, but trying to hide it was risking torture and execution. Brigade after brigade started marching. When filing past the SS men everyone who had something dropped it into the container. After a brigade marched through, it was stopped by the SS men, who, accompanied by Askaris and the Jewish camp police, checked the inmates' pockets. Those in whose pockets money or documents were found were put aside. Afterward those guilty men had to pull down their trousers and reveal their buttocks. SS men and Askaris beat them with whips with all their strength. Victims yelled in pain. Slowly, these shouts got softer and one could hear shots. It was Rokita himself who was dispatching the victims. This procedure was repeated with all the brigades. The yelling of the victims and the shots finishing them off were heard for over one hour.

Our work in the sand quarry for the Hannebeck enterprise was becoming more and more onerous. At the beginning our *Schachtmeister* was not very nasty to us during work, because he was being paid by inmate Schall, the former director of the Lwów breweries, who was receiving some financial aid from outside. Some two weeks later, the SS men, who were in need of Lwów beer, known for its quality, transferred Schall to the breweries in the city, where he was interned together with his son to help produce beer and provide it to the Germans. Once our *Schachtmeister* was not receiving money from Schall anymore, and there was nobody else to replace Schall in this capacity, he started to torment us.

Despite all this, we tried to keep our faith. On Saturday, September 12, the first day of Jewish New Year, my brigade was kept in the camp for some reason, and was ordered to clean the assembly areas. One of the inmates of our group somehow got the prayer book, *Machzor*, and many of us used this book. We were taking turns hiding in the barrack and praying, while the others took care not to let those praying be caught committing this crime.

Our group was transferred for some time to work at digging sand at a new site, closer to the Jewish cemetery. We worked hard, as much as we could, but this was not enough for some Germans. One of them, dressed half militarily, came from the airfield with the truck on which we loaded the sand we had dug. When he came, he would shout in fury that we worked too slowly. He would take out a broad leather belt and beat the prisoners who—in his opinion—worked too slowly or artlessly.

Those who knew somebody in the camp office, or who had money, tried to get into the brigades working in town-at, for instance, the *Reinigungsamt* (Streetcleaning Office), the *Vereinigte Industriebetriebe* (United Industrial Plants), *Staedtisches Schlachthaus* (the municipal slaughterhouse), and so on. Alas, I had neither money nor acquaintances in the camp office.

CHAPTER 10

JANOWSKA CAMP

Before I pass on to further events, I will describe the camp itself, its physical appearance and living conditions there. All these factors changed over time. The character of the camp varied depending upon the purpose it served in the particular periods of its existence. This variation was due to historical factors that must first be explained.

There were two courses of action those in power in the Third Reich wanted to pursue regarding the Jews. One course was the maximum use and exploitation of Jews as skilled and unskilled labor to meet the needs of the war. This included strictly military purposes and those of a more general economic nature, only indirectly related to the requirements of the German armed forces (the Wehrmacht).

The other course aimed at the absolute extermination of the Jews, as quickly as possible, by murdering them with all the means available, without any scruples. For this the important considerations were speed, accuracy, and limiting German losses. All other considerations, including, for instance, the disappearance of a large reserve of labor, so important and needed during war, were in fact deemed insignificant by the proponents of this second course.

These two directions were largely contradictory. The general opinion was that the Wehrmacht represented the first direction; the SS, the second. This line of division was of course not very sharp and distinct, for there were many advocates of immediate extermination of the Jews in the army, while there were, on the other hand, some proponents of full exploitation of the Jews in the SS. Besides that, such a division did not mean that the army was against killing Jews. The question was which method would give a greater advantage in the short run, during the war. The resultant of these two forces determined the policies of the German authorities with respect to the Jews, and these varied at different periods of the war, based on the relative strengths of the two attitudes.

The policies and tactics used, the balance between the two directions, also differed depending on geographical location. In the west, mindful of the attitudes of the Christian population of the Western countries, the Germans treated the Jews differently than in the east. They were more "humane"—that is, more cautious, more cunning. Aiming at the murder of French, Belgian, Dutch, and other Western European Jews, the Germans would not kill them in their homeland, but used the pretext of sending them to work in the east, in Poland. The Jews were allowed to take their things and were carried in passenger railway cars to Auschwitz and Bełzec, where the mask was put aside and they were murdered just as all the others there were. In November 1942 a transport came to Janowska from Bełzec with the belongings of Western European Jews murdered there. Some camp inmates at that time received clothes with trademarks of French, Belgian, and other Western European firms.

In Germany and in the western territories of Poland, the camps, with all their ruthlessness and killing of Jews, were, for the most part, still labor camps. In the Russian territories different tactics were applied. There, Jews were done away with the moment the German army invaded Russian territory. The region called District Galicia, encompassing southeastern Poland or western Ukraine, was somewhere in the middle. Here, the killing would not take place at once, but gradually, with the application of flexible tactics; there were labor camps and extermination camps, but the labor camps were in a way an introduction, a transition into the camps where extermination followed. That is why ultimately the eastern Galician Jews found themselves in the worst situation.

In the east, Jews who did not get into the German killing machine at once were completely conscious of the existing situation and were trying to save themselves in various ways, either in guerrilla squads or as Aryans (with forged documents). Jews living in the west, although in very difficult conditions, could have some hope that they would live until liberation by the victorious Allies, and some of them survived. Eastern Galician Jews did not follow the footsteps of their eastern brothers, deceiving themselves by thinking that work could save them. The Germans, though, in this region valued *Vernichtung* (liquidation) more than *Arbeit* (labor) and were liquidating not only ghettos but also camps. In fact, a pronouncement by General Governor Hans Frank, the highest authority encompassing central and southeastern Poland, asserted that Galician Jews were the worst, most harmful element for Germany.

When liquidating camps in western Poland and eastern Germany, out of fear of the coming Red Army, the Germans transported Jews from camps located there to the west, deeper into Germany. However, when liquidating camps in eastern Galicia they murdered all the Jews, exceptions not being made even for the best specialists, in some cases indispensable for the German army and enterprises. And that is why there were virtually no eastern Galician Jews in the camps in Germany, besides a few who happened to be in the western territories when taken. In Jewish camps in eastern Galicia there were no older people or children. They were liquidated at once in the years 1941 and 1942. The same, with certain exceptions, applied to Jewish women. The fate of the eastern Galician Jews was the most tragic of the tragic Jewish fates of the war. They lived through the whole gehenna in its worst variety to be then entirely exterminated.

Janowska camp expressed the German policies with regard to eastern Galician Jews. Depending upon which policy, labor or extermination, was ascendant, this camp was either an *Arbeitslager* or a *Vernichtungslager*. Thus, although it was established at the beginning of autumn of 1941 as a labor camp, it became shortly afterward an extermination camp. Things stayed like that until the middle of November 1942. Then the dispute between the Wehrmacht and the SS became sharper. The SS wanted to concentrate all the Jews in their camps so as to be able to exterminate them more easily. The Wehrmacht did not want to give away Jewish workers to the SS camps, knowing that they would quickly perish there. Even if they didn't, the labor value of Jews kept in an SS camp, conscious of the fact that they were bound to die soon, would be minimal.

This dispute ended with a transitory compromise. A small part of the Jews employed by the Wehrmacht, including those working for HKP (*Heereskraftfahrpark*—military truck park) were brought to Janowska camp. The rest were concentrated in the caserns (multistory barracks) of military enterprises and in *Julag* (literally "Jewish camp"), the new name for what was left of the Lwów ghetto after many actions, each of which had shrunk its extent. But Willhaus, the SS commander of the Janowska camp, still tried to encourage the Wehrmacht to give its Jews into his care. To this end, he made efforts to change the external look of the camp, which resulted in a radical turn for the better. He often invited higher Wehrmacht officers to visit the camp (usually, by the way, when the inmates were not there) and would tell incredible stories of how he looked after the—almost luxurious—life of his charges. He would show them a thick soup, specially prepared for this occasion, point out a room in which he said the inmates gathered to play chess, and so forth. In addition, Willhaus significantly softened the camp regime, also—temporarily —treating the privileged HKP workers much better. These had a separate barrack, the best one, special ordners (inmates assigned to clean and maintain the barrack), and individual numbered cots with pallets on them. They could also have their own blankets and covers. When they were ill, they had the right to be in the new camp hospital, especially created at this time in barracks outside the camp along Janowska Street.

The period during which the labor direction more or less dominated over the extermination direction lasted until spring 1943. It was then that the extermination concept took the upper hand and, at Himmler's orders (and, as we heard, also Hitler's), the Wehrmacht had to give up. *Julag*, the last remaining ghetto in eastern Galicia, was emptied and burned down in a final and bloody action in the beginning of June 1943, and its population was killed or sent to Bełzec or Janowska. The caserns containing Jews working for the Wehrmacht were liquidated. Now all Jews were located in the SS camps, and then the last stage of liquidation started, this stage lasting until November 19, 1943. On this day the Jews of Janowska camp were exterminated. From then on eastern Galicia was officially *judenrein* ("cleansed of Jews"), almost nine months before the Soviet army marched in, and one and a half years before the end of the war.

Depending upon the changing character of the camp, its layout changed as well. Before the war, there had been a Jewish-owned factory there, at 132 Janowska Street, making machines for mills. The Soviets nationalized it in 1939, and when the Germans came in 1941 they set up workshops on the site. Jews worked there, some voluntarily and others sent there, but they were free to go home each day; it was just a workplace. The employing institution was DAW, *Deutsche Ausrüstungswerke* (German Armaments Workshops). Rumors had it that this enterprise belonged to Himmler. At the entrance to the workshops the inscription was subtitled with DAW's three sites: Dachau, Auschwitz, and Lemberg (the German name for Lwów). Only good names.

By October 1, 1941, barbed wire and barracks had been set up, and on that date the workers were told that they must stay there from then on. A camp was established, and its name passed from that of DAW to SS *und Polizeiführer Zwangsarbeitslager Lemberg* (SS and Police Chief Forced Labor Camp, Lwów). With time, however, the leaders of the SS decided to make this small forced labor camp of 350 inmates into a true concentration camp. Hence, the area of the camp was broadened significantly westward toward the railway tracks and Kleparów station, which was just beyond the northwest boundary of the city, two to three kilometers from downtown.

When Untersturmführer Willhaus took over the camp, its previous commander, SS Hauptsturmführer Gebauer, who still was in charge of DAW, separated DAW from the camp. DAW remained, however, in close connection with the camp, using the labor of the inmates. Janowska camp continued to change, expanding more and more, for the Germans planned to make it a greater concentration camp—for Poles, Ukrainians, and other nationalities—once the Jews were exterminated. At least that is what the rumors spreading among the local population said.

During the almost eleven months of my stay in the camp, from August 1942 to the following June, its face changed dramatically. I will begin by describing it as it was when I arrived. The camp was located at the end of Janowska Street, from which it took its name, at the crossing of the railway line with the Janów highway at a distance of some two hundred meters from the railway station Lwów–Kleparów. From the northern side the camp area was surrounded by hills whose quite steep slopes were oriented toward the camp, and in front of which was the area called the Sands. From the southern side the camp was bordered by Janowska Street and the railway line going along the bottom of a ravine. To the east there were the barracks and workshops of *Deutsche Ausrüstungswerke*, mentioned before. To the west was a branch line of the railroad. The compass directions mentioned here are approximate, for the camp was aligned with Janowska Street, which did not run exactly east–west but somewhat northwest–southeast.

The camp was surrounded by a double wall of barbed wire mounted on concrete poles, along which electric cables ran. There were double electric lamps every five meters on the poles, of normal and red light, the latter used for air raid warnings. There were four turrets at key points, all guarded by Askaris. They were armed with normal rifles, and sometimes also with machine guns. Besides that there were movable searchlights in the turrets, with which the Askaris could illuminate the camp and its bordering areas at night.

The camp was generally divided into four main parts and a smaller entrance area. The first part was a large external area, let us call it Area 1, which one came to through the entrance area. The internal part of the camp, call it Area 2, into which one entered from Area 1 was where the inmates were virtually all of the time, except when out of the camp at their work sites. Area 3, at the side of DAW and the town, contained

auxilliary buildings such as the laundry and some workshops. Each of
these three areas was separated from the others by a wall of barbed wire.
The fourth part, at one end of Area 1 (to the west, farthest from town),
was a large piece of land on which vegetables were grown.

The road into the camp went through the external gate and continued
straight some fifty to sixty meters, with the camp's exterior barbed-wire
wall on the left. To the right was a compound of small one- and two-story
houses. This was the entrance area. The first of these houses, at the external gate, was a guardhouse, in front of which stood a covered booth where
Askaris and SS men were on duty, always five or six of them. At the other
end, farthest from the gate, was the largest of the buildings. On the
ground floor of this building was the *Aufnahmebüro* (admission office),
where camp newcomers were admitted and registered, and where camp
administration offices were located. These were staffed with Jews, the
highest echelon of inmates, under SS supervision. On the second floor
were two rooms where the incoming prisoners were stripped of their possessions.

In this same building, but on the side away from the road into camp,
was a suite belonging to camp commander Willhaus, and which we
referred to as his villa. He lived there with his wife and daughter on the
upper floor, and had a small balcony facing the interior of the camp. From
there, observing people working in the camp, he occasionally presented
inmates with a round from his submachine gun. His wife, Othelia, also
occasionally fired at us from the balcony.

After the road into the camp had gone past the compound of houses, it
turned right, toward the internal gate, the entrance to Area 2 of the
camp, the camp proper, which only came into view at this point. As one
proceeded to this gate, Area 1 was on the left. This was a large area,
which mainly served as a transitory stage during the various actions. Here,
the selection was made of which incoming victims were to be transported
to the Bełzec gas chambers and which were to stay in the jaws of
Janowska camp.

In addition, this area was also used for penalty courses—that is, harsh
exercises given as punishment to some brigades at different times. Also,
when the prisoners, on their way out to work, entered Area 1, this was
the place where death races were sometimes held, as well as the frequent
inspections of the brigades to pull sick or weak inmates aside for execution. On the outer part of Area 1, where it was adjacent to the railway
line, there stood garages, stables, and various sheds.

Behind the compound of houses in the entrance area, on the side facing Willhaus's villa, was a long and narrow region, Area 3. Besides the

laundry, and workshops such as those of the shoemakers and the tailors, this area contained warehouses and the camp hospital. This small building had a dispensary on the ground floor in which first aid to the inmates could be given. The hospital proper, with only twelve beds (for a camp with over ten thousand inmates!) was on the upper floor.

Between Area 3 and DAW, separated from both by barbed wire, was an additional region attached to but in some sense not a part of Janowska camp. Here there were many small houses, villas, in which the SS men and Askaris lived. Camp inmates never went there, except for the highest elite, which included the office staff, the camp doctor, and the Jewish camp police. These had the privilege of living in some of the villas here. This region also contained canteens for SS men and Askaris.

At the internal gate, just before it and on the right as one entered Area 2, there was a clerk from the office sitting in a booth and accompanied by an SS man. Here, every brigade marching out to work or coming back was registered, and the number of workers was recorded. The brigadier, who received a slip of paper from the booth, gave it to the SS man commanding the external guardhouse to check. When the inmates went out to work, Willhaus or his deputy stood next to the booth with a group of SS men. Behind them was a unit of Askaris, and finally the Jewish camp police. Across from them, to the left as one approached the gate, was one of the four turrets that surrounded the internal Janowska camp. At the foot of the turret stood the camp orchestra, which played every morning as brigades marched out to work. Just next to them was the entrance to the space between the two walls of barbed wire separating Areas 1 and 2, the terrifying "behindwire."

As one passed the internal gate into Area 2, one came into an enormous rectangular space. To the left, behind the (more or less) western double wall of barbed wire, was the second turret, near the path leading from "behindwire" to the Sands. When I arrived in August 1942 the first three quarters of Area 2 was generally empty, with uneven ground and a few trees. Construction was just beginning for new barracks. Past this empty portion was a large building that contained the old barrack, the only place where inmates could seek, often in vain, a place to sleep. This barrack could accommodate at most several hundred prisoners, while there were thousands of inmates in the camp. The western end of the old barrack was occupied by the kitchen, which had four windows facing west through which food was distributed to the inmates. The area behind this building served as the assembly ground, the site of the roll calls.

In front of the kitchen windows, at a distance of thirty paces, a pit was dug out and barriers were posted before it. This was the latrine for the inmates, where they could relieve themselves—under the open sky, next to the kitchen, in the presence of all the other inmates. One could see in this the care the camp authorities took for the health and appetite of their charges. Between the latrine and the kitchen there was a large waste box in which Gebauer once shut and choked to death an inmate caught resting during work.

Near the old barrack and parallel to it, on the side away from the assembly area, there was a trough some three meters long. A pipe that ran from the kitchen poured water into this trough. This was the wash basin for all these thousands of prisoners. That was how the Germans looked after the sanitary state of these workers.

The space between the old barrack and the external northern wall of the camp was, as mentioned above, the assembly area. Close by were gallows, somewhat north from the kitchen. Side by side with the gallows was a double barrier where offenders were attached by legs and hands and left hanging like bullocks for various periods of time. Just next to the kitchen, between it and the gallows, was a pile of beams and stone poles—a platform on which the SS man directing the roll call would stand. From this place different orders and instructions were announced. This was also the place where flogging and other forms of punishment were carried out.

Overlooking the assembly area were the third and fourth turrets. One was near the northwestern corner of Area 2, high on the hill behind the camp. The other was to the northeast, near Area 3 and DAW.

That was how things were when I came. Most of the changes that took place during my stay happened around the time that the HKP workers entered the camp in November 1942. Five new double barracks were built on the western and southern sides of Area 2. The old barrack also had two parts, so barracks were now numbered 1 through 12. Some of these were completed later, in winter and spring 1943, together with an additional barrack to house the brewery workers, including Schall (the former director of the brewery) and his son, when they were moved back into the camp.

Barracks 1 through 12 defined a rectangular open space roughly one hundred meters long and fifty meters wide. This space became the new assembly area, starting at the end of 1942. The ground here had been leveled, and the trees removed.

In the autumn of 1942 a new latrine was built at the same time as the new barracks, behind them, near the second turret. Around the same time a new *Waschraum* (washroom) was constructed near the old barrack. This facility could accommodate as many as fifty persons at a time. This *Waschraum* was the pride of Willhaus, who used to show the place to visiting guests. There were mirrors on the walls, running cold and hot water—it all looked luxurious. Hot water was, however, a rare occurrence in fact. Next to the *Waschraum* a disinfector was constructed that did not function at all. It was there that camp barbers were later located.

Although the most dramatic changes took place in Area 2, other areas also were affected by changing camp policies. Deep in Area 1, barracks were also built; from January to May of 1943, the *Frauenlager* (women's camp) was housed there.

The additions were not all for the benefit of the inmates. In Area 3, in front of his villa, a fountain was constructed for the "Duke of Janów, Sir Willhaus," together with a small garden and a bower. Also, the part of DAW that was adjacent to Janowska Street was closed in by a high wall constructed in the fall of 1942, secured with barbed wire and broken glass over the top. Likewise, in autumn of 1942, the external gate was moved farther out into Janowska Street. The road from the street to the external gate, and some way past it into the camp, was paved with stone slabs, which were gravestones removed from the Jewish cemetery by these Hitlerian barbarians. During quite some time yet one could see Jewish inscriptions when passing over this road.

Like the earlier gate, the new one had a big signboard hanging over it bearing the inscription "SS UND POLIZEIFÜHRER ZWANGSARBEITSLAGER," the official camp name, as was mentioned earlier. The letters were composed of electric bulbs, which, illuminated during the night, gave the impression of an entrance to a circus.

The new external gate looked much more robust than the old one. It was wide. Composed of enormous iron circles and vertical bars, it was hinged on both sides on large rectangular concrete structures, commonly called bunkers. This name was due to the fact that they were hollowed out, with a grille door facing into the camp. It was there that inmates caught in town after escaping; Jewish offenders encountered, for instance, in the Aryan quarter; or those who provided their relatives with food were shut in. The bunkers could accommodate at most two standing persons. People imprisoned in them had to stand all the time, for there was no room to sit. They were often shut in the bunkers naked, even without underwear, thus exposed to cold during day and night. There was usually no return from the bunker. After twenty-four hours, and sometimes after several days, a prisoner was led out to the Sands and executed. The record length for withstanding the torture of the bunker was attained by a brigadier who was caught in the ghetto after he had fled from the camp. He stood fourteen days in the bunker before he was executed. Sometimes Aryans also landed in the bunkers.

One part of the camp that mirrored the various stages of the camp closely was the hospital. The small hospital with twelve beds, in Area 3, might have been adequate before the camp grew to thousands of inmates, but at that point it was not a real hospital anymore. Rather, it was a sick bay from which patients—usually suffering from typhus—were transported after a few days to the hospital in the ghetto, which was done to some extent during the so-called good initial period.

That is how things were at the hospital in the early days; however, once Willhaus came to the camp the situation changed radically. He eventually forbade sending the sick to the hospital outside: "There is no hospital for Jews; they must drop dead," he used to say. Then the sick bay was liquidated, together with the sick there. And many, many times inmates reporting ill during roll calls were directed to the so-called hospital only to be—in most cases—led out behind the barbed wire after two days, to the Sands, to be executed.

When, in November 1942, the camp authorities wanted to persuade the Wehrmacht to give them its remaining Jews, a small camp hospital was created outside of the camp, not far, at Janowska Street as well, in the former city barracks. These had been used before the war for the contagiously ill during epidemics, when the hospitals were overflowing.

Living conditions in the camp were changing dramatically over time. When I got to the camp in August 1942, only the old barrack existed. It consisted of two stories and an attic. The only persons who had the right to sleep in the attic were brigadiers, former ghetto policemen, and a certain group of privileged relatives and friends of theirs. One could sleep there relatively comfortably. Some of these inmates had covers and blankets, some others had electric cookers, on which one could make oneself something warm to drink.

These were not the most luxurious accommodations available to inmates. Even more privileged than this elite were the highest echelons of Jewish prisoners in the camp. Included among these were the musicians, an unusual circumstance that resulted from deputy camp commander Rokita's being a musician and favoring Jews with this background. His friend and colleague in nightclub jazz bands before the war was a Polish Jew named Kampf, from the town of Tarnów. When Kampf arrived in Janowska, Rokita made him *Oberkapo*, or *Oberjude* (head Jew for the entire camp). Kampf had many privileges, including living in separate quarters, namely an apartment in the villas where the SS men lived. Rokita also put those inmates who were musicians into the camp police, which was housed jointly in another of the villas. Also living in these villas were those Jews who worked in the office.

The musicians formed a camp orchestra under the leadership of a well-known violinist and orchestra leader, Leonid Striks. This orchestra played when the other inmates marched off to work in the morning. During the day its members often performed for the SS, especially Willhaus, in the garden by his villa, instead of doing any physical labor.

Other favors were available to musicians, and also to those who had influence with the very powerful office staff. In the group that I arrived at the camp with, two, named Schlichter and Lederman, became co-brigadiers. One of them got his position through influence with the camp office; the other was a well-known conductor of a jazz orchestra and was an acquaintance of Kampf.

As I said, the garret of the old barrack was reserved for the lesser elite. Regular inmates had to spend nights on the ground floor and the second floor. There were bunks on three levels constructed there out of coarse plywood with wooden supports for the prisoners' heads. The inmates jokingly called each bunk level a "floor," so a person on the bottom bunk upstairs was said to be on the fourth "floor." This barrack could, of course, accommodate only some of the inmates. Thus, when prisoners were let into the barrack in the evening (entering the barrack during the day was punished by flogging or even death) there was an indescribable crush at the entrance. Everyone wanted to get a place for himself. Those who were too late to get a place in the bunk beds lay down on the floor or spent their nights sitting wherever they could find some free space. Those who did not find even this would go to sleep under the clear sky in the new barracks under construction. Sometimes inmates would give up the so-called dinner in order to secure for themselves a better place in the line to the entrance of the barrack.

The bunk beds were actually not individual units. Each bunk level was one long continuous layer of planking, with individual places distinguished only by the closely spaced wooden headrests. We would lie side by side like herrings in a barrel, on hard and coarse boards, with lots of dust, mud, and sand from our day's work brought in on our shoes. There was no way to get undressed. Once a week bunk beds were cleaned, and once or twice a week they were sprinkled with stinking calcium chloride. And, of course, there were no covers, blankets, or mattresses, because the camp would not provide them and it was forbidden to bring anything from town. There were no windows in the barrack, no flow of fresh air to relieve the stench. The only light source was the electric lights, and these were kept on at all times.

Later on, in November 1942, after the new barracks had been constructed, housing conditions significantly improved. The new barracks
had bunk beds of smoothed boards, and cleanliness was looked after quite
carefully by the newly nominated ordners. Bunk beds were mounted in
four to five levels, with considerable space between them. They were covered with sacks for pallets. Once the privileged Wehrmacht workers from
HKP arrived, covers and blankets, which the workers had brought with
them on special allowance, appeared. Soon a majority of inmates did the
same, following in their steps. Starting with the HKP Wehrmacht workers,
people began to fill the sacks with straw, and by the beginning of 1943 all
the bunk beds were covered with pallets. The new barracks, like the old
one, were not heated during winter, so that having come back from work
we trembled from the cold until the breathing of the crowd warmed the
room adequately. Aryans, as before, continued to have a separate barrack
that, to the best of my knowledge, was similar to ours. In the old barrack,
we were in separate parts of the same building.

At this point I would like to mention that Aryans constituted not more
than 3 to 5 percent of the roughly ten thousand prisoners of the camp.
Very few of them were political offenders. There were also only a few educated people among them. They were put in the camp on the basis of ver-
dicts for such offenses as nonprovision of the agricultural product levy,
flight from work, drunkenness in work, or theft of German possessions.
Their sentence was one, two, sometimes six months, or even a year. After
that they were let free. Their Jewish companions were getting into the
camp without any verdict and with no term, until their death. For purposes of distinguishing the Jewish prisoners from the Aryan ones, Jews had
attached to their shirts at the breast level, on the left side, yellow rag triangles; the Poles had red triangles; Ukrainians had blue; and *Volksdeutsche*
had white. *Volksdeutsch* was a term commonly used by Germans in the
Nazi era for a person of German national origin who was a citizen of
another country. Many Poles with German names declared themselves to
be *Volksdeutsch* to obtain special privileges. This was encouraged by the
German authorities. During my stay in the camp there were perhaps two
Volksdeutsche there. All camp inmates also had to carry the *Hundemarke*
(dog tag) around their necks. Mine was numbered 1455, and it is now in
Yad Vashem in Jerusalem.

The Aryans lived separately, but they ate from the same kitchen as we
did, and they had the same work, with all the harassment, whipping, kicking, and what we inmates called "vitamins": occasional additional severe
forced labor (called vitamins because they were "supplemental nutri-
tion"). They did not starve, though, as we did, for it was easier for them to

get aid from home than for us; in addition, they were getting food once or twice a week from the Polish or Ukrainian committee for the care of prisoners. Both these committees had access to the camp. The Jewish committee had no access to the camp. Aryans were punished in the camp with flogging, almost never with death, while Jews were shot for the smallest offenses. Besides that, Aryans were sent to the hospital when sick, while Jews, when sick, were shot. The Aryans did not take part in the "death races," in the selection to Bełzec, and so on.

I must note with sorrow that the distinction into Aryans and Jews was not only formal, forced upon us from above. The Aryans also separated themselves from us spontaneously. They did not feel any unity with us in this misery. It was exceptional to see their expressions of compassion and pity. Rather, the cases of harassing Jewish co-prisoners, or even beating them, were more frequent. The position of Jews who worked in brigades with an Aryan majority was not at all to be envied.

Inmates received three meals a day. In the morning there was only bitter black ersatz coffee; for lunch, watery, unsalted soup. Until October 1942 it was, in principle, unsalted water smelling of soup, in which, at the bottom of the pot, one could sometimes see a pair of grit grains or a cabbage leaf. Thick soup was eaten only by the clerks from the office, brigadiers, camp police, and people known to the cooks. This water was the whole of lunch. For dinner prisoners obtained one piece of bread weighing 120 grams (4½ ounces) and, again, bitter black ersatz coffee. Every second night two pieces of bread were given for dinner. From time to time dinner was complemented with the lunch soup, even more diluted or with the muddy sauce of boiled rotten potatoes in their skin, the latter usually causing vomiting. Once a week we would get a spoonful of butter-honey or of beet marmalade.

From October 1942 the soups became thicker—they contained turnips and barley grit. Sometimes we would get old, moldy cheese (called *kwargle*) instead of marmalade. That is how the Germans fed people working hard from dawn until night, and quite often also during night at the so-called vitamins. Consequently, those who were not secretly receiving food aid from outside died within more or less four weeks. After one to two weeks the legs would start to swell, both because of general undernourishment and lack of proteins in the food. Hunger made people going out to work jump like wild animals at the waste heap, looking there for food refuse, rotten cabbage leaves, and the like. As a result of this, inmates quickly developed diarrhea. This occurred more and more frequently. Finally, the starving victim would move his bowels involuntarily—during work, on the bed, or when marching. Stinking trousers and a dreadful smell gave away the misfortunate one at work or while marching. His face darkened and ultimately either the victim would break down at work or would be sent to "behindwire" to be executed.

The brigade in which I worked in August and September of 1942 began with 102 persons; after six weeks there were only seven of us left. The others had died from execution or from hunger. Only very few (around 5 percent) succeeded in fleeing the camp. Then, of the brigade in which I worked starting in late September 1942, originally composed of 150 persons, there remained some twenty-five after just four weeks.

Many persons had fallen victim in the night, when they were going to the latrine to satisfy their physiological needs. These latrines were much used at night, because of frequent diarrhea attacks, even more frequent urinations due to the consumption of increased volumes of liquid, and the stress due to living in constant nervous tension. This was taken advantage of by the SS men and the Askaris on duty in the turrets, who made games for themselves using the inmates visiting the latrines. Askaris were shooting out of boredom, for fun. The SS men would hide behind barracks and unexpectedly attack the victim, beating him with a whip on the head until he fell down on the ground in a pool of blood. If the victim did not die, he would be taken the very next morning out of his row at the selection as a cripple and sent "behindwire" to be executed. All these were unofficial, private activities. Besides that, however, from time to time, for completely unknown causes, leaving one's barrack during the night was totally forbidden or was allowed only in groups, accompanied by an ordner. Consequently, those in need, not wanting to risk their lives, urinated under themselves, showering those sleeping under them with warm urine. And so, for instance, in August and September of 1942, when I slept in the old barrack, frequently on the fifth "floor," I was almost regularly showered by an inhabitant of the sixth "floor." Many inmates, not seeing any other way out, used the metal bowls or cans from which they were eating or drinking coffee during the day, therefore turning them into chamber pots during the night. These chamber pots, though, were often kicked by the sleepers, pouring urine on their fellow prisoners on the lower "floors."

Life in the camp was an indescribable hell on earth. I often pinched my thighs during the night, not believing that all this was not a monstrous dream, that it was a reality. At night, having luckily found a place on the bunk, I would lie on coarse, dirty boards, amid all the other prisoners, without the possibility of undressing, for there was no place for clothes. Even if someone tried to undress, at least partially, then he would find out after waking up that his shoes or something else had disappeared.

Desperate inmates, who did not have any aid from outside, were stealing what they could during the night.

It turned out that one could pay with one's own life for lack of shoes. One day during roll call, I saw a prisoner of some forty years of age who was lamenting in distress over the fact that his shoes had been stolen in the night. He was running barefoot among the rows desperately asking for help. An SS man noticed this.

"What's going on?" he asked. The poor fellow, surprised, showed him that he had no shoes.

"Oh, pity," said the SS man with pretended compassion. "Come here. I will help you." He conducted the prisoner to the center of the assembly ground and with a shot in the neck killed him on the spot.

Theft was a pervasive problem, and it affected me as well. One day I was happy because I had gotten half a loaf of bread in a haversack sent illegally to me by my parents through a prisoner working in town. I kept this bread as the greatest treasure. At night, not wanting it stolen, I lay almost fully on the haversack. When I woke up the bread and the haversack had disappeared.

The day started early. Even before dawn, often just after four A.M., SS men and brigadiers would storm into the barrack shouting, "Get up! Get up! Go!" One had to quickly get out of bed and run to the assembly ground. Those who did not do it quickly enough were beaten with whips as much as possible. We stood in the assembly area for hours, trembling from cold, before the roll call began. During the roll call we were drilled, "*Mützen ab! Mützen an!* [Caps off! Caps on!]"—many, many times. Then every brigade was counted. The cadavers of those who had been killed the previous day, had died at work, or had committed suicide by taking cyanide, were put at the side of the corresponding brigade so as to have the number of members of a given brigade correct from day to day. When the number from the previous day was not the same as at the roll call of the current day in a particular brigade, an SS man would menacingly nod and note down the fact.

The counting of all these many brigades lasted almost one hour. Then the commander of the camp, Willhaus, or one of his deputies, came and the punishments started. Surrounded by a group of SS men, he pulled prisoners out of those brigades from which some people had escaped the previous day during work, taking two to five inmates for every escapee. He was also accompanied by Dr. Rapaport, the head doctor of the camp, who helped him choose inmates who appeared sick or medically unfit. He went from one row to another, slowly and carefully looking at individual prisoners and, according to his whims, pointed with his finger at the next victim. "*Raus!*" sounded the command. With whips and rifle butts the man was driven to the center of the assembly area, where he received the *Gnadenschuss* in his neck. People were falling down in a line, side by side. Incidentally, it always surprised me that the victim, although shot in the neck from behind, did not fall forward, but invariably backward, face up. I have no explanation for this.

This slow and lengthy review of rows with selection of victims induced maximum tension and fear, especially when the pack of SS men was approaching one's own brigade. This procedure, though, was usually not enough to frighten prisoners out of escaping, so the number of executions per escapee increased as time went on.

After the executions new niceties awaited us. Prisoners were called out of the rows if they had been informed on for having worked inadequately or evading work or being guilty of some other offense. They received floggings, just like the ones I saw on my first day in camp. In the first months, these occurred at most roll calls, but after November 1942 they were rare.

These nerve-racking roll calls lasted approximately two hours in all, including the drills, the counting, the executions, and the floggings. They took place often two times a day, in the morning and in the evening, during the first months of my stay in the camp. During the roll call the commanding SS man asked whether any inmates felt ill; if so, they should report this immediately. Those who went up were unaware that going to the small camp hospital was but a brief prelude to execution. After the roll call the brigades marched slowly out to work, and as they passed through the inner gate each brigade was again very accurately counted as to the number of inmates.

CHAPTER 11

TYPHUS AND SURVIVAL

I tried as much as possible to be with Józek and with my father-in-law. These were the two people close to me who were in Janowska. Of course, there could have been other relatives or friends of mine there as well. The number of inmates in Janowska camp varied between ten and fifteen thousand. In such a large group it was entirely possible for two people who cared deeply about each other to not know about each other's being there.

Józek and I were in different brigades, so for much of the day we could not see each other. At night his brigade, DAW, had a separate sleeping arrangement, so we could not be together then either. However, when we returned to camp at the end of the day, during the "dinner" time, we could seek each other out. Since the brigades came back at various times, and sometimes quite late, we only were able to have some time together every other day, on average. We eagerly looked forward to these moments. I especially felt that I could help him, give him encouragement and support.

My father-in-law was also in a different brigade, but we were together every night. Although brigades generally slept together, this was for most brigades an informal arrangement, not a requirement. Maurycy and I slept in adjoining places on the fifth bunk level in the barrack. Whoever got there first would save a spot for the other.

When my brigade was temporarily sent to work in the sand quarry that was farther from camp and much closer to the Jewish cemetery, I relayed this information to my family through an inmate working in the vicinity of the ghetto. This was an opportunity for one of them to take a chance to contact me by pretending to visit the grave of a relative.

One day my mother appeared there, standing on the side with a food parcel for me and for my brother. This was my first meeting with my beloved mother since the time of my arrest and detention in Janowska camp, and it was a joyful surprise. She looked pale, undernourished, and sad, but I was moved to see how stoically she seemed to be bearing all the hardships and heartbreaks she had to suffer. Our meeting was brief and furtive, however, for both of us risked beating or worse if we were seen talking to each other. On this day I did not feel very well; I had a light fever and symptoms of a cold. My mother noticed this at once and was very concerned. I comforted her by saying that this was only a common cold and that it would pass over quickly. I kissed her hand as she left, and hid the package in my haversack.

It turned out, though, that it was not a common cold. I constantly felt that I had a fever and was weak, but I tried to somehow fight back this sickness. The next day my group was transferred to the airfield to work, as usual, for the firm of Hannebeck. The German supervisors of this firm ruthlessly bullied the prisoners, showering them with curses and insults, like *Schweine Jude* (Jewish pig) and the like. Our group had to collect boulders and throw them into carts being rolled on trolleys. We tried, of course, to spare ourselves and to carry smaller stones. The Germans who were supervising us, though, made us carry large boulders. One of these Germans picked me out especially. He boiled with fury, ordering me to carry the largest boulders. I still had some fever, and was weakened, feeling that I did not have the strength to lift these stones and carry them to the carts. The German took his pistol and, aiming it in my direction, looked to see whether I had fulfilled his orders. With desperate last efforts I lifted these great boulders and transported them to the carts. The German, with his gun in his hand, observed me constantly. My strength withered away; I thought I would soon fall down exhausted. Luckily for me, soon our work time was over and we were brought back to the camp. It was Saturday, September 19, 1942. I was convinced that another day of such work in the airfield would be the last day of my life.

On the following day, September 20—Erev Yom Kippur was on that day—deputy commander Rokita was at the Sunday noon roll call in place of Commander Willhaus. (On Sundays the inmates stayed and worked in the camp, since the various industries were closed that day.) Rokita murdered by his own hands more Jewish inmates than Willhaus did—at least during my stay there—but while Willhaus did not care at all for the sanitary state of the camp, food, or clothing of the inmates, Rokita liked *Ordnung* (order). He liked to drop into the kitchen, to see whether the inmates regularly got their soup, and he would kill on the spot those who were pushing their way through, skipping the line to the kitchen window. For *Ordnung* must be!

On some other occasion he would express his dissatisfaction with the fact that inmates were wearing rags and direct us to the *Wäscherei* (laundry), where we were given assorted clothes of doubtful quality but, still, better than the ones we had been wearing. These clothes came from the victims of the actions conducted by the SS men in provincial areas.

Thus, on this day, Sunday, September 20, during the absence of Willhaus, Rokita ordered doctors, ex-ghetto policemen, and barbers to step out of the rows. He assigned one medical doctor, one policeman—as *Vorarbeiter* or foreman (assistant to the brigadier)—and one barber to each brigade. Their duty was to take care of the health and appearance of the brigade.

I was assigned as a doctor to the Ostbahnhof (east railway station) brigade for the next day's work. It was a true miracle from heaven. On the very day of Yom Kippur! For one thing, going to work several kilometers from the camp, at Ostbahnhof, I would have the opportunity to communicate with my family still in the ghetto. But—most important—as a doctor I would not have to do physical work, which, given my health condition and the work of carrying heavy boulders, I would probably not have been able to withstand for a single day. This was simply a miracle.

My joy, alas, was short-lived. In the afternoon my fever went up and in the evening it was already 42° Celsius (108° Fahrenheit) and I had diarrhea. During the night I was lying half conscious on my bunk bed. As if through a haze I heard fellow inmates praying on their bunks, under their breath, crying the *Kol Nidre*. Half asleep, I was delirious. Besides fever, the fear—or, rather, the certainty—that I would be killed the next day did not let me sleep.

In addition, from time to time I had to climb down from my bunk on the fifth "floor" and run to the latrine because of my diarrhea. On the way to the door I had to make my way among the inmates lying or sitting on the floor because of the lack of room on the bunks. One could also see excrement next to some of them, for those in need were afraid to go out to the latrine. As I was coming back from one of my trips to the latrine, I understood why they were afraid. Two SS men, Blum and Schubert, had invented a night game for themselves. They were hiding behind the barrack and when someone went out, they jumped upon him with no warning and beat the victim until he fell in a pool of blood on the ground and

did not move anymore. Then they would go away, hide again, and wait for
a new victim. I had to wait for a proper moment to go back to the barrack. When I returned, I stayed there, lying on my bunk, half asleep, with
high fever and fearing what would now happen to me.

Suddenly a terrible shriek: *"Raus! Raus!"* Roll call! Everybody jumped
up and ran into the assembly area to stand there in rows, by brigades. I
went down from my bunk bed and tried to reach the assembly ground.
I had to stop in front of the barrack. Terrible dizziness and weakness. I
could not move. I could not make a step, my legs were as if paralyzed. Roll
call! Roll call! I heard the voices of brigadiers. From the direction of
Willhaus's villa a submachine gun sounded. Warning shots. It was
Willhaus or one of his deputies, approaching the assembly ground. And
me, I was utterly desperate. I could not move. I was paralyzed. If any of
those rulers of ours had seen me in this state outside of the assembly area,
I had no doubt that he would have beaten me to death, and, to finish me
off, shot me like a dog. O Lord! I looked imploringly up to the sky. O
Lord! Save me. O Lord! Help me. I tried to take a step and all of a sudden
I could, very slowly, move. I was still in deadly fear, not knowing whether I
would be in time to be with my brigade in the assembly ground before
the commanding SS man arrived. With my last effort I reached my
Ostbahnhof brigade and, out of exhaustion, I sat on the ground.

"Have you gone crazy?" my brigadier shouted at me. "Please get up at
once!" I got up, but my legs bent under me. This roll call lasted, luckily, a
short time, and the march out to work started. It was my first day of working as a doctor with my brigade. I was wearing a red arm band on my left
arm as the sign for my employers that I was a medical doctor. I was told
not to wear it when I came back to the camp, however, because Willhaus
would not confirm Rokita's decision to assign doctors and others to special status in the brigades. He was said to have explained, "Doctors or not
doctors, all Jews are trash and dung."

We marched to the east railway station very slowly, in order to spare
strength. I was barely dragging myself on, often falling behind my brigade.
The brigadier was furious, asking me, "What's going on with you?" I
answered that I had caught a cold.

When we came to our place of work, the chief of works in the station,
a Ukrainian, accepted without enthusiasm the information transmitted by
myself and the brigadier that I was the brigade doctor. Not being obliged
to physical labor and not having patients at that moment, I looked for a
place where I could hide and rest. I had a high fever. Still about 42°
Celsius. I looked around. A lot of locomotives, numerous Polish and
Ukrainian workers, and supervisors from the *Ostbahnpolizei* (eastern rail-

way police), who observed the working men. Large banners with inscriptions reading, "RÄDER MÜSSEN ROLLEN FÜR DEN SIEG [Wheels must roll for victory]," reminded everybody that they should work with zeal for the Sieg and for the Führer. These watchwords evidently did not convince me. I found a large tree somewhere nearby and, exhausted, I sat at its foot. Tired, I fell asleep.

Suddenly a strong kick in my breast woke me up. There was a German standing in front of me in the *Ostbahnpolizei* uniform and shouting at me. He tried again to kick me with his boot. I sprang up quickly and ran to the WC. It was quite a large lavatory for the workers. I hid in one of the booths and locked myself in. Polish and Ukrainian workers were going in and out, relieving themselves. They noticed, however, that one of the booths was constantly occupied. One of them remarked, "There must be a Jew inside. There must be a Jew sitting in there." Somewhere they found a rubber hose leading from the water supply and directed a strong jet of water into my booth. They chased me out and laughed heartily at their achievement. When marching back to the camp I was going groggily, dragging myself with great effort behind my brigade. I felt that these were the last hours of my life, that SS men would dispatch me as a sick prisoner.

I had already said good-bye to the world in my thoughts; I said farewell to my family, to those still alive. When we were marching through Janowska Street to the camp, a group of Jewish women was going in the opposite direction from their work in the *Wäscherei* in the camp, back to the ghetto. I saw as if through a haze my cousins Teresia and Nusia, who came up to me, marching, and—wishing me a Happy New Year—pushed a piece of cake into my hand. I had tears in my eyes.

In this desperate and hopeless situation someone dear to me wished me a Happy New Year. I was deeply moved and something heartened up in me. I looked at the cake given to me, a cake of white flour, stuffed with fruits. I had not seen something like this for so long, so long . . .

Having come back to the camp I went to the dispensary. The doctor who worked there, known to me from the University Clinic, gave his diagnosis—typhus. My legs bent at this piece of news. This was a death sentence. I would in no way get to the hospital in the ghetto, for I knew well that Willhaus's motto was "No hospital for Jews; they must drop dead."

What to do? What to do? My doctor friend told me that he could admit me to the camp hospital, located above the dispensary, which then had twelve beds. There were at that time more than ten thousand prisoners in the camp. But every few days SS men would come storming into the hospital and pull out the sick to be executed in the Sands. There was no other way out but to go to work every day; perhaps I would manage somehow and make it past the daily check during the march out to work; perhaps my body could withstand and I would fight back this dangerous sickness. Perhaps? Perhaps?

The only help he could extend to me was an injection of caffeine and strychnine for strenghtening my heart and blood circulation. He told me to come to the dispensary in the evening after returning from work and, if possible, also before the roll call. If I became unable to walk by myself, and Willhaus's substitute, Scharführer Kolonko, was at roll call in place of Willhaus, then I could report sick to the hospital and wait for a miracle. (Scharführer was an SS rank roughly equivalent to sergeant. We inmates used this title in addressing all SS men at the camp other than the higher-ranking commander and his deputy, however. We didn't know the ranks of each individual and erred on the safe side.)

Typhus took thousands of victims in the ghetto, and even more so in Janowska camp. This was caused by the terrible sanitary conditions and the impossibility of isolating the sick from the healthy in the crowded human mass of the camp. Spread through lice, this disease was endemic in the camp. It could not be fought back in these horrendous, indescribable hygienic conditions; lice could not be eradicated, prisoners could not wash themselves well (except for the rare trips to the city bathhouse), and, of course, we could not change underwear.

Many of us tried to preserve personal cleanliness and avoid contact with others as much as was possible. This, however, did not help in any case, neither the other inmates nor me.

In the winter of 1941–1942, Willhaus's predecessor, Hauptsturmführer Gebauer, had invented a novel and radical method of dealing with typhus. On a frosty day he ordered prisoners to undress completely and kept them like that during the whole night out in the assembly square under the frosty sky. Numerous inmates got pneumonia then and died.

In the first half of 1942 the director of the hospital in the ghetto, Dr. Kurzrock, used his influence to convince the authorities of Janowska camp to transfer inmates suffering from typhus to the ghetto hospital, to the specially established ward for contagious diseases. It was located at Zamarstymowska Street. Many sick prisoners had their lives saved there, and sometimes, due to a lucky incidence, those who were cured avoided the return to the camp due to efforts of the same Dr. Kurzrock.

After the August 1942 action the sick inmates were no longer allowed to go to the hospital in the ghetto. Even then, Dr. Kurzrock was occasionally able to help. He came a few times to the camp with his hospital personnel, treated as many inmates as he could in the limited time he was given, and also used this opportunity to provide some medical supplies to those inmates who were doctors. Other than this, however, the usual treatment for sick prisoners now was being put "behindwire" to be shot in the Sands after the roll call.

Such a fate awaited me also if I reported sick or if the SS men noticed that I was unwell. I tried with all my strength to keep up, and, with fever remaining at around 42° Celsius, I dragged along to work, trying not to be left behind when marching either to or from work. I was regularly getting injections of caffeine with strychnine every day.

My mother, when she learned of my route from the camp to Ost-bahnhof, would stand on the side almost every day, together with other families of prisoners, as we passed to work. Risking her life—or at least a beating—she tried to sneak some food parcels for me and for my brother, Józek, as well as medicine I had asked for in the letters I had smuggled from the camp—for example, digitalis, needed for strengthening my heart.

After a few days, cerebral complications accompanied my sickness. Besides dizziness and a strong humming in my ears, I had temporary deafness and an inability to read—alexia. I could not read a letter smuggled from my parents—I saw characters, but I could not understand their meaning. And then came apraxia—I wanted to write a letter to my parents, but I could not write. My hand was simply incapable of writing what I wanted. I also lost appetite, which—with our starvation diet—was simply unheard of.

When Józek and I were talking one evening, he grew increasingly upset that I wasn't hearing him properly. "What's the matter with you, are you deaf?" he asked me. When I explained to him that the typhus was affecting my hearing nerve, among others, he apologized. He knew that I had typhus, and was very anxious about me, but hadn't realized that it would cause hearing problems.

Day after day dragged on, my fever was still very high, and my physical strength was withering away, but my inner strength was supporting me in my struggle for life. I was constantly in fear, especially during morning roll calls and during selection at the march out to work. When going from the camp to work I would pray fervently, imploring God not to let me be dragged to "behindwire" and to keep me from breaking down suddenly during work or during the march out to work, which would have been my death. In my prayers I begged for God's help.

During the first week of my sickness, upon returning from work one day, we were called to assemble in the evening and were told that we would be conducted to the public baths in town. Fear overtook the whole camp. The bathhouse meant death for many. The camp did not have its own bathhouse, so once every few weeks we were led out to the public baths at Szpitalna Street, next to the ghetto, a few kilometers from the camp.

A cordon of Ukrainian police closed the streets—Janowska, Kazimierzowska, Karna, and Szpitalna—that led to the baths. Prisoners were driven with whips, *im Laufschritt*—that is, running—through the middle of the streets, while SS men and Askaris surrounded us, beating us with whips, and shouting, "*Schneller, schneller* [Quicker, quicker]." Whoever did not have the strength to run quickly enough was knocked down on the ground with whips and rifle butts.

I was in despair. I knew that with my typhus, with the high temperature I had, and being physically weakened, I would not be able to run through the streets, and this would be my end. In my despair I ran to the dispensary and pleaded with the head doctor of the camp, Dr. Rapaport, to allow me to hide there, since all the barracks were being meticulously emptied and shut by the ordners.

Whoever tried to wriggle out of this bathing procedure was shot on the spot by the SS men. Dr. Rapaport was unyielding—he did not even want to speak to me, but I saw how he talked in a low voice to two young men about something and I was certain that, in exchange for large sums of money paid to him, he offered them refuge in one of the rooms of the dispensary.

I asked again and, almost kneeling, I begged Dr. Rapaport, but he was simply merciless. When he left I got under the bed, thinking that perhaps this might work. After a while Dr. Rapaport came back, found me under the bed, and shrieked, "Get yourself out of here at once!"

I implored him to let me stay, for I would certainly die on the way to the baths, being sick with typhus, and if some SS men found me hiding, I would take the whole blame upon myself and say that I had done it without his knowledge.

He went out, impassive, and came back a moment later with my brigadier, who ordered me to immediately report to my brigade, in my place in the row. Despairing, I had to obey this order. I was convinced that I was heading for certain death.

Brigade after brigade started marching out and then running down Janowska Street. I was muddled, but I ran. As if in a haze, I saw my fellow prisoners running side by side with me, the cordon of Ukrainian police, and the SS men and Askaris, who were shouting, "*Schneller, schneller.*" I could hear the yelling of victims, beaten to unconsciousness—those who could not run adequately "*schnell.*" I ran as if in a waking dream. I survived as far as Karna Street, next to the building housing the Brygidki prison. The SS men ordered us to sit down in the middle of the street,

keeping the brigades in order. SS Untersturmführer Rokita, who supervised the whole expedition, from time to time came out from the baths,
where he was taking care that everything was "in *Ordnung*." On one such
occasion, he noticed that not all the inmates were sitting on the road in a
row, which made him shoot a series of shots from his submachine gun in
our direction.

Sitting in the street lasted for hours. We suffered from cold through the
whole night. The baths were not big. There were about ten thousand prisoners, and so we moved forward very slowly. The SS men who were
watching us searched for some entertainment, so as not to get bored. At
one point, I saw on the upper part of the wall of a building opposite the
prison, in a circle of light, the shadow of a man who seemed to be doing
knee bends. It was hard to believe that someone was performing calis-
thenics in the prison so late at night. After a while this riddle was
explained. Coming nearer and nearer I heard the voice of an SS man saying, "*Eins, zwei* [One, two]. *Eins, zwei*." A moment later I recognized the
approaching profile of SS man Brumbauer. With his rifle hanging from his
arm he would approach a group of us and ask a chosen man, "*Kalt?*
[Cold?] *Kalt?*" And if the inmate responded affirmatively, he ordered the
man to stand up and perform knee bends—"*Eins, zwei*"—until the man
was sick and exhausted. Brumbauer illuminated the exercising man with
his flashlight, which was what produced the image I had seen on the wall
opposite Brygidki.

Late in the night we reached the baths. When we entered the facility, a
terrible sight came into view. Along the wall bodies of prisoners were
lying, killed by Rokita in his frequent fits of fury. He required everything
to go smoothly, in order, and quickly. Inmates entering the baths had to
undress quickly, give their clothes and underwear away to the Poles and
Ukrainians working in the baths, take a quick bath and a hot shower, take
back their clothes and undergarments, quickly dress, and go out into the
street to their row. The people working in the baths were taking advantage of the situation. They kept the clothes and underwear of better quality to sell on the black market and gave the prisoners rags instead. When a
cheated prisoner demanded his good clothes be returned, he would get a
blow on his head or hands with a wooden shovel and an order to move
on. When Rokita noticed any commotion, he came running at once and
killed the prisoner with his pistol for causing a disturbance in the *Ordnung*.

Those who passed through the baths were allowed to approach a table
prepared by the ghetto's Jewish Committee for helping the prisoners of
Janowska camp. They provided baked rolls and bread that were distributed among the prisoners. Then we had to go out in a hurry to join the

ranks in the street. We had to stand like this for a long time before we were ordered to march back to the camp. It was cold in the streets, and our bodies, not wiped dry after the hot bath, were steaming.

When we came back to the camp, there was not much time left for sleeping, for we soon had to get up for the morning roll call. The consequence of the visit to the bath was a significant number of dead and beaten prisoners, and also a significant number of those who, instead of their more or less decent clothes, had received rags and underwear in which there were more lice than before the bath.

My brother had had clean underwear before the bath, received illegally from the ghetto, and was given different underwear in the baths, underwear in which lice were moving. He threw it away and remained without any underwear at all.

I survived this escapade to the baths by a miracle. After two weeks, in early October, the desired climax of my typhus's course suddenly came. My fever decreased, the humming in my ears started to cease, and the cerebral symptoms receded. Only a strong physical exhaustion was left. This could not have been possible during peaceful times—to survive typhus with a high fever while still walking!

After my recovery from typhus, I decided not to stay in the horrible barrack anymore. The construction of the new barracks had progressed to the point where there was some shelter to be had there. I began spending my nights, as others also did, on the construction sites, under either a clear sky or the overhang of the roofs. Cold as it was, it was much cleaner and better for the soul. I have no idea why, but we were also much less subject to SS harassment there than in the old barrack.

New transports of people were still coming to the camp—people brought from the incessant actions conducted in the provincial towns of Przemyśl, Sambor, Stanisławów, Stryj, Tarnopol, Buczacz, Monasterzyska, and the like. People brought to the camp were selected by the SS men, who kept some of them in the camp and directed a vast majority of them to the transports going from Kleparów railway station to the gas chambers in Bełzec. Women, irrespective of their health, appearance, or profession; children; and men over forty-five were automatically sent to Bełzec. In order to accelerate this process of extermination, Willhaus simultaneously performed selection procedures in the camp every few weeks, and joined those whom he had selected with those transported to Bełzec. The death mill of Janowska camp and Bełzec worked nonstop with German accuracy. Everything went according to Hitler's plan for the extermination of the Jews.

While in the first selections only the weak and sick were taken out to die, less account was made thereafter of the health and appearance of a prisoner. Sometimes healthy and strong prisoners were also pulled out of the ranks so as to have the numbers of the murdered be according to the plan. And typhus was spreading ever more in the camp. Almost no one succeeded in avoiding this dreadful sickness. As I mentioned before, the Germans found only one method of dealing with this disease—shooting.

My Ostbahnhof brigade became smaller and smaller. Prisoners either died or were executed in the Sands, while some succeeded in fleeing the camp. One day, when we were marching back to the camp from Ostbahnhof after work, our Askari escort noticed that two of us were missing. He became furious, banging his rifle butt to the left and right under any pretext, because he knew that he was responsible for the integrity of our group. When we came to the camp he immediately reported to the SS men that two from our group had escaped. We were soon informed that there would be a general camp roll call and an execution would take place. At that roll call our group got the place of honor, in the first row. Two from our group were picked to be hanged. Two other inmates were chosen as well, to help in the hanging; they were to place under and then to pull away the box on which the executed men stood.

This was the desired opportunity for SS man Fox, whose specialty was hanging. Fox, said to be a *Volksdeutscher* from Silesia, relished the procedure of hanging. When somebody was to be executed this way, he would storm into consecutive barracks shouting in a mix of German and broken Polish, "*Raus! Raus! Chodźcie! Chodźcie! Będziemy wieszać żydków* [Get out! Get out! We shall be hanging kikes]." He personally took part in the hanging, and when the hanged prisoner still twitched, Fox would squeeze his throat, delighting in choking his victim. He was in a kind of frenzy.

As I mentioned already, the number of prisoners in the Ostbahnhof brigade decreased quickly—after four weeks, of the initial 150 there were only twenty-five of us left. Around mid-October the brigade was dissolved, and the rest of the inmates were assigned to various other brigades. I was assigned to Thomas enterprises on the airfield; as it turned out, I was there only one day. Unlike my time at Ostbahnhof, where I worked as a doctor, at Thomas I did physical labor, similar to what I had done at Hannebeck. But although the work was as hard, there was no tormenting of the prisoners as there had been in Hannebeck.

Two scenes from that day stuck in my memory. One was the sight of a young boy, who, after being flogged in the camp by SS men, had bleeding buttocks from which blood or serum trickled. These injuries had been covered with paper, and the poor boy was still crying from pain. The second scene involved a Polish woman working in the firm. She was bringing out a bucket with potato peels to throw them in a waste container. She was quickly surrounded by camp inmates asking her for the peels. I was among them. When I stretched my hand out for some peels, bitterness overtook me. I felt so humiliated that tears appeared in my eyes. I thought, O Lord, what have I lived to see?

On the next day a new brigade was formed, a second one, for the *Heereskraftpark* (HKP), and I was reassigned to this group. We worked in the military caserns of the HKP at Pieracki Street. My work with the HKP was much easier than in the previous brigades—I again worked as a doctor, although half legally. What's more, while my status as a doctor at Ostbahnhof had been barely tolerated and had not spared me harassment, here I was accepted as a doctor. It was very important that we were surrounded by the German military and not by the SS, or similar scoundrels like those at Hannebeck or other such work sites. These soldiers from HKP did not in principle torment prisoners.

At the beginning I had to be with my fellow prisoners out on the work site under the clear sky, often feeling cold during cooler days. Later I succeeded in getting permission to sit in the room meant for HKP doctors. It was a tremendous help for my survival that I was a doctor, for I was spared physical labor and had a warm room to be in. I also took satisfaction in being able to help people somewhat in this awful time.

Unfortunately, I was not able to help my father-in-law. In October he also came down with typhus. Being older, he was more in danger, and my efforts to save him with the limited tools available were not succeeding. One day, Dr. Kurzrock came to the camp on one of his rare visits when he was allowed to treat inmates and take patients to his hospital. I ran to him and begged him to include my father-in-law. He knew me well, and was glad to agree, but my father-in-law was nowhere to be seen. Dr. Kurzrock waited as long as he could, but finally he had to leave.

Fifteen minutes later, my father-in-law's brigade came into camp. I asked him why he was so late, and told him how close he had come to getting real help. "What can I do?" he said. "It wasn't my fault. Anyway, I am dying. Please, take my boots." These boots were of very high quality, and I needed boots, but I simply could not do this. I felt it would be like being a hyena to take them. He again urged me, "Please, take them. Somebody else will take them, anyway, if you don't." I thanked him, but repeated that I could not do this. That night, October 20, 1942, he died.

One day shortly afterward, news went through the camp that the commander-in-chief of the SS and German police for the District of Galicia, General Katzmann, would come to visit the camp. Katzmann's visits to the camp always meant the death of many inmates. Normally he would not enter the internal part of the camp. His black limousine stopped in front of Willhaus's villa, where he conferred for a brief time with our ruler. After his visits major selections followed and many paid with their lives.

On that day, however, he was to review the inmates personally. All barracks were emptied and were watched by ordners while the inmates were arranged in brigades, standing on the new assembly square. They stood for hours until finally Katzmann's black limousine appeared. After having been greeted by Willhaus, General Katzmann, together with his whole SS pageant, went on to the internal square of the camp. He was short, with a pockmarked face, a pale typical face of a murderer. He walked slowly from row to row looking carefully at the inmates. Those to whom he pointed with his finger were dragged out of the ranks by the SS men. I was glad that I was in the HKP brigade, for we felt somewhat safer since we worked for the Wehrmacht; and indeed, our two brigades were virtually untouched. After a long review General Katzmann drove away. Prisoners chosen by Katzmann were conducted to a large shed next to the old barrack. On the same night they were all led to the Sands and shot.

Changes were introduced in the camp. Prisoners now had rectangular patches, about ten by fifteen centimeters, sewn on. These were white patches with large black numbers that they had to wear on their chests and backs. The numbers were the same as those on their *Hundemarken*. Under this numbered white patch on the chest was attached the small triangular patch that had been worn before, with the color, as previously, denoting nationality.

The SS men also took care to make sure the inmates kept their hair cut very short, down to "zero." The aim was to make the escapees easily recognizable by their shaved heads. Woe betide him whose patches were not well sewn, or whose head was not shaved. SS men would beat such an inmate until he lost consciousness. Sometimes they called the camp barber to run his cutting machine down the middle of a prisoner's head, forming a belt in the middle of the head. An inmate with such a belt would be beaten ruthlessly, so he would try to get to the camp barber as soon as possible in the evening after work, to have his head shaved completely and avoid further tortures.

Working for HKP had many advantages. One of these was that, because prisoners were not harassed there, they had an easier time communicating with their families. My mother visited me from time to time, bringing food parcels for me and for Józek. One day in November she came holding back tears. I noticed a big bruise around her right eye. Some Ukrainian militiaman had struck her with his fist in her right eye when she was on her way to the HKP caserns. Tears came rolling down her cheeks.

In my short talks with my mother I kept asking what was going on in the ghetto and at our place. I learned of the tragic death of my uncle Adolf, the husband of my aunt Andzia, both of whom I loved very much. During the August action, when SS men and Ukrainian police entered our house, my uncle remained alone in the room, for he had a card saying that he worked as a menial laborer for the Gestapo, while my mother ran quickly to the basement. An SS man called my uncle and ordered him to follow him to the basement. Uncle Adolf obediently went with him to the cellar. The SS man conducted him to the cellar and in one moment, when they were about to approach the far end of the cellar where my uncle knew that my mother was hidden, he apparently refused to go farther. My mother heard a shot and then silence. When she came out of her hiding place, she saw my uncle still standing, against the wall, shot dead by the German. His gold wristwatch had disappeared.

I also asked about my little daughter, Sylvia. I was always thinking of her, whatever else I was doing, every day. My mother repeatedly reassured me, as had my father-in-law (who received frequent communications from his son Zyśko), that Sylvia was safe, with Poles. The knowledge that I had a living daughter motivated me in my struggle for life. I had someone to live for, someone for whose sake to try to save my life.

In the middle of November 1942 a new action broke out in the ghetto, the so-called November action. Crowds of people were again brought to the camp and sent, after selection, to Bełzec. Using this opportunity, Willhaus carried out a greater selection among the prisoners during the march out to work. Nearly eight hundred inmates, after their shoes and dixies had been taken away, were included in the transport to Bełzec.

I suddenly noticed my uncle Zygmunt, my natural father's brother, among the condemned, running around barefoot in despair, looking around as if trying to find help from somewhere. I had not known that he was in camp. He might also have just been brought with those from the ghetto. It was heartbreaking to see his pitiful state. My colleague Dr. Keller went to Bełzec as well. Willhaus pulled him out of the row because his number was not well sewn on the back and front of his jacket.

Two days later, my uncle Joseph came to see me. He was another brother of my natural father. When my mother remarried, some of her siblings took offense and rarely saw us. Joseph, on the other hand, kept close contact, and I loved him dearly. He was now heartbroken. He told me that the SS had come to his home during the November action and wanted to take his daughter and her child. Her husband had a valid card, but when he offered resistance to his wife's being taken they shot him on the spot, as well as his wife and child and her mother, Joseph's wife. Joseph was taken to Janowska camp, where he found out that I was there and sought me out.

I tried to console him, but his despair was beyond reach. He had lost everyone, for his lovely daughter was his only child. I told him to keep in contact with me, that I wanted to see him again soon. A few days later, some inmates came to me. They were from Joseph's brigade, and told me he had died. They didn't say, but I guessed that it was suicide. Probably at his request, they brought me some few belongings of his, including photographs of his family that I have kept to this day.

After the November action Willhaus and the SS attained their goal. For a long time the SS had been trying to concentrate all the Jewish employees working for the Wehrmacht into Janowska camp. The Wehrmacht had until then opposed this, since people from the ghetto who worked for them were very useful for the military. There were many skilled craftsmen there and the army people were very content with their work. The military were quite aware that if these Jews got into Janowska camp, into this death mill, the German army would soon lose them completely, or at least the productivity of these people would be significantly lower.

Willhaus promised the Wehrmacht special privileges for these people, but the Wehrmacht did not want to agree to this, until an order came from the highest German authorities. Consequently, after the November action, the HKP people from the ghetto were marched out into Janowska camp. In order to satisfy the Wehrmacht a special barrack, one of the newly constructed ones, with bunk beds covered with pallets and selected ordners who were to take care of the cleanliness and order of the barrack, was given over to the new HKP workers. Jews from HKP were not deprived of their own clothes; they only had to have the numbers sewn on, front and back, and they were also given "necklaces" with the *Hundemarke*.

A special hospital was organized for workers from HKP. It was located in former city barracks beyond the camp, on Janowska Street. What's more, this hospital was not under the control of Dr. Rapaport, the head camp doctor who ran the so-called camp hospital from which patients went to "behindwire." Instead, the helpful Dr. Kurzrock, who was director of the ghetto hospital, also became director of this newly created one, so the patients there could get some real treatment. Eventually, inmates from other brigades could sometimes get into this hospital.

Our two HKP camp brigades were included with the big one from the ghetto and also placed in this barrack number 9. In addition to these three HKP brigades there were two others also housed in this barrack. They were the Opel-Damke and Lueg brigades. The firms at which they worked were associated with HKP, so these brigades were affiliated with HKP as well, although they didn't go to work at the caserns.

When workers from HKP, from the ghetto, were brought into the internal part of the camp, they were guarded by the SS and stood aside, waiting a long time for registration. They were of course very depressed by this turn of events. Someone called me to help them. I put on my doctor's red arm band, took my small case with medicine, and went to them. I explained to the SS men that I had come to help someone needing medical aid. The SS men did not oppose my contacting these people.

Many of the newcomers secretly put into my pockets small parcels containing money and other valuable objects, because during registration all valuables and money were taken away from new inmates. If I had been caught doing this it would have been my end, but the SS men did not notice, and in the evening of the following day the owners of the parcels came to me, taking their belongings back and thanking me for my help.

Camp life improved suddenly for me. I slept in a clean barrack, on a pallet, of which I had only dreamed. I had my numbered place, on the bottom level of one of the individual bunks, and nice neighbors (two brothers who were engineers; I don't recall their names).

The brigadier of the main HKP brigade, Dr. Schwarz, was a very nice man, really looking after his people. He also had some influence with the chief of the *Judeneinsatz* HKP (Department of Jewish Labor at HKP), Captain Hartmann, who truly cared for his workers. Dr. Schwarz and his brother—both of them lawyers—soon became my grateful patients.

After the Jewish workers from the Wehrmacht, and especially from HKP, had been incorporated, life in Janowska camp improved to a degree. Roll calls with executions became much rarer, Willhaus only seldom appeared during roll calls, and camp soups became thicker, less watery than before. Tortures, harassment, beating, and killing still occurred, but not on such a scale as before. It seemed that perhaps Janowska camp would become a labor camp and not an extermination camp.

Around this same time, in late November, many inmates were reassigned to different brigades, including Józek, who was now in the Wäscherei brigade. He again was lucky to have a brigadier who helped him a lot and was protective of him. However, his work in the laundry kept him in the camp, so he still was dependent on me for any contact with the outside.

Life went on relatively peacefully, with some exceptions. Trade in the camp flourished. It was illegal, of course, and conducted in a clandestine manner, at some risk of discovery. Inmates working in town, cleaning at the *Reinigungsamt* (Sanitation Department), or in various other German factories, would bring soups and other food products they had received in the city from pitying Christians and sell these in the camp. They set up in barrack number 8, and sold to those who worked in the camp itself or in its vicinity and who therefore did not have the opportunity of contacting the outside world, but who could still have money smuggled in from outside. Those inmates who sold soups and the like would then use this money to buy, in town, various goods that were in demand in the camp, and then sell them there. That is how commerce really flourished in the camp. We were full of awe at how Jews, in the worst conditions possible, like here in the camp, could still engage in trade.

Winter was approaching and the cold became increasingly a nuisance, especially since the barracks in the camp were heated only by our bodies. Fortunately, we now had blankets. Still, when coming back from work, we felt acute cold, at least for the first hour or so.

Before marching out from the camp to work we were not harassed as before. However, the SS men who checked us as we marched out and came back demanded that we sing. Those who did not sing were beaten at the camp gate by the SS men, and were turned back in order to march out again singing. No matter what songs were sung, singing there had to be. A song, called the "camp anthem," written by an unknown author, was created in the camp. It was sung to the popular melody of the Krakovian dance tune "Are we this or are we that, boys from Kraków—is what we're at." The song went this way:

> Are we this or are we that,
> From Janowska labor camp;
> The world will someday hear of us,
> Sonovabitch, fuck your ass.
>
> Morning coffee, evening coffee,
> This is a full day's nourishment,
> From such nourishment you feel like pissing,
> Sonovabitch, fuck your ass.
>
> For the dinner one liter of soup,
> One liter of water and one grain;

> And you go to sleep in the Sands,
> Sonovabitch, fuck your ass.
>
> Action in January, action in February,
> Wife and children—behind the wire;
> Your heart is breaking from pain,
> Sonovabitch, fuck your ass.

Later on two more stanzas were added. One was in Polish, like the rest of
the song, and the other one, put in by the demand of SS man Brumbauer,
was in German. The Polish stanza joked about the director of the camp
orchestra and went like this:

> Our conductor, very good chap,
> Reports to the officer,
> Too cold and frosty, it's impossible to play,
> Sonovabitch, fuck your ass.

The German stanza had to be sung as in a choir on those occasions when
SS man Brumbauer, bribed with vodka, chocolates, and the like, allowed
some inmates an illegal excursion to the ghetto. These inmates, who
wanted to go to see their families, had to stand in a row and sing:

> *Gehst du in das Ghetto ficken*
> *Mit der Nummer auf dem Rücken*
> *Halt dein Maul, mach kein Quatsch*
> *Huj czi w dupe, kurwa macz.*

This roughly translates to:

> You go into the ghetto to fuck
> With the number on your back,
> Keep your mouth shut and make no fuss,
> Sonovabitch, fuck your ass.

The last line, a sort of a chorus, was repeated in broken Polish.

After the November action, the Lwów ghetto was reduced in size. New
Meldekarten were issued, with either a *W* (for Wehrmacht) or an *R* (for
Rüstung, arms industry) on them. The intent was that only those working
for the army or for arms manufacturers would now have a valid card. In

addition, those with valid cards got a patch with W or R on it to sew on their clothes. Anybody without such a patch was very much in danger of being rounded up and taken to Bełzec. My mother did not have such a patch, so she could no longer risk visiting me. My stepfather did have one, but was working. So, if I wanted to see my family, I would have to try to visit them.

One day I had a chance to do this with the help of the HKP brigadier, Dr. Schwarz. He liked me a lot and was also very grateful to me for providing medical help to him and his brother. He used to bribe Brumbauer to allow small groups from his brigade to go to the ghetto, and on this occasion I was included, without even being asked to pay for it. While Brumbauer supervised an excursion to the baths, the chosen group was pulled aside in the bathhouse, sang for him, and then left. We had to be back in an hour, to join our brigade when they returned to camp. It took about fifteen minutes to walk through a semideserted section of the Aryan quarter, then into the ghetto. The gate was guarded by Jewish police, who let us through. The apartment where my parents lived was not the one we had lived in before. Shortly after I was taken to Janowska, when the August action had finished, the ghetto had been reduced in size and my family had to relocate. That apartment now was inhabited by Aryans.

When I arrived at the new apartment, I had less than half an hour with my parents. We embraced and talked. I learned that Gina was staying in the countryside with Mr. Faliński's family, using her Aryan papers. They also told me many sad things about various relatives. They asked about me and Józek. Much too soon, it was time to go.

These excursions to the ghetto, though, were illegal, and when somebody got caught there and sent back to the camp, the unfortunate one could pay with his life for the expedition. Nevertheless, numerous camp prisoners risked the expedition, even without Brumbauer's help, to see their families while working in town, or to meet their friends on the Aryan side. Woe to him who was caught by the camp SS men, or by Willhaus himself, when in town illegally. The prisoner was transported to the camp, beaten until unconscious, and finally shot dead.

Once, when a group of us prisoners were talking about those inmates who took such a risk, my colleague, Dr. Pliskin, told me, "If you do not risk, you will not survive." This statement suddenly convinced me that the risk was worth it, and from that time on I repeatedly risked illegal excursions, when the opportunity arose, both in the ghetto and outside it, to see my family and for other reasons (like getting food).

Time was passing. Our fate still looked hopeless, but in late November and December 1942 rumors started to go around that in the area of

Stalingrad, on the eastern front, the Germans were having large losses and were not advancing. Once, when we were marching to work, several German soldiers, apparently opposed to Hitler, passed by us and, looking compassionately at the emaciated camp inmates, shouted to us, "Children, do not be afraid, there is one big shit on the eastern front." Another time, French POWs called in our direction, "Courage, courage!"

The mood in the camp, in spite of a certain improvement in conditions, was still very depressing. The loss of dear ones was painful and not to be overcome. On top of this, every one of us had an unwritten death sentence over our heads. The execution of this sentence was hanging over us like the sword of Damocles, and could take place any day, any hour.

Still, many of us would not give up, and everyone tried with all his strength to fight for survival. Those who gave up died quickly, of exhaustion and diseases, or as victims of the frequent selections. When we talked things over in groups after work, discussing our tragic, hopeless situation, the fronts of war were still far away while Willhaus and his pack of Germans were close by. I repeated again and again that I believed, in spite of all of this, that I would be at their—the Nazis'—funeral. Others admired my optimism and tried to get closer to me, as if they wanted to take some of this optimism for themselves.

Typhus raged in the camp nonstop; one could not get away from it. Since the camp authorities simply executed those with this disease, the sick had either, if it was possible, to hide, or to go to work, receiving injections of caffeine and strychnine from the camp doctors.

When I was coming back from work to the camp, I was frequently called to help people sick with typhus. Since I had already had this disease I was now immune to it, and could do so safely. Besides me there were several other doctors busy with attending to these patients. In the evenings, we were often discussing with each other our common experiences and observations. I had such experience with typhus as is rarely encountered. I saw hundreds of typhus patients, and therefore after a first glance, I could diagnose a patient with typhus at once. I saw repeated symptoms of this disease that were not mentioned in the medical handbooks. Besides this, I observed a phenomenon I had not encountered in normal living conditions, namely, an unheard-of resistance of the human organism when fighting for life in such abnormal conditions as those in the camp. Not only I, but also many other inmates went through this terrible sickness, walking around with a constant fever of more than 40° Celsius lasting for more than two weeks.

I observed, as well, an immunity against secondary infections. Coming back from work to the camp, I had syringes with me, which I had secretly received from the ghetto, and ampules of caffeine and strychnine. Before returning to the camp, at our workplace, I boiled my needles and syringes. In the camp I was attending sick people who were lying in the barracks on dirty bunk beds. In order to get to them, I had to climb and crawl on these bunks. The first patient got his injection with a clean, boiled syringe and needle, but the next ones were getting their injections with the used syringes and needles. Also, my hands, after having crawled upon these bunks, were not too clean.

There was, however, no other alternative. We had to help these sick people and risk infection, or leave them to die. I was very often called to attend to the sick. I had hundreds of patients, but I did not have even one case of a secondary infection in the location of the injection, in spite of the used syringes and dirty hands. This would be unbelievable in normal conditions. I really cannot explain it, but it seems that the human mind and body have unexpected inner strength that comes out at such times of struggle for existence.

My other observations were that the younger and thinner patients withstood typhus much better and had a greater chance to overcome this disease. Older and athletically built patients had poor prognoses. They often died of cardiovascular insufficiency, or contracted complications such as pneumonia, phlegmons, and so on.

Dr. Falik, previously an assistant at the University Clinic in Lwów, told me about his amazing discovery of how one could cure pneumonia—by striking the patient on the head with a rifle butt! Apparently, one of his typhus patients had gotten pneumonia and was hiding in the barrack. That is, his brigade was letting him stay there when they went to roll call, and had some arrangement with people in the camp office, perhaps bribing them, so that the number of persons in the brigade was fudged so his absence would not be noticed. In this way he could miss roll call as well as the day's work.

That evening, however, the inmates were called to come for their vitamins—a march after work, at double time, down to Kleparów station, to bring materials such as bricks, beams, crossbeams, and the like from there to the camp. Unlike the usual morning routine, when barracks were not checked thoroughly, the SS men went into each barrack and made sure everyone went out, including this patient of Dr. Falik. Prisoners were driven and beaten with whips and rifle butts by the SS men and Askaris, who formed a kind of lane along the route from the camp to the station.

When someone did not run quickly enough or did not have enough strength to carry their load, they could be beaten to death on the spot.

This patient, having pneumonia after typhus, could of course only barely move, let alone run, and was therefore beaten to unconsciousness. He was left lying in a pool of blood on the road, while other inmates were hurrying to the camp carrying various materials. He was considered a corpse and left on the road. At dawn the next day the victim woke up from unconsciousness. He looked around—there was nobody in sight. At first he did not know what to do, but then he decided to go along the way taken by his brigade when marching to work. He joined his brigade and the very same evening, when Dr. Falik examined him, he found that the symptoms of pneumonia had disappeared completely. So this was the method for curing pneumonia—with a heavy club on the head! This was presumably autohemotherapy.

This term literally means "own-blood treatment," and it refers to a practice commonly used before there were antibiotics, and fairly effectively. A patient would have some blood drawn and then injected into his muscle tissue to build resistance to his disease. This wasn't quite what happened to Dr. Falik's patient, but it was as good a guess, half in jest, that we could make to explain this amazing medical mystery.

Some of my typhus patients, who still had money, would requite me with a small sum. I bought food products with this money—for myself and my brother Józek—and once (in January) I brought two pounds of barley to my family in the ghetto.

In the beginning of December 1942, I received very sad news from the ghetto. My beloved uncle Nahum, my mother's brother, from whom I had received my religious and cultural upbringing, died of typhus. He could not get proper medical treatment in the ghetto. According to my mother, his last words before dying were, "Milek [my nickname] is not here. Nobody can help me."

CHAPTER 12

"BEHINDWIRE"

When new HKP inmates came to the camp they quickly contracted typhus. According to the promise of the SS given to the Wehrmacht, sick Jewish HKP prisoners had to be taken care of in the specially created small hospital outside the camp, on Janowska Street. The sick HKP inmates were taken there upon the recommendation of an HKP doctor, once confirmed by Captain Hartmann, the army chief of the Department of Jewish Labor at HKP. He was a very good man, and was friendly to the Jewish prisoners. Alas, in the meantime, he also fell sick with typhus, so his place was taken by his deputy, Feldwebel (Staff Sergeant) Feroli, a fierce anti-Semite. He would very carefully check and question any list of sick men he was given to confirm.

The main doctor of HKP was Dr. Tendler, who was assigned to the HKP brigade that originally was in the ghetto. The other three HKP doctors were Dr. Eck (brother-in-law of Dr. Tendler), myself, and yet another doctor who came later. Of the two HKP brigades in the camp that predated the move of the larger HKP brigade from the ghetto to the camp, Dr. Eck took care of one, while I had the other. We wondered what diagnoses to give these sick people in order to get them into the hospital. If we diagnosed typhus, the military authorities could, out of fear that the German soldiers would get this infection from the Jewish prisoners, throw all the Jewish workers out of the military caserns. In view of this, we decided to give false diagnoses. Doctors may, obviously, err—diagnosing flu, fever of unknown origin, et cetera.

But this seemed suspicious to Feroli. One day we reported two sick men, the next day eight, then twelve. After the end of work on this third day, which was now the beginning of December 1942, my brigade and I, and Dr. Eck with his brigade, came back to the camp. The main brigade, formed of former ghetto inhabitants in HKP, were still at work. In the evening, in the camp, the news suddenly spread that Feroli, deeming these daily increasing numbers of sick to have been made up artificially by the doctors, had loaded the sick onto a lorry—together with Dr. Tendler, who was served a rifle butt on his back. The lorry went in the direction of the camp, carrying Dr. Tendler and the sick inmates and escorted by Feroli. Dr. Tendler then jumped out of the moving lorry and escaped. Feroli brought these sick inmates, whose sickness he refused to believe, and had a meeting with the camp's SS leaders.

On the next day, during the morning roll call, Dr. Eck and I were called out. We stood in the middle of the roll call square. My HKP brigadier, Dr. Schwarz, ran to Rysiek Axer, the chief of the Janowska camp office. He asked Axer and the others from the office what would happen to us. The reply was that we were accused of sabotage and nothing could be done about it. After the roll call, as always, brigade after brigade marched out to work from the camp. Dr. Eck and I were put behindwire—that is, to be executed.

It was a sunny day in December. The earth was covered with snow, but the sky was clear and sunny. I was aware, not for the first time, that these were the last hours of my life, and I prayed in a whisper. I felt sorry for my mother when she would learn of my execution. I saw her despair with the eyes of my soul.

The brigades marched out, reporting at the SS control before leaving the camp. The two of us were joined by the twelve "allegedly" sick; then two others were selected from a brigade from which two inmates had escaped while working; and several more for unknown offenses—all meant for execution.

My brother's brigade, *Wäscherei*, passed by us and I saw the pale, terri-fied face of Józek. Now the last brigades were leaving the camp. Our turn came—we shall be escorted to the Sands to be executed, I said to myself. Sorrow, great sorrow, overtook me. In my thoughts I said farewell to the world.

Suddenly, the camp commander, Willhaus, appeared. He looked at us and asked the commanding *Scharführer* what was going on with us. The other explained in a low voice who we were and for what reasons we were going to be taken to the sand pit. Willhaus looked again at us, sarcastical-ly, and nodded his head. Our fate was decided.

Just then a black limousine turned around the corner and stopped in front of Willhaus's villa. It was the director of the Todt organization camp, a paramilitary organization formed by Reichsminister Todt. The director, Graefe, was a friend of Willhaus. Both were from Saarbrücken and had certain common interests. Graefe was getting workers from Willhaus, and these workers formed a special brigade, *Betonwerke*, which was going out every day from Janowska camp to the camp of Organization Todt. In return, Willhaus received gasoline for his limousine and concrete tubes for Janowska camp, which Willhaus was planning to expand to the scale of Auschwitz. Graefe was a good man who treated his Jewish workers well. They constructed his villa with a fountain, acquainted him with a Polish woman who later became his lover, and they did not spare gifts of money for him.

On this occasion Graefe had come to Willhaus to ask him for additional workers, because he had gotten a new transport of uniforms, shoes, and various military equipment that had to be unloaded and put in place in the warehouses at Kordeckiego Street in the western part of Lwów. Willhaus looked around. All the brigades had already marched out to work; there were no more brigades, no more people at his disposal. He decided, then, that our group of convicts would go to work at Kordeckiego Street. Before we were loaded onto a truck, Willhaus turned to the Askaris who escorted us and said, "These two doctors"—he pointed at me and Dr. Eck—"these two doctors, saboteurs, deserve your special attention!"

We went onto the truck and then Graefe came up to us and said in a low voice, "Do not have fear, nothing will happen to you." I was miraculously snatched away from the claws of death; I was extremely happy—and then a new thought—for how long?

We set out to work in Kordeckiego Street. We were guarded during work not by SS men or Askaris but by the Germans from Org. Todt (the common abbreviation for Organization Todt), who were, in principle, not the worst ones. They had no guns or whips, and would generally not torment Jewish workers, but one of them nagged me as if he had special instructions. He would follow me and watch that I worked sufficiently eagerly, kicking me from time to time, though I tried to deftly avoid these kicks.

After work we returned to the camp and, to my great happiness, as well as Józek's, found that we were not taken for execution. We were to continue working in Kordeckiego Street as the additional Org. Todt brigade.

After a week or so there was much less work in Kordeckiego. During the morning roll call, half of the workers, including myself, were separated from the Org. Todt brigade and directed to the SS *und Polizeiviertel* brigade, whose task was cleaning the streets and similar work in the elegant quarter of Lwów, where the headquarters of the SS and the villa of General Katzmann were located. Those prisoners who had worked for a longer time in the *SS und Polizeiviertel* were telling us with fear how SS Scharführer Keil sadistically tormented Jewish workers who, in his opinion, did not work diligently enough. Rysiek Axer from the camp administration bureau, who tried to save whomever he could and who especially tried to help educated people, nominated me the *Vorarbeiter* (foreman) of this small group, so as to spare me the hard physical work and limit my duties to the supervision of the others.

When, however, Keil caught some worker relaxing or working badly, he would beat the *Vorarbeiter* even more than the worker himself. Time passed. Dr. Schwarz from the HKP brigade, who liked me very much, was trying hard to get me back to HKP, but he was informed at the bureau that this was impossible, for my file now said that I was a saboteur.

On December 24, 1942, we finished our work earlier than usual because of Christmas Eve. However, those of us in the *SS und Polizeiviertel* brigade got additional work. We were transported to the train station in order to unload lorries of coal meant for the *SS und Polizeiviertel*. Our work was supervised by Untersturmführer Fichtel. As he was in a hurry to go to the Christmas Eve dinner, he was rushing Jewish prisoners with his whip, shouting almost incessantly, "*Los, los, los!* [Move on, move on!]" His whip struck to the left and to the right. Although I was appointed a *Vorarbeiter*, and was therefore not supposed to work but to supervise, I knew that this would not have any significance for Fichtel. I knew he would beat me with his whip in the same way, shouting, "*Los, los!*" I therefore inconspicuously disappeared from his sight and hid in the neighboring railroad lorries.

There was, on a side track, a passenger train in which Romanian soldiers were packed, most probably heading for the eastern front. Sitting gloomily, they did not turn their attention to me. Looking at them, I envied them. I would rather have been a soldier and even go to Stalingrad, and be treated as a human being, than stay here in Janowska camp to be treated much worse than an animal, with death menacing at every moment—not less so than in Stalingrad.

The night was dark, but not too cold. The monotone shrieking of Fichtel's voice—"*Los, los*"—did not end until all the coal was unloaded. When we came back late to the camp all the brigades had already been in their barracks a long time. My friends had been anxious about me.

Around this time, I had not seen Józek for a while, but made little of it because my brigade often returned late. One evening he came to my barrack to see me, and told me that he had contracted typhus. Fortunately, it was a mild case, possibly because of his youth, and his brigade had covered for him, letting him hide in his barrack and not go to roll call or work. He was now recuperating, and I gave him a few injections to help.

A few days later I was informed that the HKP brigadier, Dr. Schwarz, had finally made a deal to have me transferred to HKP. However, I would not join the main brigade located in the Wehrmacht military barracks at Pierackiego Street, where I had worked before. Instead, I would go to the Opel-Damke firm, which worked for HKP. It was located much farther from the camp, at Kazimierzowska Street, in the central part of the city.

This was a great relief to me, for my function—albeit unofficially—was to again be a doctor. Also, being in town allowed me to be in touch with the outside world. I could get and read newspapers to find out, more or less—reading, of course, between the lines—what was happening in the war. And, yes, I had a greater opportunity to illegally enter the ghetto, since I was much closer to it now.

Brigades working in town were in a more advantageous situation than those working in the camp. They could communicate with their families in the ghetto or with friends in the Aryan quarter. These Aryans, being relatively safe from the Germans, kept money and valuables of their Jewish friends and could supply them from time to time with necessary money.

Those who worked within the area of the camp and in the neighboring DAW were constantly exposed to tormenting and beating by SS men; the SS men considered it their special duty to persecute the Jewish prisoners as much as possible, harassing them at every occasion.

On Sundays the German firms were closed, of course, so we stayed in the camp. The SS men, however, would call us to report, ordering inmates in the brigades to do various jobs within the area of the camp, sometimes to do senseless work. We were ordered, for instance, to take bundles of wire, bricks, or beams lying in some place in the outside square and carry them to some other place, located one hundred to two hundred meters away, and when this was done, to carry all this back, and again the same, just to prevent us from resting and relaxing. Brigades working in town in firms whose directors had a positive attitude toward Jewish workers, or who were bribed, were given, when asked by the camp inmates, certificates that workers were also needed on Sundays. Thus, these brigades could spare themselves the Sunday in-camp harassments and could instead relax in the plants in town.

Some German institutions were also issuing certificates stating that they needed a certain number of workers for the night shifts. In this way, people from these brigades were taking turns having a safe sleep in town instead of sleeping in the camp, where there was constant danger. Captain Hartmann from HKP had been willingly issuing certificates for Sunday work in the military barracks at Pierackiego Street, and this was already taking place every Sunday. When Feldwebel Feroli replaced Captain Hartmann during his long illness, and learned one Sunday that prisoners came to the caserns to avoid camp labor, he ordered them to go back to the camp and informed the SS authorities in the camp of this illegal, inso-lent behavior of the Jewish prisoners. When the HKP brigade returned to the camp, the SS men decided to take care of them. They gathered the HKP people, and especially the brigade foremen, in the external camp square, covered at that time with quite a thick layer of snow, and ordered them to fall down, stand up, crawl forward, stand up again, fall down, and so on, until they became completely exhausted.

CHAPTER 13

LOSS OF A MOTHER

It was the morning of the New Year, 1943. During the morning roll call, having listened to the normal report from the brigadiers giving the number present in each brigade, two SS men who were commanding the roll call shouted to us, "Happy New Year wishes from the SS." We did not believe our ears and eyes. This was unheard of, simply unbelievable. Thousands of inmates enthusiastically shouted, "Hurray!" Was it a sign of a change in attitude toward the Jews, especially in the camp?

There were optimists who believed it was. There were also pessimists, skeptics who maintained that those SS men were probably still drunk after the New Year's Eve feast. The future proved that the skeptics were right.

Two days later, on Sunday, January 3, 1943, during my Sunday shift, I sneaked into the ghetto to see my parents. We were happy to at least be together this short time. My parents were also happy with the package I brought, which contained a kilogram of barley, for they were often hungry. They were worried because they had heard gossip about a new action that was supposed to happen soon. I comforted them, saying that this was only gossip and that since our morning roll call had been acccompanied by New Year wishes from the SS men, this indicated an improvement of the situation instead.

The next day, Monday, January 4, 1943, the SS and police troops unexpectedly entered the Lwów ghetto and started another action. Working in the Opel-Damke enterprise at Kazimierzowska Street, we saw the streetcar lorries carrying victims toward Kleparów station. We were constantly under stress and fear for our families. From our workplace, which was relatively near to the ghetto, we saw smoke from a burning building in the ghetto, where—as we learned later—SS men had driven selected victims and then set the house on fire. One member of our brigade, named Kolman, a skilled auto mechanic, was desperate. His wife and children lived in the house that we assumed was the one burning. At that point a German army *Schirrmeister* (supervisor) came to our auto repair shop to check on the work. Kolman, in tears, said to him, "Mr. Schirrmeister, how can I work when the house in which my family lives is on fire?"

The *Schirrmeister* replied sympathetically, his voice full of anger at the outrages committed by the SS, "Those damned dogs! But the day of vengeance will come."

A few hours later that day, I had a conversation with Mr. Kotlarski, a Pole who was employed by Opel-Damke as a salaried bookkeeper. He was an educated man with whom I had several times discussed the political and military situation and related matters. I had the impression that he was sympathetic to our tragic plight. As we were talking about this day's events in the ghetto he made a statement that shocked me, especially in contrast to the earlier reaction of the German *Schirrmeister*. "Look, Doctor," he said, "we Poles are Christian Catholics. We couldn't murder men, women, and children like the Germans do. But we are very glad that they are doing this job for us." I was speechless and left the room.

The January action lasted two days, and thousands of people were killed. Those who had not been killed on the spot were transported to Bełzec.

I learned from Józek that our mother had been taken with the transport to Bełzec. He had been told this in the *Wäscherei* by some women who worked there and lived in the ghetto. Our despair was without limits. We were broken down. We wept and could not pull ourselves together.

A few days later Józek received news that brought us some hope. A young boy (a nephew of our aunt Rachel), who had been taken in the same transport to Bełzec with our mother, returned after a few days to the ghetto. He told our father that the transport had been thrown into disarray on its way, either by the resistance forces or from within, he did not know, and many prisoners had jumped from the railway cars and tried to escape. He and our mother were among these.

On that frosty day in January, the SS men had taken their victims in the transport to Bełzec with only their shirts on. The young boy who had escaped had a scarf with him also. Pitying our mother, he gave her his scarf and wandered back in the direction of Lwów. After two or three days he was back in the ghetto. We waited with hope for news of the return of our mother. Alas, she did not come back. They had certainly killed her on her way.

At the nearest opportunity I sneaked into the now smaller ghetto in order to see my stepfather, whom I loved like a true father. From him I learned that my mother had been taken not by an SS man and not by a Ukrainian policeman, but by a Jewish one. My mother had offered him a golden chain, asking him imploringly to leave her in the ghetto. The rascal took the golden chain, but still brought my mother to the SS men.

After the January action the Germans renamed the shrunken ghetto, calling it *Julag*, short for *Judenlager* (Jewish camp). The implication was that the ghetto itself was to be considered a camp, and those who did not have the *W* or *R* patches were considered "undesirable elements," living there illegally and in constant danger of arrest. Julag was under the command of the notoriously sadistic SS officer Grzymek.

News, passed secretly by word of mouth, indicated that the Germans had been beaten by the Soviets in Stalingrad, which encouraged us. The Germans did not admit their defeat, but then, at the end of January 1943, there was, on the front page of the German newspaper, the portait of Field Marshal Paulus surrounded by a black frame, and a note announcing that this commander in chief of a German army had been killed in battle in Stalingrad—"*für den Führer und das Vaterland* [for the Führer and fatherland]."

It was only after liberation that I learned about Marshal von Paulus, that he had not been killed "*für den Führer und das Vaterland*" but had surrendered and been taken prisoner by the Russians, and soon afterward became the head of the German committee against Hitler in Moscow.

CHAPTER 14

ENTERTAINMENT SS-STYLE

Despite the defeat in Stalingrad, which was a tremendous trauma for the Germans and their leaders, the extermination process continued. Even though the SS now faced the possibility that the war might be lost and they would be held accountable for their deeds, the anti-Jewish policy was unaltered.

Our "masters" arranged for themselves an unusual show. During a liquidation action in the town of Jaworow and its vicinity, these brave fighters against unarmed people, women, and children, captured a rare spoil—two bearded Jews. During the German occupation the pious Jews cut their beards and side curls in order to avoid giving a pretext for being derided, abused, and tortured. There were, however, some pious Jews who stuck to the religious orthodox rules despite the frightening consequences. And in Jaworow the SS men found two such pious bearded Jews. One of them was a rabbi and the other a *shohet*, or rabbi's assistant. The SS men did not kill them but decided to bring them alive to the Janowska camp for amusement, to play with them. When the SS men brought them to our camp with other young Jewish men who had been captured during the action in Jaworow, they separated these two from the others, who were destined for our slave work.

The SS men ordered that the rabbi and his assistant should remain in their clothes and that their beards and their side curls should not be shaved. They were not attached to any brigade; they were not to work, but to stay in the kitchen the whole day. This was an unheard-of privilege in our camp, especially now, in the wintertime. However, early every morning when the brigades started marching out to work and the camp orchestra, situated outside the internal gate near the entrance to "behind-wire," played various marches, the rabbi and his assistant were ordered to report to the SS control post. Then they had to get up on a platform consisting of wooden boxes, close to the orchestra, and, holding a completely torn umbrella, had to dance to the marches that were played.

The rabbi was an old man of small stature, gaunt, with a whitish gray beard. His face was pale and his eyes expressed goodness, wisdom, and deep sadness. He was wearing, as many orthodox Jews did, a black capote and a plushy black hat. His assistant was taller, a middle-aged man with a jet-black beard, black hair, and black eyes, wearing a black capote also, and a black fur cap. He was also pale and scared. Because the old rabbi was frail and could hardly dance, his assistant would hold the umbrella and with his other arm support the rabbi in steady motions to the marches that hardly could be called a dance. But the SS men were laughing and enjoying themselves tremendously.

For us, marching by, the view of the dancing rabbi and his assistant was shocking and frightening, especially on the first day of the "performance," when the rabbi and his assistant, like we all, were convinced that after the end of the show they would be murdered. They were scared, pale, trembling from the freezing February winds and from fear. One could see their lips moving in prayer and their eyes looking up to the Lord, begging for mercy. It was heartbreaking, and the SS men were laughing, full of endless joy.

The brigades were marching out one after another. It took about one and a half to two hours, and the orchestra played marches continuously; these two victims, partly covered with snow, had to dance all the time. After the "show" they were not executed but were sent back to the kitchen, and the next day, early in the morning, the rabbi and his assistant had to perform again.

When some German officials, directors of different German institutions, came to visit the camp commandant Willhaus, they were also invited to this show, and they too laughed and had a good time.

So it went on for about ten to fourteen days. Finally, the SS men became bored. One day, when the rabbi and the assistant were marching exhausted to the kitchen, the two SS Scharführer Siller and Brumbauer followed them and shot them in the backs of their heads. The bodies of the rabbi and his assistant fell down like puppets in a puddle of blood. We were shocked, but at the same time we envied them for being killed so unexpectedly. Sudden unexpected death without torture was what we were wishing for ourselves.

Life in the camp went on "normally." It was February or March 1943. In the countryside, the extermination of the Jewish population was being carried out according to plan, exactly and mercilessly. The clothes of the murdered were brought by trucks to Janowska camp, where, in the *Wäscherei*, under strict control, inmates scrupulously searched the clothes, picking out gold, dollars, and the like, which were then carefully gathered and sent to the Reich. Appropriation of even the smallest object could be punished by immediate death.

After a careful search, good clothes were sent to the Reich, while worn-out or shoddy garments were left in the *Wäscherei* for inmates in the camp. I learned from my brother Józek, who worked in the *Wäscherei*, that transports of clothes from the countryside and from provincial towns were coming regularly. It was also frequent that groups of Jews, meant for liquidation in the Sands of Janowska camp, were brought with these transports.

One evening, after work, Józek came to my barrack pale and trembling with fear. He told me that on the same day the brigadier from the *Wäscherei* brigade, Schleicher, who had before the war been a wealthy owner of a soda water plant, got an order from the SS men. He was to immediately come with a cart to get the clothes of some recent victims who had been murdered on a site located between the camp and the Jewish cemetery. Schleicher took Józek with him; they harnessed a horse and set out for the place indicated. When they got there, they saw a terrible sight. There were still traces of blood from the victims just buried in the sand. Heaps of clothes were lying aside, still warm when touched, some stained with blood. A group of SS men with an SS man named Büttner leading them were joking noisily, laughing, and drinking. Büttner, imitating the female voice of a young murdered girl, shouted, "I am still young, please, I want to live yet, I am still young, I want to live yet." And he roared with laughter. The SS men were having fun.

Suddenly Büttner saw my brother and, keeping his submachine gun in his hand, called out at him, "Come here, come here," with an obvious intent to kill him. The bloodthirsty hyena was looking for a new victim. Józek's legs became weak from fear. Schleicher, seeing what was going on, came up to Büttner to talk him away and whispered to Józek, "Drop off, quickly." Józek fled rapidly, not noticed by Büttner, and ran to my barrack trembling with fear.

One day, after coming back from work to the camp, we heard astonishing news about Scharführer Keil, terror of the Jews, who was supervisor of the Jewish inmates in the SS and police quarters, where I had worked for a week in December. Keil had been killed by a Jewish SS *und Polizeiviertel* brigadier named Tadek. Tadek was a tall, muscular young man of less than thirty years, always joyful, very helpful, and liked by other inmates. He was also a favorite of the SS men, and especially of Scharführer Keil, for whom, just as he had for other SS men, he served as a chauffeur, driving passenger cars and trucks. At this time Keil bought himself, or got, a new car, and gave it to Tadek for a test drive. When Tadek returned from this test drive, the fender of the car was, unfortunately, somewhat bent. Angry, Keil jumped at Tadek and hit him strongly on the face. Shocked, Tadek, who was not accustomed to being beaten, grabbed an iron bar lying about in the garage and struck Keil on the head with it. Keil was killed on the spot. Knowing what to expect, Tadek took the SS uniform off Keil and ran for his friend. Both of them got into the SS truck and, not recognized by the SS guards, fled into the unknown.

The next day, the SS authorities learned of the killing of Keil and resolved to immediately take revenge on the Jews for his death. An SS detachment marched into the ghetto and there, during the march out to work, took more than one hundred Jews to be murdered. Simultaneously, at the morning roll call in Janowska camp, the SS men who directed the roll call were taking out inmates from the rows standing in the square, also to be executed. The son of one of the selected inmates was a brigade foreman. He came running up to the SS men, asking them to let his father go. At this moment SS Scharführer Schönbach appeared. When he was informed what was going on, he took out his pistol and shot the father on the spot. When he turned to the son with the same intention, the man started to run quickly, zigzagging through the grounds. Schönbach ran after him, shooting from a distance several times, and finally hit him. When the victim was lying in a pool of blood, still alive, Schönbach dispatched him by shooting him in the mouth.

Soon, camp commander Willhaus appeared in the roll call square with his submachine gun. Accompanied by SS men, he walked up to the inmates standing in rows and, with a gesture, he ordered the prisoners he had chosen to step out of the rows and turn their backs to him. He shot each victim in the neck, killing one after another. Those who did not want to step out of the row, or who lingered, asking to be spared, were beaten with whips and rifle butts by the SS men and were forced to stand in front of Willhaus to be killed. Dead bodies were falling one next to the other.

When Willhaus had partly satisfied his thirst for blood, he ordered inmates to go out to work. He stood at the exit control post and started anew to select, for liquidation, inmates from the marching brigades. He selected more than one hundred inmates, who were transported to Bełzec to die in gas chambers, joining those who had been taken from the ghetto.

Thus, Willhaus and the SS satisfied their desire for revenge. When, during the following days, we marched to work through Janowska Street, next to the Janów Christian cemetery, we saw from far away a grave covered with flowers and wreaths with lily ribbons. People said that this was the grave of the SS man Keil.

Some time later, marching to work down Janowska Street, we saw yet another scene of SS men tormenting Jews. Jews could not use sidewalks, but only the middle of the street, just like cattle. Ukrainian militiamen often beat Jews who dared to go on the sidewalk. On that particular day, another brigade was marching ahead of us, led by brigadier Kweller, a man whom I knew from our high school times. Kweller, acting in the same way as the other brigadiers, commanded his brigade from the sidewalk, while the brigade marched in the middle of the road. There had been no problem with this until then. Brigadiers used to wear special arm bands that distinguished them from other prisoners. Two SS men, though, who coincidentally were walking down Janowska Street, were not pleased that Kweller was marching on the sidewalk. They started to mercilessly beat him and kick him in the face. When Kweller, his face covered with blood, had bent over so as to avoid further blows, both SS men took turns kicking him in the nose. Blood was pouring out of Kweller's nose like water from a faucet, which did not stop the SS men from continuing to kick him in the face and nose. When Kweller, in blood, swayed and fell down, the SS men, satisfied with their deed, went away.

CHAPTER 15

TRAGIC NEWS

In March 1943 I received word from my brother-in-law, Zyśko, Frania's brother. He wanted to see me. He had been put in the Wehrmacht caserns at Zamarstymowska Street and worked there. I decided to take the next opportunity to meet him in these caserns and get from him the most important information—the name and address of those Poles who, as I was told, were hiding my daughter, Sylvia. Both my father-in-law, in the camp, and my mother had assured me that Sylvia was being safely kept by Polish friends. As I mentioned before, I did not have any reason to doubt this.

Since my father-in-law had died of typhus in Janowska camp in October 1942, and my mother was killed in January 1943, Zyśko was the only person who could tell me something about Sylvia. I was constantly comforting myself with the thought that she still was alive. In these terrible conditions, the awareness that Sylvia needed me encouraged me and supported my conviction that I had to fight for life and endure everything for her.

When I met Zyśko, he was very happy to see me. He brought me to his room and handed me photographs of Sylvia, of myself, of Frania, and other family photographs he had taken from our house before he had to leave it when the ghetto was reduced after the August action. I was glad to have these, and have kept them to this day. They include seven photos in this book.

I asked him where Sylvia was. Zyśko first lapsed into silence and then started to stammer. I was overtaken by a horrible foreboding. "Tell me where she is!" I shouted. Zyśko became pale, and after a while I learned the terrible truth—Sylvia was dead. This innocent, beautiful, little two-year-old girl had been murdered by those bloodthirsty Nazi bandits.

Sylvia at eleven months.

Zyśko told me that during the August action, on Thursday, August 20, 1942, the SS men rushed into our apartment. Since Zyśko had a card saying that he was working for the Wehrmacht, they left him alone. But when they saw Sylvia, who had been with him since the time when Frania, my wife, and her parents had been taken five days earlier during the same August action, they took the child. Zyśko implored them to leave Sylvia with him, saying that she was his child. They struck him with a whip on the head, and threw her into the hands of some Jewish woman on a truck on which victims were being transported to Kleparów railway station to find their death in Bełzec.

Zyśko was justifying himself, saying that he could not in any case have helped, but already I did not hear his words. I was broken; something collapsed inside of me and was weeping constantly. Zyśko felt awful, and was apologizing. I certainly did not blame him. I quickly said good-bye and went away. I had with me the only mementos of my family, the photographs that Zyśko had given me. I returned to my work in Opel-Damke and there, among friends who were also prisoners, I cried. Like Niobe from Greek mythology, I was receiving blow after blow; I was losing my beloved ones, my dearest—one after another.

A few days later I again broke away from work and illegally went in the direction of the ghetto. One of my friends, a pharmacist, worked there in a pharmacy that had initially been in the ghetto and then, after the August action, found itself outside of the ghetto. I was looking for this friend in order to buy cyanide from him. This poison was then very much sought for by the Jews and bought by them for very high prices. People buying it on the black market were frequently cheated and got something else instead.

After all that I had lived through, all I had seen, and facing what yet awaited us, I urgently wanted to have cyanide. I was not afraid of death, I did not care much for life when my dearest ones were dead; I was only afraid I could be buried half dead. Unfortunately, I did not find the pharmacy, nor my friend. Apparently, the Germans had liquidated the pharmacy.

About two weeks later I got a message, through someone else, from Zyśko. The Wehrmacht from Zamarstynowska Street, where Zyśko worked, had handed over all their Jewish workers to the SS, who transported them to the prison in the ghetto. Zyśko implored me through the messenger to save him. I went to the ghetto as soon as possible—illegally, of course—and went to the prison. There, incidentally, I knew a man who worked in the administration. I obtained assurances from him that in two days, at most, they should be able to get Zyśko out.

On the next day, the Germans carried out an action in the Schwarz enterprise. It was a large German firm at St. Martin's Street that produced materials for the Wehrmacht and employed quite a number of Jewish workers. Until then these Jews had been safe from any action in the ghetto.

From our place of work in the Opel-Damke firm, we saw trucks loaded with men and women, escorted by the SS and Ukrainian police, speeding quickly down Kazimierzowska Street. Trucks passed, one after another, in the direction of Kleparów station, for transport to Bełzec.

I then learned that during this "Schwarz action" the prison in the ghetto had been purged. This meant that all those imprisoned there were sent by the Germans, together with the workers from the Schwarz enterprise, in a transport to Kleparów railway station and from there to Bełzec.

While transports were passing by our firm, one of the inmates who worked on the second floor and who could see better what was going on in the street, told us the following: when a truck loaded with people was passing by our building, a young woman jumped off the speeding truck and started to run. SS man Hahn, whom we knew from Janowska camp and who had an amputated right arm, also jumped out of the truck, in order to catch the escapee. He could not have done that, though, if not for the "gentlemanly help" of some German soldier or officer, who ran after the fleeing girl, caught her, and gave her back to Hahn. The SS man pulled the miserable victim by her hair into the truck and the transport moved on its way in the direction of Janowska Street.

I learned later that also among the prisoners taken from the ghetto to Bełzec was my colleague from medical studies at the university, Dr. Ochsenhoit. I was told that he had been hiding in the apartment of Professor Nowicki, a professor of pathology and the ex-dean. Professor Nowicki had been shot by the Germans together with other professors of the university and Lwów Polytechnic, in July 1941, just after the Germans captured the city. The professors were shot at a site on the outskirts of the city. Several dozen Polish professors in Lwów were killed by the Germans at that time.

The family of the late Professor Nowicki had been hiding Dr. Ochsenhoit, but in March of 1943, for some unknown reason, could not keep him there any longer. And so Dr. Ochsenhoit had to leave their apartment. As he was going down Piłsudski Street, in the center of the city, he was noticed by a former Polish patient, who immediately reported him to the German police. Dr. Ochsenhoit was arrested and, as punishment for having stayed illegally in the Aryan quarter, was put in the ghetto prison. Consequently, in the Schwarz action, he shared the fate of the other prison inmates.

CHAPTER 16

HEINEN THE HUMAN BEAST

When we came back to the camp after work, each day of my stay there, we were not allowed to enter our barracks immediately. We were let in only around seven-thirty in the evening, shortly after "dinner." We therefore had to bivouac in the roll call grounds. This provided an opportunity for SS man Heinen to fulfill his plan.

Friedrich Wilhelm Heinen was the worst of the SS beasts. He was not of high rank—a mere SS man, as far as I know—but that did not stop him from being a mass murderer. He came to the camp at the beginning of 1943. Various SS men of different ranks came and left from time to time. Rokita, for instance, I did not see after December 1942; I learned after the war that he became commander of his own labor camp in Tarnopol. Janowska camp was a training ground for SS officers.

Once an inmate, mistakenly or through lack of knowledge, addressed Heinen as "Herr Scharführer Heine," whereupon Heinen burst out in anger, shouting, "You idiot, I am not the Jewish poet!" referring to Heinrich Heine, the famous German poet of Jewish origin. Then he took his whip and beat the worm who had dared to insult his name. His sadism, bestiality, and insatiable thirst for Jewish blood were greater than those of any of his other colleagues in the trade. Heinen was young, some twenty to twenty-five years old, tall, thin, blond, with an almost feminine face, regular features, and kind blue eyes. He limped slightly with one leg. Looking at his gentle face and kind blue eyes no one could expect that in this so-called human there lurked such a horrible beast.

During the whole day, and sometimes even during the night, he would circulate around the camp like a ghostly specter, with death following him. Woe to whomever was caught by the gaze of this young blue-eyed beast. The poor inmate's fate was done.

Heinen approached calmly, as if the matter was an entirely innocent one, waved his finger, and muttered, "*Komm mit* [Come]." His behavior, facial expression, Olympic calm, and his "*Komm mit,*" uttered in a low voice, made the victim drop his guard, not expecting anything wrong. The chosen one was conducted by Heinen behind the camp kitchen and there killed with a sudden pistol shot to the neck. Then, as if nothing had happened, Heinen would come back to the camp and, wandering about, would look for a new victim to satisfy his desire for Jewish blood.

It was told that when he appeared in the camp, he announced that he had up until then killed only four hundred Jews with his own hands, but his self-appointed goal was a thousand. He was making every effort to fulfill his vow as soon as possible. He was in a hurry, as if he were afraid that he would not have enough time and that there would not be enough Jews. Heinen also was not satisfied with mere numbers of murdered people, but took care to avoid monotony in his work. He was constantly inventing new methods of physical and psychological torture for his victims before killing them. He would also economize by trying to use as few bullets as possible, for they were so needed by the thousand-year Reich. That is why he preferred to use the gallows whenever possible. In their free time, Heinen and his comrades perfected their shooting skills by aiming at empty bottles near the kitchen.

One day he was on duty, guarding prisoners in the Jewish cemetery at Pilichowska Street, where a brigade from Janowska camp worked to dismantle the graves and dig up the corpses to search for gold teeth. The cemetery brigade employed many prisoners who had previously been dentists. Extracted gold was sent by the SS to Germany in order to enrich, in this cultivated manner, the German treasury. Stones from the graves were thereafter used in road construction. The road leading into Janowska camp from the external gate contained these stones, with the Hebrew inscriptions still visible.

Heinen, as usual, was going like a specter among the working prisoners and was, from time to time, shooting selected victims for fun, as if they were hares. Once, when one of the prisoners whom he had shot was lying in a pool of blood and writhing in pain, an Askari approached Heinen asking whether to kill off the victim with the so-called *Gnadenschuss.* Heinen answered that it would waste a bullet. "Take the boulder lying nearby and throw it on his chest." The Askari obliged and the victim yelled under the weight of the stone and died.

In a short time Heinen gained the reputation in the camp of being the worst of all murderers and sadists. He was nicknamed Jack the Ripper, after the infamous character whom we had known about from before the war, whose deeds were described by the newspapers. It must be admitted that Heinen surpassed the authentic Jack the Ripper in all respects.

It was late evening in April of 1943. This evening was the Seder evening, the first one of the Jewish Passover holiday. Each of us had very painful feelings that night, which was, like Christmas for Christians, a family feast day, when whole families would sit down to dinner. A feeling of despondency mixed with that faint hope at the bottom of the soul for the coming of liberation. It was already after the Stalingrad defeat; we knew armies were already fighting over Kharkov, a large industrial city in eastern Ukraine. People were saying that the Russians were approaching the Dnieper. In northern Africa, the German army led by Marshal Rommel was a step away from ultimate defeat. Soon, any day, any week, the desired second front in the west would be established. We told ourselves that we would have the next Passover feast in our own homes—not all of us, perhaps, but many of us.

Nuchim, ordner of the ninth barrack, belonging to the HKP brigade, was one of those who believed in this deeply. Nuchim was a pious man and his emotions on this Seder evening were deeper than in anybody else. He was smiling, satisfied, and his good, always sad, eyes glittered with festive brightness.

On this night of the Seder he was, together with two other ordners, on duty. Lights in the barrack had gone out, according to the rules in the new barracks, at nine P.M. In the adjacent corridor, where the lights were on, Nuchim was talking in a low voice with his other colleagues. He was not paying attention to what was going on around him. He did not notice that every once in a while the door to the barrack would swing open and groups of crouching silhouettes with terrified faces would sneak into the ninth barrack. Everybody in the barrack proper was caught up in the wave of anxiety and expectation. I, like the others, was in my bunk bed, but not asleep, when they began to come in.

We learned from the newcomers, who had come to us from the eleventh and twelfth barracks, that nightmarish scenes were taking place there. We learned that two prisoners coming back from the latrine had stopped in front of their barrack door and engaged in a low-voiced conversation. Suddenly, from nowhere, Heinen's silhouette had appeared before them. As if they had seen death, both had fled into the barrack. Heinen had quietly followed them inside. At his command the ordners had turned on the light. Heinen had looked around the bunk beds and announced that the two who had been standing in front of the barrack should immediately report to him. If they did not report within five minutes, twelve persons would immediately be shot. The prisoners had started to look for the two escapees. Since both were wearing light-colored trench coats, Heinen ordered all those wearing such trench coats, and there were many of them, to appear before him. Everyone was aware that whoever reported to Heinen would see his fate sealed. Lamentations started, and those who had light-colored trench coats were sneaking out one after another through the back door to other barracks. Shouts and shrieks were heard, and after a while Heinen walked out with his prey, which he shot.

This was, however, not enough for him. The smell of blood had obviously excited this scum, so he looked for more victims. At a certain moment, the entrance door to the corridor of our barrack opened with a thud and shots sounded. Shouts, groans, the noise of people fleeing, and then silence. After a while Heinen's voice was heard, sounding innocent: "Have I hit anybody? Have I injured anybody?" He went out of the barrack smiling and satisfied. Several prisoners ran to the corridor, and one prisoner shouted, "Nuchim, Nuchim." "Nuchim, Nuchim," someone wept loudly.

After a while one of the ordners came to me with a wound in his hand. While I was dressing his wound he told me that Nuchim, who had been talking to him, not expecting anything, had been killed by one of Heinen's bullets. Heinen had appeared suddenly in the door and shot in their direction. A bullet hit Nuchim in the mouth and caused instant death. He fell, inert, into the hands of my interlocutor. It was probable that Heinen was using dumdum bullets, for a fragment of the bullet that killed Nuchim had injured this ordner in the hand. Heinen walked out content that even before going to bed he had succeeded in recording new victims on his account.

One day in the second half of April, I myself also had an encounter with Heinen, in the washroom, in one corner of which was the barbershop. As in many, many other cases, I was lucky that time as well, for I avoided death—or, at the least, a bloody beating. On this particular day, I went to the camp barbers in the evening, after returning from work, for there had been a barber check that morning. When we had gone out to work, we marched between two rows of camp barbers who were meticulously checking whether or not our hair had grown. Every prisoner was obliged to have his shaven pate shine, so as to facilitate recognition in case of escape. Anyone who tried to have even a trace of hair was suspected of preparing to escape. With this in mind, the camp authorities ordered occasional barber checkups. Anyone who had some hair had a haircutting machine driven through the middle of his head so as to leave a visible shaven strip. In this way one was branded.

If one did not have his head completely shaved, erasing the stripe, the SS men would mercilessly beat him with whips on the head and face. The only privileged ones were the brigadiers and medical doctors. They had the right to have some hair showing, although it must be short and even neatly parted. This privilege was not granted by the camp authorities but was created by these people themselves, who managed to talk the others into believing that that was how things should be. And, somehow, this was accepted. Every SS man heard repeatedly that this was an order from the superior authorities, and believed it.

I was, at that time, a medical doctor with the Opel-Damke brigade, one of the HKP brigades. While going to the camp barbers that evening, I deliberated whether to risk still having my short parted hair, or to have my head shaved. It was possible that someday this little cheating would be uncovered, which could end tragically for me. On the other hand, I had to be constantly prepared for an escape.

Still perplexed, I entered the camp barbershop. The room was filled with inmates standing in line to get served. I stood next to our brigadier from Opel-Damke, Neustein. The shop was noisy and swarming like a beehive. Suddenly there was silence—almost dead silence. Heinen appeared in the door with a whip in one hand and a pistol in the other. He looked around the room searching for a victim. Our hearts stopped when Heinen directed his steps to us. He found here two victims with hair, providing him with a pretext for his blustering. First he turned to Neustein. "You dog, what is that? What?" he asked, pointing with the whip to Neustein's hair.

"I am . . . I am a brigadier," answered Neustein, stuttering.

"What? Brigadier?" snarled Heinen. The whip swished in the air and struck with a crack in Neustein's face. This good man of athletic build moaned and bent his head between his shoulders in expectation of further blows.

Heinen spoke again, in my direction: "And you?" My soul sank; I felt that my blood flowed from my face to my legs, but I responded energetically, pretending self-assurance with my tone.

"I am a medical doctor."

"What? Doctor, doctor?" shouted Heinen.

"In HKP," I added, knowing that this firm, belonging to the Wehrmacht, enjoyed certain privileges in the camp. The upraised hand with the whip went slowly down. My assured voice had apparently disconcerted him.

"Doctor in HKP," muttered Heinen. He hesitated for a while and then moved on. As soon as Heinen turned around I sneaked out and disappeared into thin air, fearing that this beast Heinen might change his mind and not let me go unpunished. From the barbershop I hurried with all my might in the direction of the barrack, turning back to see whether or not he was following me. After that time I tried to avoid Heinen like fire. I always calculated so as not to find myself within the reach of his beastly sight.

There was one other occasion that I knew of in which Heinen let his victim out of his claws. This was in May 1943, when the inmates were waiting to be allowed to enter the barracks after their day's work. As they were sitting on the grass or walking about the roll call grounds, Heinen prowled around the camp looking for victims, as usual. At a certain moment he dragged out of some group a young, sixteen-year-old boy, told him to bend over a log and to pull down his pants. Heinen called for a camp policeman and told him to beat the boy with a rubber club on the buttocks. He threatened the policeman, saying that he would shoot him if he did not beat the boy with all his strength. Heinen took out his pistol and pressed the barrel against the boy's neck. The policeman was forcefully striking the boy's buttocks with the rubber club, the boy whined in pain, and Heinen was keeping his pistol pressed to the boy's neck all the time, threatening to shoot if he moved.

We were looking at this scene from a distance, blood freezing in our veins. We knew that after twenty blows Heinen would, as always, shoot his victim. Some of us turned our heads away, expecting to hear the shot. After twenty blows, to the great surprise of all, Heinen pulled the pistol away and let the victim go. This was simply incredible. Heinen had let his victim go? When Heinen walked away, everybody went with joy to console and help the crying boy.

CHAPTER 17

THE STORM APPROACHES

I had not seen my stepfather since visiting him in the ghetto shortly after the January action in which my mother was killed. It was now the second half of April. We kept in touch, however, and so I knew that Faliński had helped him find a hiding place in Łyczakowska Street, in the Aryan section. My stepfather was now there all the time, no longer working in Faliński's laundry. I decided to see him, leaving my workplace at Opel-Damke (which on Sundays was loosely enough supervised to allow such an excursion with my brigadier's help). It was a long walk through the Aryan section, so I removed my patch (which I had attached with snaps so it would look sewn on but could easily be taken off). On the way there, I saw an SS man from the camp. I was terrified lest he recognize me, but kept walking and luckily was not noticed.

When I arrived at the hiding place, my stepfather was overjoyed to see me. As we talked, he tenderly bathed my back, as a father would for a young boy. He told me that Gina, who was still living as an Aryan with Faliński's family in the country, would soon return to Lwów for a while. She was arranging, through Faliński, to have Aryan papers made up for Józek as well. She would then try to arrange Józek's escape from camp.

A short time after my visit, Józek told me that he had heard, from a co-worker in the *Wäscherei* who lived in the ghetto, that Gina had come back. She was now living with my stepfather in a new hiding place, in the same building as Faliński's laundry, on St. Martin's Street.

A photo of my sister Gina, given to me after the war
by Mr. Faliński.

About two weeks after my visit to my stepfather, I went to St. Martin's
Street to see him and Gina. She was unhappy living in the country, and
was not sure whether she would go back there. She missed our family, and
she did not feel safe. She had been blackmailed by someone who threatened to reveal that she was a Jew. Gina told me that Józek's Aryan papers
were ready; she would soon go pick them up. She also said that she had
acquaintances in the Janowska camp office with whom she was negotiating Józek's escape. First he would be transferred to a brigade that went far
into town to work. They had already decided on Betonwerke, a brigade
that worked at the concrete plant in the Org. Todt camp. The brigadier,
Rosenblüth, would be bribed to let him get away, and the office staff also
would get paid to arrange it and cover it up. Gina had gotten together the
money for this. All I had to do was contact the brigadier and confirm the
deal.

I was elated that things had already progressed so far. Once Józek got to
the hideout he would go to a small town in the country. With his Aryan
looks and papers, he would be relatively safe. I was worried for my stepfather, however. There were over thirty other Jews hiding in the same build-

ing he was in. I felt uneasy, for this greatly increased the chance that the hideout would be discovered. He had no better alternative, though.

As for myself, I could probably manage to escape camp, but where to? I could not pass as an Aryan, even if I had false papers. The hideout was risky. I would much have preferred joining partisans in the countryside, if that were possible. I decided to wait until the Russian front was nearer. I could survive in the country, somehow, for a short time, maybe a month. Until then it made no sense to escape unless some other opportunity arose. If the situation in the camp got worse, I could still try to make it to the hideout on St. Martin's Street.

A week after my visit with Gina and my stepfather, Józek was transferred from the *Wäscherei* brigade to Betonwerke. He was happy to now be able to get out of the camp during the day, and we were waiting for the best moment for him to make his escape. He also told me that he had made a friend in his new brigade, a man named Mechel Pfeffer. He was helpful to Józek at work and Józek shared his food with him.

Around this time, in the first week of May 1943, a very unusual event occurred in the camp. We were awakened by a hellish shooting. We rushed to the barrack windows. There was nobody in the roll call square. On the other side, beyond the camp, we could see fire and smoke. Something was on fire in the neighboring DAW. Askaris were shooting from all the turrets, as if they had been given orders to fend off a possible mutiny in the camp. After a while SS men with their pistols drawn appeared, headed by Scharführer Schönbach and Willhaus with his submachine gun, and accompanied by Oberjude Oremland.

We quickly jumped out of our bunk beds and were pulling up our pants when we heard, next to our barrack, the order of Oremland and Schönbach, "*HKP raus, raus* [HKP out, out]." We ran out of the barrack in a hurry and we stood in a row. The order came: "Forward, quickly, on the double," and we were driven in the direction of the exit gate of the camp and from there to the neighboring DAW. Several SS men and an SS officer were already there. The officer obviously had not yet had the chance to dress completely, for he was standing in officer trousers and boots, in a shirt, but without a jacket. He was holding a pistol in his outstretched hand and was, with his shouts, driving all the people to the burning buildings, to the workshops. The purpose was to save the tools, equipment, and whatever else was possible, from the fire. Meanwhile, the fire was growing; flames were consuming an ever greater part of the workshops. Burning beams were falling with noisy cracks and prisoners were trying to save whatever they could from the flames. I took a look around and decided that I did not want to go into the fire for the good of the Reich and the SS.

I quickly noticed that in the meantime a chain of prisoners had been formed to speedily pass buckets of water from the fire hydrant in the street to the fire. I pushed myself into that row of people and in this way avoided being fried in the fire. We worked in transporting water so quickly and effectively that finally, when the fire trucks arrived, we had already extinguished the fire. Was this fire caused by an act of sabotage, as was said then, or not—we did not know.

Willhaus was very satisfied with our achievement, and we were told that he expressed his pride to Captain Hartmann of the HKP, who had just then arrived. Referring to the uprising in the Warsaw ghetto, which took place in April 1943, Willhaus said, "This is not Warsaw, these are my Jews."

"This is a doubtful compliment for us," I said in a low voice to other inmates.

Willhaus also expressed his acknowledgment to Oremland for having chosen us, HKP, to do this work, and for the results of our work. Some half an hour later Oremland, a simple country man with no education, but cunning, appeared suddenly in our HKP barrack and, with his arms akimbo, made a pathetic speech: "Venerable gentlemen of the HKP, I thank you very much for what you did for my personality." We laughed heartily at this "personality."

All signs on the earth and in the sky indicated that the transitory period of leniency was about to end and that the last stage of the Jewish tragedy was approaching, the ultimate extermination. In the first half of May, the weekly *Das Reich* published an article by Goebbels titled *"Der Krieg und die Juden* [The War and the Jews]." This minister of propaganda of the Third Reich foreshadowed the radical solution to the Jewish question in the very near future. Obviously, Goebbels did not write explicitly that a decision had been taken to murder, down to the ground, all the still-surviving Jews; he wrote only of the necessity of separation and isolation of the Jews so as to make them harmless, but one could find in the article the following sentence: "In the fight over our being or not being, we have to get rid of our enemy in our hinterland." Then, Goebbels wrote that this must be done "without pity and without mercy."

The purpose was to prepare everyone beforehand, so that during this ultimate liquidation of thousands of innocent people, no remorse should, God forbid, awaken in the German soldiers; rather, they would be able to withhold even the smallest sign of compassion for those being bestially murdered—in other words, to make the operation go smoothly and painlessly.

For us in the camp, who on our own selves had been experiencing all the ups and downs and nuances of anti-Jewish politics of the German rulers, each such enunciation (or visit from some of Hitler's henchmen) meant a new wave of markedly increased persecution or an outright massacre, and so this article in the semiofficial newspaper *Das Reich* caused strong despondency and anxiety.

This anxiety got even more tense when soon afterward, in the German daily for Lwów, *Lemberger Zeitung*, the governor-general of occupied Poland, Dr. Frank, was quoted as saying, in his major annual address on plans for the upcoming year, "If you ask me for the watchword for the near future, I tell you, our watchword is—Jews, Jews, Jews."

For the thinkers in our inmate society, everything was clear. A new wave; new actions were coming, most probably the liquidation of the rest of the ghettos. Those camps that still remained had their days numbered as well. It would begin in a matter of weeks or at most months. This new direction was soon felt in the camp. Instances of shooting and prisoners' being tormented under the slightest pretext appeared anew.

One day, after we had returned from work to the camp, we noticed a strange phenomenon that, initially, alarmed us. Almost all the SS men were wearing helmets, and the watchtowers and posts were manned with SS men and not, as usual, with Askaris. In the outer portion of the camp the Askaris were standing in two rows, unarmed. In front of them stood the camp commander, Untersturmführer Willhaus, making a speech, surrounded by SS men. We worried that, as had often been the case, they were going out for new actions in provincial localities and that Willhaus was giving them his final instructions before they set out.

This anxiety lasted for almost one hour, at which point it gave way to relief, and even a feeling of satisfaction, for it turned out that the Askaris, whom we hated no less than the SS men, had been disarmed and, as a punishment, transported away in some unknown direction. There were people who said that they had been sent back to the prisoner of war camp from which they had originally been recruited; some others said that they "went to waste" (had been executed).

Only six Askaris were kept, the ones who were trusted by the SS men. For several days one could not see Askaris in the camp, which was greeted with joy by all of us, and was even enthusiastically commented on by some incorrigible optimists as the sign of a change for the better.

After just a few days these optimists found themselves wrong again, for a new detachment of Askaris appeared in the camp. These Askaris turned out to be even worse than the previous ones. They tried to be even more zealous than their predecessors in beating and tormenting us. Later, it turned out that in connection with the new era, our rulers had decided to replace the old detachment of Askaris who, in their opinion, were unreliable. There had been occasional cases of escapes from work of armed Askaris together with Jewish prisoners. Our rulers could rely on the new detachment with more certainty, insofar as these Askaris had not yet entered into deals with the Jews.

The new Askaris had the opportunity to display their zeal during the very next "vitamins." When transports of various materials meant for our camp came to the Kleparów railway station, located several hundred meters away, the Askaris and SS men would storm into the barracks, where we had not yet had time to rest after work, and would drive us out, beating us with whips and rifle butts. We had to run in groups to Kleparów station and, taking these materials, had to run back to the camp carrying them. We were often obliged to make such rounds several times. When carrying beams, we called them "vitamin B" (from the Polish *belki*); bricks were "vitamin C" (from the Polish *cegła*); boards were "vitamin D" (from the Polish *deska*); iron crossbars were "vitamin T" (from the Polish *trawers*); and so on. Those who did not run quickly enough or could not carry such heavy loads were often beaten until they were unconscious. After such vitamins the road from the camp to Kleparów station was frequently strewn with the dead bodies of such camp inmates. This had always been the case; however, these new guards beat the running prisoners with sticks and rifle butts under *any* pretext, and even with no pretext whatsoever. These vitamins had a much more brutal character than any in the past four to five months.

Once, when we were taking vitamin D (boards), we made one round and put them down in the camp. We were happy because the camp police did not send us on a new round to Kleparów station. It turned out, though, that this was a misunderstanding, for two or three railway cars had been left unloaded. Soon, the SS men were running into the barracks, shouting *"Raus, raus,"* beating us blindly with their whips. Like a herd of sheep, we ran out of the barracks, and our panic increased even more when we saw Willhaus at the entrance to the roll call square, with his "saxophone" or *gragier* (a wooden noisemaker toy used by Jewish children during the holiday of Purim), as his submachine gun was called in the camp. He used to parade with this gun especially when he was thirsty for blood. Willhaus fired a series of shots aimed at the barracks, after which he went with a quick pace toward the kitchen, where some prisoners were still standing in line for soup, not suspecting anything. At this moment, an inmate walked out of barrack seven. Seeing Willhaus at a distance of some hundred meters, he quickly turned on his heel back toward the barrack door. Willhaus noticed him and turned his *gragier* toward him. This all lasted for a fraction of a second. The *gragier* roared, the inmate somersaulted like a clown and collapsed in a pool of blood in front of the door. This, however, was not enough to calm down the beast. Soon after, we heard a new series of shots beside the kitchen. Some more corpses fell down, and only then was "Willie," as we called him, calmed.

A few days later, we learned on the way back to the camp that there were vitamins anew. We tried, therefore, to go slowly to the *lager* so as to arrive as late as possible. On the way, we met other brigades returning from town that were trying to do the same. Suddenly, a truck full of SS men from the camp arrived and a dramatic scene took place on Janowska Street in front of the passersby. Inmates, in chaotic groups, were hurrying with all their might toward the camp in the middle of the street and on the sidewalk. We were followed by a truck with SS men who, when they caught up with a victim, would jump off the truck and beat him with whips on the head and face. Everyone was running blindly with their last strength in order to avoid being beaten or, even worse, being run over by the truck. The street was hellishly long, and one could not see its end. Fortunately for me, my brigade was able to avoid most of the attacks, which came largely to the brigade in front of us.

Some two hundred meters in front of the camp, one of the victims got under the wheels of the truck and had both legs broken. The rest of the inmates, bleeding and beaten, reached the camp with difficulty. But more vitamins awaited us. We barely had time to get over this one game when another scene shook us up. We went to the railway station and not far from the vitamin transport there stood a freight train. German and Ukrainian police were chasing people out of the cars and putting them in the order known to us as *zu fünft* (by five). As it turned out, this was the transport of people from the action in the town of Stryj or in its neighborhood. Apparently, some plans had changed and instead of being sent to Bełzec, the victims were unloaded in Lwów and brought to Janowska camp.

Soon a death parade moved on in the direction of the camp. How well we knew this view, which opened our wounds anew—this march of pale, depressed people, broken down physically and mentally, looking about vaguely, with mute expressions of despair on their faces. The silence was a hundred times louder than shouting, than human yelling. This mute cry should have shaken the earth and heaven.

Leading the march was, among the others, an elderly woman with silver-gray hair on her head. Against this silver background of hair a great red stain of blood stood out more distinctly. Clotted blood together with her tangled hair formed something that looked like a red cap on her silver head. Apparently, one of the fighters of the *Neue Ordnung* ("New Order") had offered her a blow for not being quick enough. But we knew that silver-haired older people deserve respect. That was what we had been taught during our childhood. Perhaps these uniformed executioners here had been taught the same, though everyone, it seemed, understood this in a different way.

The elderly woman had apparently not been considered a human being. Were she, however, an animal, who would dare to strike her calmly with a rifle butt on the head? Conscience would not allow him to do it. And besides, an animal protection society could step in. Yes, but this elderly woman was not even an animal in their view. She was something much worse, for she was a Jewess. She was a mother and grandmother of some Jewish children. There was, alas, no Jews protection society. And there was nobody who could stand up for her and for those thousands and millions of people like her. She had to simply drop dead.

Behind the marching procession we could see young men pulling dead bodies from the cattle cars and throwing these bodies onto a truck. These were the people who had not survived the transport in the stifling cars filled to the limit with people deprived of food and water, or those who had tried to resist the order of beastly death and save themselves with an escape.

There had to be orderliness in the new Europe, and because these people were to have died together with the whole transport, the truck carrying their bodies followed the marchers to the camp. Here they were all kept in the outer square to await their common fate.

The next day, Saturday, May 22, 1943, we received some news from the ghetto—that is, from the so-called *Julag.* The ghetto had been surrounded by German and Ukrainian police. All the columns of workers going out from the ghetto to work in the city were stopped at the exit gates. The whole elite of the Lwów Gestapo, with all the main officials responsible for the Jewish department, with Inquart (brother of the notorious Dr. Seyss-Inquart), Sawicki, and still other Gestapo men, arrived in front of the gate. They gave a speech to the Jews, calling for calm and no panicking. Nothing wrong would happen to anyone, for workers were needed for the work in the forest, in afforestation. Thus, as usual, columns of people went marching out to work in fives. Every third group of five would be drawn aside and directed to work in the forest. The officers assured everyone that nothing would happen to these people. After having finished their work, these chosen people would return to the ghetto.

In the Jewish ranks there was more calm then. After all, it was not just anybody, it was the high-ranking German officers who had assured the

Jews that nothing bad would happen to them, that they were only going to work in the forest. It was known that the word of an officer always meant something, and the word of a German officer should be even more valid, since the Germans treated *Soldatentum und Ehre* (a soldier's life and honor) with the highest sanctity—so the naive ones believed. . . .

After the selection was finished, the chosen ones were loaded onto the trucks with the accompaniment of beatings with whips and rifle butts, and then were escorted by guards and brought to Janowska camp. There, in the outer square, they were joined with the people from the transport from Stryj, and waited for further orders from the SS authorities.

The situation was ripe for action. In the evening, my brother and I decided that on the next day he would escape, either from work or on the way to work, to the hideout in St. Martin's Street. Our father and sister were waiting for him there. After just a few days, he would go away as an Aryan to one of the small towns in the eastern Galician countryside. My brother had bought vodka and cake somewhere, in order to celebrate the very next day in St. Martin's, his day of escape and liberation from the camp. We bade each other farewell, drinking some of this vodka in a corner of the corridor of the twelfth barrack, where his Betonwerke brigade slept. We each had one small glass, wishing each other to live to the day of final liberation, soon. My brother was in a very good mood, but I was overtaken by a strange melancholy.

It was a strange thing—over nine and a half months we had been together in the camp, and in the first five months my situation had been much worse than his. Death had looked into my eyes much more often; I had been beaten more frequently, and still it had been me who had always been full of optimism, while he had been gloomy. I thought for myself and for him, I trembled for his life not less than for mine, I had been taking care of him like a brother and a son—he was eleven years my junior; I could say I almost brought him up. I always had been keeping his spirits up, comforting him, and assuring him that we would soon be liberated. And now, in the moment when it seemed that we were halfway to the goal, that he, a part of my own self, should be free the very next day, after my long efforts . . . I had helped Gina to prepare everything for his flight, negotiating with his new brigadier and delivering five thousand złotys to him for covering up the affair of Józek's escape, and still something was haunting me, some subconscious bad apprehension. My brother took it as resulting from the fact that it was he who was escaping while I was to be left in the camp, and now it was he comforting me and calming my bad thoughts, saying that my family were all awaiting me and I could join them any time in the hideout. He misunderstood, however. For my own part, I still wanted to wait until the Russians were close, and not risk staying in that hideout. My uneasiness was something else, hard for me to explain. On this night I went to sleep in my bunk bed with a heavy heart.

On the next day, Sunday, May 23, 1943, when we stood up for the roll call, we noticed with anxiety that the band wasn't at the internal exit gate of the camp as usual. Tense, we awaited the further course of events. Soon, Willhaus appeared before the gate with the whole pack. The first brigades started marching in the direction of the inside exit. "Stop, Aryans back." Yes, the apprehension became reality. The death race selection started. Everyone's nervousness and anxiety reached their peak. Whereas every day there was some selection of those who looked ill as we went out to work, the death race was an additional selection, based on our running strength as compared with others in our groups. These took place only every few weeks or so, and in the "good" times had been even less frequent.

I came up to my brother, who was extremely nervous. He could not stand in one place, his nerves were strained to the utmost limits. What bad luck, just today, when he was about to escape, just today was the death race. Why had he not escaped earlier? I tried to reassure him and to explain that his self-control would decide whether he would pass through the sieve of selection or not. I tried several times to remove the smallest faults in his clothes, his cleanliness, and other aspects of his appearance. I stated that everything was correct. I reassured him once again and went back to my brigade.

From there I started to observe the situation. It was important, very important, to do so, for on many occasions the smallest matters could have great significance in determining one's chances for survival, matters such as starting the death race a few minutes earlier or later. Being an experienced camp inmate, I also had some knowledge of these races, and knew how crucial it was to note what was going on ahead of us. What made us especially nervous was the fact that, for the first time, the authorities did not care whether one was a skilled specialist or what the victim's appearance was. Everything depended only upon the whims of Willhaus and the SS *Scharführer*, and I now understood that the ultimate liquidation had come. The issue now was the numbers, the quota ordered from central headquarters, and not the value of a given victim, so that it was just a question of a short time before these survivors would again be sorted out. *Usque ad finem* (Till the end).

Meanwhile, the group of those put "behindwire" was growing almost with every second. As usual, during the death race the SS men and Askaris would trip those who were running and beat them with whips.

The ones put "behindwire" had their shoes pulled off and their utensils and haversacks taken away. At the moment when Willhaus went out for a while, we moved on toward the gate and set out for the race. Our brigade was small; altogether there were nineteen men. Four were taken out of our ranks even before the death race started. The race itself went well; there were fifteen of us left.

After having passed the outside gate checkup, we marched quickly to town to work. We were saved, but for how long? This question haunted us incessantly. I was, beside this, still extremely anxious about my brother, wondering whether he had gotten through the sieve and whether he had managed to flee to the city. After a few hours, I received good news— Józek telephoned me at Opel-Damke! He had miraculously passed selection: SS Scharführer Siller had wanted to put him "behindwire," but after a while of hesitating, he let him go. On the way to work, Józek escaped and was calling from Faliński's office in the laundry at St. Martin's Street, downstairs from the hideout.

I was very, very happy, but after just a few hours I was overtaken by a wave of depression. What now? And how long would we still be tormented? Would we withstand it? I looked at the newspaper that I had bought from a newsman on the way—no bigger changes in the east. The same in the west. When, finally, would the second front be created? They were not hurrying there, and here thousands of innocent people were perishing every day, here the earth was burning under our feet. The noose on all our necks was getting tighter and tighter. If I could only get through somehow to the forests, to some guerrilla groups. But in our neighborhood around Lwów, the guerrilla was some fantastical notion. People spoke of it, but no one could see or meet it. It existed only in the propaganda disseminated through rumors and in the illegal press.

Here and there acts of sabotage occurred, certainly, but they were apparently not the deeds of the "forest people." A group of young men, armed Jews, had recently left the ghetto during the night to go to the forests and join any kind of guerrilla group whatsoever that they might find there. After some time they had encountered Poles or Ukrainians, who had led the Jews into an ambush, taken away their weapons, robbed them, and driven away. These Jews had barely saved their lives and were forced to come back to the ghetto.

The tragedy of Golus (the Diaspora) became apparent to the Jews. To fight with the enemy openly was to fight the sun with a hoe. To conduct guerrilla warfare, or at least to hide oneself, was impossible without the help, or at least the mere neutrality, of the local population. But this local population not only did not want to provide help, they would not sell bread to a Jew, even for a lot of money. Without food one could not survive in the forest. Even worse—the locals, wherever they could, would themselves attack the Jews in hiding, who just wanted to fight against the common enemy. They would rob the Jews, murder them, or, in the best of cases, inform the Gestapo of the places where Jews were hiding. In this sea of hatred, the shipwrecked Jews could not keep their heads above water, and sooner or later they fell into the hands of the Gestapo or Ukrainian police.

On the day after Józek's escape, Monday, May 24, 1943, all those selected—meaning those put "behindwire" in Sunday's death race; those from the transport from Stryj; and those brought to the camp from the ghetto on Saturday, except for a small group of those who had been reselected to work in the camp—were loaded, with beatings by whips and rifle butts, into the cattle cars in Kleparów railway station to be transported to Bełzec. The road from the camp to the station was closed for pedestrian and vehicular traffic, guarded by a double row of police. The transport was completed with all the ill prisoners from the camp hospital, which had been totally purged. All the victims were either naked or in shirts only.

In the afternoon of that day, we were coming back from work in a pessimistic mood. In our barrack, where all the HKP brigades lived, we did not encounter a better atmosphere. Everybody was commenting on the events of that day. For instance, one could hear how the daughter of an engineer, one of the HKP brigade foremen who was a much esteemed older man, was taken during the selection. She was trying to resist in Kleparów station, where all victims were ordered to undress and stay only in their shirts before being loaded into the cattle cars. This beautiful girl, approximately twenty years old, had not wanted to follow this order. One of the SS men shot her dead on the spot with his pistol. This had a "pacifying" influence on the others who hesitated.

Suddenly those who were telling us this all stopped and we all looked in the direction of the barrack windows. Our eyes saw an extraordinary scene, which resembled the images from the times of Emperor Nero. A group of people was marching through the center of the square. Most probably these people had been caught during their flight from the Bełzec transport. A man of thirty to forty years of age was leading. He was barefoot, in black trousers and undone shirt, with a child in his arms. Side by side with him was a woman, also barefoot, in a ragged dress, and behind them two men and two women, all of them without shoes. The men were wearing only slacks and shirts, and then, behind all the others, an eight- to ten-year-old boy, who was naked, wrapped in a sack, and driven by a big German shepherd dog.

This procession had the rear brought up by three SS men armed with rifles, and among them was the terror of the camp, the notorious Heinen, with his submachine gun. The dog incessantly attacked the boy, and was tearing away pieces of the sack with which the boy was wrapped. The boy cried out at the top of his voice, sometimes stopping and sometimes trying to run away. The dog was biting away piece after piece, so that finally everything was taken away and the boy was completely naked. Then the dog ran for the naked boy, who shouted piercingly, but nobody paid attention. The group ahead of him tried to accelerate its steps in order to get to the place of destiny as soon as possible. The SS men following the boy were laughing heartily and telling each other funny things. They were going along as if for fun.

Finally, the whole group reached the square behind the kitchen, where the gallows stood and where, beside hangings, executions of a smaller scale were carried out. Here all of the victims were ordered to undress. They obediently complied with the order. The man who was carrying the baby did not want to get separated from it, and pressed the child more strongly to his chest. Shots from the submachine gun roared. Bodies tumbled. Subsequent victims were hanged. One married couple was left, but there was only one place left on the gallows. Heinen then decided to hang them on one rope. The rope, however, did not withstand the weight and broke. They tried a second time, but with the same effect. Heinen then had an ingenious idea—he ordered them to immediately lie down and have sexual intercourse. The victims looked at each other for a while and, obviously fearing further torment more than death, tried to do what they were told. The SS men were beside themselves with laughter. Fantastic fun. What ideas! For some moments they enjoyed this funny view. Finally the game became boring for them, and with shots in the necks of both spouses the entertainment was finished. The SS men went back through the square to their mess hall, as if from a splendid show, joyfully laughing and happy.

On the next day, in the morning before the roll call, disturbing news spread around. People were whispering that small brigades were to be liquidated and only big ones were to be left. Nobody knew what and how, but anxiety was growing. The orchestra did not arrive. Time passed. The sun was rising. We were all standing in ranks for the roll call, but roll call was not taking place. Different, often conflicting, rumors crossed each other in the crowd. Suddenly there was news that caused panic. Namely, someone had learned somewhere that our camp policemen had been sent away to the institutions where our workers had been left for the so-called *Nachtdienst* (night service), with the order to immediately return all inmates to the camp. What would happen? Would it be liquidation?

Tension was rising. Soon, a table and three chairs were brought to the roll call square, and Hilda, the main secretary from the *Aufnahmebüro*, and another clerk, both German Jews, together with SS men, came to the square. They brought files and ordered individual brigades to come to the table to be registered. A wave of relief passed through the crowd. So, it was not liquidation but a checkup registration. Thank God. Those from the night service would be full of fear when they arrived. They would have fantastic faces when they came and then saw that it was only registration. And, indeed, after an hour or so, groups coming back from the *Nachtdienst* started pouring in. People were pale, scared. When they learned what this was all about, they started to hug each other in joy. They had been so depressed; there had been rumors circulating in the city that there would be a liquidation in the camp. They had been wondering whether to come back or not. Yes, but it is easy to say that you would not come back; however, where to go then? What next? And, thank God, everything ended well.

See, though, what sort of situation we were in. We suspected that we were going to be executed, and still we had little choice about returning to the camp. This was our bloody Jewish situation, in which, even knowing that we were probably going to die, we had to come back, for there was no other way out for us. We were sentenced to depend upon the grace of our torturers.

Our moods were slowly improving. We only wanted this registration to end as soon as possible, in order to go to work in the city, to get out of this damned camp. But time passed and we were not sent to work. We in the HKP brigades were more hopeful than others, for whatever happened our brigades would not get dissolved, since they were some of the most important ones. But we had less and less hope for going out to work on that day.

In the meantime, the sun got higher and it got hotter and hotter in the roll call square. Heinen was circulating like a vulture among the brigades, doing his usual routine, but much more so, since we were now standing there for hours at his mercy, instead of being exposed for just the usual short time going to or returning from work. He singled out his victims, and seemed even more calm and unthreatening than usual, for his hands were free—no submachine gun, not even the whip, with which he usually never parted. The victim, even more assured, thinking that the purpose of the order was to do some work in the kitchen, would follow Heinen, who did not look back. When the SS man and his victim were already behind the kitchen, Heinen would pull out his pistol. He would order the victim to undress completely and, after having meticulously put down his clothes, turn his back to Heinen. With a shot in the neck, the victim would fall down and the game was over. Over and over, this same ceremony was repeated. Still bloodthirsty, Heinen continued with this procedure until he was tired. Fear overtook the inmates, for they finally guessed what was going on. Heinen, a death symbol, wandered around incessantly.

Then a sigh of relief—a limousine was noticed stopping in front of Willhaus's villa. An officer got out of the car. Some people recognized that he was from HKP. Accompanied by his aide, he went in to see the camp commander. Joy reigned in our ranks. It was an intervention on our behalf. And, indeed, about ten minutes later, SS Scharführer Schönbach came out of Willhaus's villa with a list in his hand, and we heard his order from afar—the call for HKP. So we would go to work. All the other brigades envied us enormously. We stood in double ranks. Schönbach took out the list and started reading names. Those people whose names were read out loud, after having proven their identity, had to form new ranks on the side. Anxiety overtook us again. A new selection. And nobody knew whether to be happy or sad about having one's name read, for among these were both skilled and unskilled workers. There were also some who had died or had been killed long ago. The list was therefore old and put together in a hurry.

Finally Schönbach ended the reading. Out of some four hundred people in all the HKP brigades, a little over one hundred names had been read. The reading would continue at two P.M., though, he said, and went away. Astonishment, disappointment, and anxiety grew among us. There were numerous first-class specialists among those not read out yet, but there were specialists in the other group as well. What did this mean? Nervously, we waited for two P.M. to come.

After two o'clock, Willhaus himself arrived with the manager of the Lueg firm, one of the private firms that worked for HKP. The largest of the three HKP brigades was the one that worked at HKP itself, at the caserns. The other two were Lueg and Opel-Damke (my own brigade, the smallest of the three). The Lueg manager was a good friend of Willhaus.

Again HKP was assembled. From these, the entire Lueg brigade was called out to stand on the side. Turning to the rest of us, who had not yet been called out from HKP, the Lueg manager asked who among us were specialists and of what kind. Various specialists started to call out eagerly. It was clear by now that it was better to be in the selected group. After several were chosen to join the Lueg brigade, one of the associates of the Lueg manager whispered something to him: "Opel-Damke." My brigade! It was mainly composed of specialists in car repairs. Both rulers of our lives now looked at us. "Who are you with this case?" the Lueg manager asked me, pointing toward my medical bag.

"Medical doctor," I said.

"Doctor? I do not need any doctor," he replied. Willhaus ordered me with his whip to move aside. Others begged to be taken, giving their area of skill. Only some of them were accepted. The rest were also being waved at with Willhaus's whip. Willhaus turned to his friend, saying loudly, "This goes to other enterprises." I did not know then what kind of "enterprise" Willhaus meant.

My situation was desperate. I was without a brigade assignment, and I did not know where they would assign me, to what brigade. I didn't think of any worse possibility, but feared I might lose the relative freedom I'd had and my contacts with family and the outside world. I walked about the roll call square looking for my friends and acquaintances in order to share my worries with them. I encountered everywhere the mood of uncertainty and nervousness. Rumors said that only a small number of bigger brigades would be sorted out, while the rest would be transferred to a camp somewhere in the countryside, supposedly to Jaryczów (a small town in the province around Lwów). Despair overtook me. I was aware that going into the countryside meant death for me. I would not have any assistance from the outside. I would lose contact with my family and with the hideout to which I could eventually flee, in case of emergency. One of the pessimists offered the idea that perhaps the rest would go "to waste." But he was laughed off and scolded as a croaking raven.

Willhaus, in the meantime, walked up to the registration table and, having looked at the clerks' work for a while, started to berate them, apparently unhappy with how it was being done. New registration! The previous one was not valid. The news spread like lightning, and after a while the desk, together with the employees, moved over to the outer camp square. The people who had been selected from HKP that morning, followed by the enlarged Lueg brigade, and then the ZELA 19 (*Zentralersatzlager* 19) brigade, were called to register there, which caused general commotion. The latter brigade was known as the worst, quasi-penal brigade, because its Jewish workers were very badly beaten and tortured during work.

Hence, the information that this brigade had been included in the selected elite caused astonishment. We experienced even greater surprise when the brigadiers of the two best brigades—VIB (*Vereinigte Industrie-Betriebe*, the United Industrial Enterprises) and the *Reinigungsamt* (street-cleaning brigade)—were called forward. These brigades did not have the influence that HKP had, but their employers treated them very well. These two brigadiers—Muszkat and Birnbaum, respectively—had both enjoyed the grace and support of the SS men, often giving them bribes and gifts. They were now called forward by the SS, and upon their return from this audience they chose thirty friends and protégés from VIB and forty from Reinigung, and then marched to the first square in order to register to ZELA 19. This was an incredible scene—from these privileged brigades, on the advice of the SS, to that penal one? This, however, resulted in even greater anxiety among us.

A general roll call was now ordered, to be held in the roll call square at five o'clock in the afternoon. The whole elite of the SS, headed by Willhaus and Gebauer (SS Hauptsturmführer and the DAW commander), came as well. Willhaus ordered the three brigades selected so far to stand on one side of the roll call square. These brigades were HKP, Lueg, and ZELA 19. Then he called out the *Betonwerke* brigade (which went to work in the concrete factory in the Org. Todt camp), followed by the Ostbahnhof brigade and DAW, after which Willhaus walked from row to row of the remaining inmates. He assigned parts of some brigades to Ostbahnhof, and then he called out, as he stood in front of our ranks, asking for particular skills and trades. Those who reported were assigned to DAW, the third worst brigade. We were waiting, anxious, wondering what would happen to us. I especially wondered what would become of the rest of HKP.

"What kind of brigade is this?" asked Willhaus, approaching VIB with all his pack. VIB had until then been a privileged brigade. "VIB." Willhaus smiled ironically, and, having tipped his cap, bowed sarcastically. "Who of you is a locksmith, a blacksmith?" Not many answered, for nobody wanted to go to DAW. They waited for a better brigade. "All this to the wall," Willhaus said, waving his hand at them, telling them to retreat by a few steps toward the wall of the barrack standing behind them.

At this moment, it was as if something touched me. I was already a long-term inmate. This gesture of Willhaus's, to which others did not pay attention, alarmed me. I could not, neither then nor afterward, explain this to myself. But something moved within me then and pushed me to do an unprepared, strictly risky move. This move decided my life. Not waiting for our turn, before Willhaus passed in front of our HKP group, I retreated stealthily behind the rows, took off my doctor's red arm band, moved over to the left, and in the instant when Willhaus with his whole SS group turned in the opposite direction, I quickly paced through the empty ground in the middle of the square to the *Betonwerke* brigade, standing some fifty to sixty meters away in front of us. This was an extremely risky step. If any of the SS men had turned back and noticed me, I would have been lost. I would have been beaten with whips until

unconscious and then killed. But I felt as if some invisible hand was pushing me in this direction.

Frightened to death, I crossed the distance to the concreters. I immediately turned to their brigadier, Rosenblüth, asking him to hide me among
his workers. But he announced that he did not need a medical doctor and
told me to go away. I promised to be a concreter like everybody else, and
besides this I promised to pay him, as I had done for my brother. This latter promise convinced him. Everything went on in a flash. I barely had
time to position myself in the ranks when Willhaus turned in our direction and ordered Hilda to continue the registration, beginning with
Betonwerke. In a short while I was a concreter.

My colleagues and acquaintances admired my boldness and determina-
tion. I was reasoning logically. It was possible that by waiting I could have
become a doctor in a brigade, perhaps even in not a bad brigade. But all
this was uncertain, I had thought to myself. I wanted to feel ground
beneath my feet. They would probably leave this *Betonwerke* brigade
alone, because Graefe, the director of Org. Todt and the one who had
saved me when I was put "behindwire," was a friend of Commander
Willhaus. In a few days I would examine the situation, and if things went
badly, I would escape.

The sun was setting, and dusk came. Soon Willhaus stopped the selection, announcing it would continue the next day. That evening in the barracks there were long discussions on the subject of what had happened.
Many boasted that despite being skilled mechanics they had kept this
secret in order not to get into the bad brigades. Tomorrow there would
certainly be better ones, so they said. They were satisfied that they had
succeeded in avoiding those bad brigades so far.

CHAPTER 18

DAY OF DOOM

May 26, 1943. A day to remember. During the roll call, the brigades selected on the previous day were ordered to go out to work. The band was playing joyful marches. The internal gate was not, however, wide open as it usually had been during the march out to work, but closed. Suddenly the gate was opened, and the first brigade to be called out was the HKP brigade that had been selected on the previous day. Contrary to usual practice, after this brigade went out, the gate was closed again. Similarly, contrary to usual practice, a very accurate check of the brigade was carried out as its members went through the gate, by calling out names and numbers while checking prisoners. All this, of course, took a lot of time. Finally, HKP marched out to work and the gate closed.

The gate opened again and the Lueg brigade started marching out next. Again, there was a strict check. Suddenly Heinen, who had been standing by and was looking melancholy at the whole procedure, jumped up from his place. He had found something for himself. Namely, during the check of the Lueg brigade, it turned out that one of the inmates present, a saddlemaker named Hoffmann, a boy some twenty years old, was not on the list. The boy's desperate explanation—that he had been on the list selected by the Lueg manager, and that it had only been the brigadier who crossed his name out and replaced it with somebody else's name out of favoritism or for money—were of no use. Nothing helped—neither explanations, nor supplication, nor begging. SS Scharführer Schönbach, who was directing the control together with other SS men, trusted only the brigadiers, as did all the SS. Having received a few strikes with a whip for the way, Hoffmann had to return to the roll call square.

Here, however, Heinen already waited for his victim. "Come here." He waved his finger. Hoffmann understood what was in the air and started to beg Heinen to let him go. Heinen pulled out his pistol. "You come here at once." Hoffmann gave in. Heinen sat in a chair and ordered Hoffmann to lie at his feet, and kept his pistol in his hand in case the victim was disobedient. He looked around, searching for new victims. Hoffmann slightly rose and, taking a kneeling position, put his hands together as if to pray and started to implore Heinen: "Let me go, please, Sir Scharführer, I am innocent, I want to work." It was one of the very few cases during almost a year of my stay in Janowska camp that someone asked Heinen to have his life spared. Heinen scolded him, directing the pistol toward him, and barked, "Be quiet, you dog. If you say one more word you will be shot at once." Hoffmann lay down again like a dog at Heinen's feet.

In the meantime, the ZELA 19 brigade was let out. Heinen got bored with waiting and called Hoffmann to follow him. Hoffmann went obediently, trying on the way to beg Heinen to let him go. Heinen was, however, unyielding. After a few minutes a shot was heard from behind the kitchen. We knew what this meant. Hoffmann's sister, who was standing nearby in the women's brigade, cried out and burst into spasmodic weeping. Soon, Heinen's silhouette appeared in the distance from behind the kitchen. He came back alone, calmly, as if nothing had happened.

Meanwhile, the Ostbahnhof brigade had gone through. Now it was our turn, the *Betonwerke* brigade, which I had joined at that fateful moment the previous day. But time passed and the gate remained closed. We were nervous. We wanted so much to find ourselves beyond the gate already. The band played marches on and on. A quarter of an hour passed, half an hour, one hour, and the gate was still not opened. Suddenly, a lively commotion in all brigades, and all heads turned toward the outer square, where Willhaus's black limousine appeared.

Willhaus stepped out of the car, holding some list in his hand. Upon his gesture, Rysiek Axer, from the office, and head Jew Oremland rushed to him. Willhaus made some arrangements with them, and they ran quickly to the roll call square. "Gentlemen, a new order: everything will go on as before. All of you go back to work in your original brigades."

A frenzy of enthusiasm overtook everybody. "Hurrah! Hurrah!" Caps went flying in the air. People hugged each other. Thank God! So we were to go back to our previous workplaces. One had gotten accustomed to things there, and already had acquaintances and contacts. In a few words—we could manage somehow. It was better to have the old bad place than a new unknown. Anyway, we could not expect anything better.

In a flash, those chosen for DAW, and for the *Betonwerke* and other brigades, ran back to their previous brigades. Obviously, I also went back to my old brigade, HKP. My old companions surrounded me. There was endless joy.

"Laokoon brigade, forward march!" After them, *Verschiedene Firmen*, *Luftpostkommando*, Kommando Charkow, and finally the HKP brigades were called out. We moved over in the direction of the gate. The brigades ahead of us had gone out already. We did not pay attention to what was going on at the checkpoint during the march out. Willhaus stopped us at the gate. "Are specialists here?"

"Yes sir," said Rysiek Axer.

"Damn you, go back," shouted Willhaus.

We retreated quickly, not understanding what this was about. In a short while Axer ran into the roll call square and ordered, "Those who were assigned yesterday to other brigades have to stay with them. Understood?" Nobody moved. The specialists did not want to leave their old brigades. "No one will go to work until they return to their assigned brigades," said Axer. When this still had no effect, Axer jumped into the ranks and pulled out the resisting inmates with force. He was desperately trying to save these people, but at that time I was puzzled by his actions. Apparently he had misunderstood Willhaus, and wrongly told us to return to our old brigades. Willhaus had not wanted this, and Axer didn't either because he realized now what was happening. The camp police followed his steps. This lasted for almost ten minutes.

"HKP, march out." I hesitated. Should I go with them or with the concreters?

"Come with us, my friend," said Dr. Halpern, a known specialist in joint diseases in Lwów, whom I knew well and who also marched in the ranks of what remained of HKP.

"Come, we'll talk a bit, come, come with us," called Dr. Ginsberg, who also went with the HKP brigades.

"Doctor, come back," shouted Rosenblüth to me from the *Betonwerke* brigade. "I will have trouble because of you, for you are registered with the concreters."

I hesitated again. HKP was just passing through the gate and was almost past the exit; now was the point of no return. In almost the last second I stopped. No, I thought, I could not be unfair to Rosenblüth by leaving *Betonwerke*. He had accepted me to Betonwerke and therefore I should not repay him like that, even if I was to work with him as a concreter and not as a doctor. Reluctantly, I returned to the concreters, waving my hand with a gesture of resignation to my friends from HKP, who had already gone to the outer square. I returned to the *Betonwerke* brigade.

Brigades were going out one after another. We still had time. We were busy talking among ourselves when someone suddenly called out, "Hey, gentlemen, look what's going on." We looked toward the outer square. The procedure of marching out to work was taking a somewhat different course than normally. Once out in front of the booth, the brigades waited longer than usual. Then SS men assigned Askaris to escort a brigade. This had not happened for some time. Askaris loaded their rifles, as usual, and surrounded the brigade, which set out when ordered. What was entirely new, though, was that each brigade was followed by SS men with helmets on and with submachine guns in their hands. The whole group soon disappeared around the turn of the road leading toward the external gate, invisible from our location.

Was it not for "goulash" (execution), asked one of us, an ex-foreman. No, it seems impossible, answered the others. They would have been seen on the road leading toward Kleparów railway station, from where transports to Bełzec would go, and the road was a bit visible from our camp. In fact, I had very sharp vision and could see no group on this road. Even so, one grain of anxiety, having been sown, started to grow among us. Nervousness increased, because there was something abnormal in this day's march out to work.

After some time two clerks from the camp bureau appeared nearby. "Hey, friends, what's going on?" we asked. We got no answer, but from their pale, gloomy faces one could guess what was going on at the external gate. Soon, news reached us that at this gate, not visible from the inside of the camp, there stood trucks with SS men and *Sonderdienst* (Special Service) in helmets, with submachine and machine guns. The brigades, believing they were on their way to work and not expecting anything, were driven with whips and rifle butts to the parked trucks. Everybody had to sit and bow their heads. The escorting Askaris, Ukrainian police, *Sonderdienst*, and SS guarded the trucks, pointing the barrels of their rifles toward those sitting inside. The trucks sped along down Janowska Street, toward town and not the railway station, turning into Pilichowska Street in the direction of the sand pit behind the Jewish cemetery. There, enormous pits had already been prepared and a firing squad waited, commanded by SS Scharführer Schönbach. Execution went on with true German efficiency.

Every once in a while, a limousine would appear near the camp office, bringing Gestapo and SS officials, including General Katzmann. The whole road from the camp to the execution place was densely manned with German and Ukrainian police, and was entirely closed to foot and vehicular traffic. Even if someone were so bold and lucky as to succeed in jumping from the speeding truck, he would not be able to break through the police cordon.

Brigades went one after another. Not all of the inmates were aware of what was going on. Axer was running from one brigade to another and pulling out his acquaintances, skilled people, and those few educated people that were there, and tried to put them discreetly into DAW. This brigade had been selected the day before, and was to be spared, no doubt because Gebauer wanted to keep his workers.

Axer often encountered resistance. He was aware of what was going on, but the others did not know it. "You are a specialist," he roared, so as to make the SS men hear. "No," was the answer. Finally, Axer would push them with force out of their brigades, which were marching to their death, and bark in a low voice between his teeth, "You are a specialist, damn you, you idiot."

Once again, the figure of Heinen appeared. He was standing at the internal gate, together with two other SS men. Heinen could not stand idle; he was searching for victims with his eyes. Suddenly, he noticed a short young boy with a pale, emaciated, freckled face and red hair. The boy was pushing a wheelbarrow, busy with some earthworks inside the camp. Heinen calmly went up to him and stuck his rifle barrel to his neck. The boy, terrified, turned around. "Go on, you dog," shouted Heinen. The boy looked around desperately with helpless eyes and started to push the wheelbarrow anew. But Heinen would not let the boy go. He followed the boy like a shadow, keeping the barrel of his rifle at the boy's neck. The victim still tried a number of times to turn his head and beg to be let go. "Go, go," was the answer. They went like that some fifty meters. They went past the tenth barrack. A shot was fired. The frail figure of the boy dropped to the ground.

I knew the boy by sight. He used to often come to our barrack begging for bread or for just one złoty. He almost never said anything. It was enough to look at the pale, emaciated, precociously aging face of a teenage boy, his eyes expressing deep sadness, to have one's heart bleed. Words were unnecessary. Whatever I had on me, I would give it to him. But now he lay like a heap of rags beside the wheelbarrow. He still twitched. Heinen looked at him with contempt. After a while, he killed the boy off.

The sun was shining brighter and brighter. We still had not eaten anything. But we could not move, even to relieve ourselves. The number of brigades gradually diminished, and the band still played marches. All of a sudden we again saw a car driving in, from which Willhaus got out. He had a submachine gun in his hand. He walked up to the Jewish camp police standing in double rows in the outer square. They were his favorites. He had always promised them, "You will be the last ones" (presumably, the last to be killed, though he never said that explicitly). From such a distance, we could not hear what he was saying. We could only see a stir in the police ranks. Abruptly, Willhaus turned to the Askaris, who loaded their rifles and surrounded the Jewish police. Willhaus directed his submachine gun toward them and the whole detachment of police moved on toward the external gate. Those victims who resisted were driven with rifle butts by the Askaris.

Some Jewish policemen tried to step aside at the turn of the road, but without success. Willhaus personally, with his gun, led them all and left alive only his favorites, Commander Fluss and his deputy, Kessler, as well as the band, which was composed of police members.

We were overtaken by terror. Police "to waste"? This meant that the total liquidation of the camp had now come. Our legs felt weak from tiredness and fear. Death looked into our eyes.

In the meantime, a group of SS men came into the roll call square in the camp. They searched through all the barracks and pulled out all those hiding there, most of whom were convalescents weak from typhus. They were conducted behind the kitchen and shot dead there.

In front of the twelfth barrack a known Lwówian cardiologist, Dr. Glaserman, was sitting on a step. He was pale, for he had just recovered from typhus and from complications, namely pneumonia. One of the SS men noticed him. "Come," he said, and led him toward the kitchen. They passed by us. I shall never forget his face, white as chalk, with hopeless despair in his eyes, goggled from fear. The SS man was in a hurry, and even before he got to the kitchen, he shot Dr. Glaserman in the neck.

Afterward, Jewish women working in the kitchen were also driven out and joined with the women's brigade standing just outside the exit of the roll call square. Willhaus appeared in the square. He looked through the remaining brigades, kept some kind of list crossed with red pencil in his hand, and was calculating something. "So," he said loudly to the SS men surrounding him, and to Axer and Oremland, "this is yet to go." He pointed out the groups standing ahead of us. "And then the general roll call with the women will take place." After these words, he left the square.

At this point, someone tried to move more to the rear in a brigade. Across the roll call square, Heinen noticed this and approached that brigade. Since he could not find the culprit, who was wearing light-colored slacks, he selected fifteen men in light-colored slacks for execution.

The sun shone so as to burn us. It was noon already. There was greenery, sunshine—nature was full of life around us, and yet here death was mercilessly raking people, without a break. And the band was just playing fine waltzes from Lehar's operetta *The Merry Widow*. The band was directed by the very well known Lwówian musician and director Striks. On that day the orchestra seemed to play even more beautifully than ever. The heart of many a musician bled when someone from his own family was passing by in the brigades led out for execution, but, alas, they all had to play. They were ordered to.

The groups standing ahead of us slowly disappeared. It would soon be our turn. After a while, the women were ordered to go. "But Willhaus just told us something about a roll call with the women!" somebody whispered. Lies, all lies, I said to myself. It's our end. Today is total liquidation.

Despair and helplessness overtook us. And we will go like that, like sheep for slaughter? Something in me revolted, a wave of blood rushing to my head. I looked at my comrades. They were all either pale or blushing, looking forward with restless eyes, but after that anxiety had passed, there remained despair and resignation.

My legs bent under my body. I looked around. It was so beautiful that day, as if out of spite, so as to make us want to live and not leave this world behind. The orchestra was playing a known tango: "Yesterday my happiness was so near, yesterday the world smiled at me, but today everything is gone, happiness is gone with the wind." The violin wept tenderly. Only when facing death, it seems, can one play so sadly and so straight from the heart. I recalled, at this moment, a fairy tale heard somewhere, of a musician who by playing on a violin was able to placate a beast that wanted to tear him apart. Yes, but that was only a fairy tale. And nothing would appease these beasts. World, oh world. Why? Why? For what faults are these thousands going to die? Will our tormenting not have any end? And there was no answer to these questions.

Spring was in full bloom. The sun looked down and didn't turn pale, but in the Sands bodies bathed in blood continued to pile up in the large pits, beasts raged about, and nowhere was there rescue, nowhere was there a way out. I looked around: barbed-wire walls, one behind another, kept us in a cage. We only had bare hands, while they were armed with the most modern guns. And in the hideout in St. Martin's Street my stepfather, my sister, and my brother waited for me. I would never see them again. I pictured their tremendous despair as they learned of my death. My thoughts became tangled, my head was breaking apart, something

choked me, and my legs became weaker and weaker. Sitting down was forbidden. Heinen roamed about and still looked for victims. Only two
brigades were left ahead of us. Then it would be our turn.

Suddenly an extraordinary view appeared before our eyes. From the
outside gate a detachment of *Sonderdienst* marched into the outer square
in helmets and with submachine guns in their hands. Some of them, in
pairs, carried ammunition cases. Now even the most ardent optimists lost
their hope. Fear seized us by the throat, for the *Sonderdienst* had never
entered our camp before. Death seemed to be approaching us with a swift
step. We felt its breath on our faces. Everyone muttered something quietly. We prayed, each of us in his own manner. The bandits from the
Sonderdienst surrounded the camp and manned the watchtowers, where
previously only Askaris had served.

Only one brigade was left ahead of us. We were less than five hundred
remaining in the square when suddenly a limousine was driven into the
outer square and Willhaus got out and gave some orders. In a while, Axer
and Oremland ran into our roll call area. They managed to utter, "The
quota has been fulfilled, the rest will remain. You can go for lunch."

Out of approximately 10,000 inmates, more than 75 percent had been
liquidated that day, over 7,500 prisoners. The survivors were the roughly
1,500 who had gone to work and the 500 or so of us left in the square. We
were told to go to lunch because the quota was apparently fulfilled.

In the first moment we felt a great relief, but after a short while doubts
overtook us. Was this not a new ruse? Lunchtime—so they were taking a
break from their work and they would finish us off in the afternoon. We
did not believe them anymore. And even if not on that day, certainly the
following day or the day after. We were still despondent.

I solemnly promised myself that if I survived and got out of the camp to
work, they would never see me alive again. They would bring me back as
a dead body, but not as a living man. They might kill me during escape,
but would not get me alive. This possibility, however, was still far away.

I was standing in line for lunch, which was barley soup. Although my
stomach was empty, and on the previous day I had eaten almost nothing
at all as well, I could not swallow this soup. I barely ate two spoonfuls of
it, and then offered it to somebody else. I met Lonek Wilder, a friend from
childhood. We looked at each other with a woeful smile. We understood
each other without words.

After lunch we were all ordered to do some earthworks in the camp. SS
men, headed by Heinen and Siller, bustled among the prisoners looking
for opportunities to kill people. No, I will not go there, I told myself.
Instead, I decided to take the risk and hide in the barrack. If they found

me it would be certain death, but no matter. I ran into the barrack of the breweries brigade, where Wilek Becher, an acquaintance of mine and a master of philosophy, was the ordner. He let me in. We had once been together at a summer camp for (primarily) medical students in Kosow. I found several other shirkers in the barrack, and we talked over the things that had happened. Every once in a while one of us would go up to the window to see whether any SS men were approaching.

We were not at all sure that the massacre had ended, and in any case felt that we would likely not live much longer. Among the group hiding in this barrack was the camp police chief, Fluss, whom Willhaus had spared. Fluss had been very wealthy before the war. He said, "Gentlemen, these are our last hours, but at least I can say that I have lived, I have had a good life." I thought to myself, But I have not, my life was still in front of me! In that moment I promised myself that if I should somehow survive, I would try to live fully, and enjoy life to the utmost.

"Attention, Heinen is coming!" someone suddenly whispered. Fear came upon us. We pressed ourselves to the wall and peered out of the window. We could see Heinen in front of the barrack. He was leading two women, aged twenty to twenty-five years. One was very beautiful, tall, the other a bit shorter. Their faces could not be seen at all. We did not know how they got there. They all stopped on the lawn beside the barrack.

"Undress," Heinen ordered. Both obediently executed the order. In a short time they were in only their panties. "Undress completely," shrieked Heinen. They followed the order. "Lie down." They lay down, I'm sure wishing quicker, quicker to die. Heinen pulled out his pistol, aimed at the first one, and after a while changed his position, aimed at her face, then at her heart, approached, then moved away, but did not shoot. He played with his victims. After an instant, he got an ingenious idea. He ordered the tall one to spread her legs. She obediently fulfilled the order. Heinen aimed for a while in the direction of her vagina and shot. The victim yelled with pain. The beast looked on and laughed. For an instant, he still enjoyed the view of this woman writhing in pain, and then he killed her off with a shot in her mouth. The procedure with the second woman was shorter. In a short time two men from the gravediggers brigade took both victims on a stretcher to the Sands. The Nazi superman had shown what he was capable of.

A dozen minutes passed. We had not yet had time to recover from this horrible scene we had just witnessed when we heard a voice. "Komm her." We saw in front of the barrack another show. A prisoner was standing between our barrack and the one opposite, a tall man of some twenty years of age. If not for the yellow patch by his number, one could take him for an Aryan. He held a shovel in his hand. He had obviously been digging out earth behind the kitchen and, apparently wanting to rest a bit, hid beside our barrack. He was noticed by SS men Siller and Schönbach, the latter having just come back from the executions in the sand pits. "*Komm her,*" repeated Schönbach to the unfortunate fellow, approaching him. "What are you doing here, what?"

In slow motion, he pulled out his pistol and pressed it against the left side of the victim. The boy mumbled something incomprehensible. For a few moments, they both stood motionless. We thought that Schönbach would be satisfied with scaring the boy and that he would let him go, having beaten him with his whip. But the beast was still thirsting for blood, in spite of all the blood spilled not even one hour before. There was a shot. The boy's long body fell down on the ground with a thud. Scarcely audible yells blurted out of his mouth as he lay there. Schönbach brought his pistol to the back part of the boy's head and delivered the shot of mercy. The body twitched and tensed, then moved no more. Both SS men returned to their interrupted talk.

Time passed and we did not see prisoners coming back from work. We were anxious. Until they came back we could not believe that the liquidation had ended. Some of us were convinced that those brigades selected as the first ones to march out had also gone "to waste." In any case, if they were still living we should envy them for not having gone through all that happened in the camp this day.

At about four P.M. the first brigades appeared. All the inmates in them were anxious and nervous. They had already heard in the city about the massacre in the camp. Everyone was looking and asking about those close to them. The joy of those saved was drowned in a sea of despair and sorrow for the others lost. They listened to our stories with the deepest sadness.

After four, a new group of women appeared in the camp. They had been working until then in the *Lagerwäscherei* (camp laundry) and living in the ghetto. Presently they were brought to the camp to replace the women's brigade liquidated before noon. From that brigade, besides the Polish women, only the three most beautiful Jewesses were left, having been turned back by Willhaus before the external gate.

At five o'clock, the general roll call was ordered. During this roll call, we could see what devastation had been brought about in our ranks. The human walls that outlined the square in the roll call area had become very, very thin. In addition, one and a half walls had disappeared entirely.

Willhaus came accompanied by SS men and a dog, with his "saxophone" hanging from his arm. Willhaus never spoke more than a few words or a brief barked sentence to us, but this day I heard him for the first time speak to us like this: "So, starting with today, the action is finished. From now on there will be no more resettlements [this was the standard euphemism for execution of individuals or groups] in the camp. You have, though, to work well and honestly, because we Germans, we work as well. After work you will all come back here to the camp. If, however, any of you escape, then for any such one I will shoot ten or even fifty. Watch out, then! Here is your homeland; you can live here in peace as long as fifty years—and what might yet happen, nobody knows."

We stood astounded. We had not heard anything like it yet from Willhaus—neither as to the contents nor as to the tone. His last comment was a clear reference to Germany's suddenly uncertain position in the war and the consequent possibility of our survival somehow.

It was now May 1943. The Germans were still sitting well in all of Europe, from the Atlantic to deep in the Soviet Union. However, they had already been defeated at Stalingrad and were retreating. Willhaus certainly wanted to assure us, to give us some hope lest we all tried to escape. He knew that this day had had a shocking impact on us and that escapes would multiply significantly. The herd would diminish, and his kingdom would start to shrink.

Rumor had it that Willhaus was not pleased with the day's massacre, at least with its dimensions. That was quite probable. Willhaus could be upset, but not because of sudden unexpected remorse or in sorrow for these innocent victims. Not so, not at all. The cause was completely different, an entirely personal reason. Willhaus had until then been the only ruler of tens of thousands of Jews. Upon a single gesture of his finger, or upon his humor, the lives of an incredible number of men, women, and children depended. Whatever he desired and whatever wish he expressed, he had it fulfilled. Although he could not ride a horse well, he received a beautiful race horse as a gift. He had three limousines, and nobody knew how much gold he was reaping every day. On her birthday, his five-year-old daughter was showered with gifts from many sides. Not only from Jews, for not only Jews depended upon him, but also those few Aryans who were in the camp, as well as German directors of the various big enterprises, who depended on him to supply labor. And Willhaus was the owner of thousands of slaves, both unskilled and first-class specialists, whom it was harder and harder to get. For these directors, the question of the supply of labor was often of crucial importance. Without an adequate number and quality of workers their *Betriebe* (enterprises) could not work, which entailed the possibility of closing their institutions and going to the eastern front. And that is why, in spite of the fact that

Willhaus was just an SS Untersturmführer, the Hitlerian big fish would seek favors from him.

Willhaus saw that his kingdom was starting to disappear. Reserves from the ghetto, which had until then been abundantly replenishing the losses resulting from his work, were getting exhausted, and the ultimate liquidation of the Jews was approaching. When that occurred, not only would it bring the end of his royal role, but it might well mean he would have to go to the front, to the eastern front, which would by no means be a pleasure. Willhaus was brave and valiant—with his machine gun in his hand, accompanied by armed SS men, Askaris, and Ukrainian police—against unarmed people, the elderly, women, and children. But at the front, where one would not only shoot but also be shot at, no, this was better for someone else. Here in the camp, he received favors, awards, immeasurable riches, which he regularly and diligently sent to the homeland, while there in the east, he could at most obtain the wooden cross (at the cemetery) and a black-framed announcement in a newspaper saying, "He has found the death of a hero in the fighting in the east for the Führer and the Fatherland." No, this was decidedly not a pleasant prospect. That was why Willhaus was so depressed that day about the massacre. And that was also why he spoke to his Jews that day, to these *Dreck und Mist* (dung and trash), differently than before. He wanted to pacify them. He wanted to possibly prolong his reign and not allow a premature dethroning.

"And what might yet happen, nobody knows." Willhaus's words were falling into emptiness, for not one of us had illusions anymore. And if there were no mass escapes during the following days, it was not because anybody believed Willhaus even to the least degree, but because there was nowhere to escape to. Besides these walls of barbed wire, there were hundredfold worse invisible walls that surrounded us everywhere at every step and forced us into passive waiting for our martyrdom. These walls were even more impenetrable than the densest net of barbed wire, and they were built of material stronger than concrete. These walls were built of Golus the bloodthirsty, the local population, unfriendly and frequently hostile to the Jews. Anyone who has not gone through this would not understand it.

Having pronounced that short speech of his, Willhaus announced that our Betonwerke group would be transported on the very next day to the Org. Todt camp, where our brigade would be stationed. He promised us, though, that he would be visiting us several times a week, and therefore that we should watch out. So we were doubly lucky. We were saved from the massacre and we were bidding farewell, although only for a certain period, to our "mother camp." A few days later, the ZELA 19 brigade was also to be stationed at its place of work.

For us, however, even a temporary transfer was reassuring. After the roll call we returned to the barracks. We only then became even more aware of the things that had happened. The barracks, until then jam-packed, were suddenly almost empty, which gave us a wierd sensation. Empty places on either side of us, below us, above us, and behind us, were all shouting with this emptiness—making us conscious that our companions from the previous day had found another place to rest. In spite of physical and nervous exhaustion, I could not sleep.

The next day, after the roll call, our *Betonwerke* brigade was loaded onto two trucks and, guarded, was brought to Persenkówka, behind the Stryj tollgate in the suburb of Lwów, to the Org. Todt camp. Willhaus was following us in his limousine, apparently fearing that we might escape on the way. When we passed by the external gate of Janowska camp, I bade it farewell by cursing. I had spent ten months in that slaughterhouse, but it was not capable of absorbing me. And I promised myself that this camp would not see me alive again, at least not before its current rulers were liquidated. But would I live to see this? My hopes were meager.

CHAPTER 19

ORG. TODT

We rushed down Janowska Street, along which in the same trucks our comrades had been driven on the previous day to their martyrdom. Along the same road, these victims had been marching yet two days before, singing camp songs put together by some homegrown poet: "Are we this or are we that, from Janowska labor camp, the world will someday learn of us"; or the other song: "Listen you civilian men, how nice life is in the camp."

I was looking in the direction of our camp where life had been so "nice." Soon, the camp disappeared from my eyes behind a turn in the road. After my ten-month stay in Janów, the OT (Org. Todt) camp seemed to be a leisure sanatorium, in spite of the fact that, as in the first period of my time at Janowska camp, I had to work physically again, and very hard indeed. But the very fact that in place of SS men I saw only OT men, who were far removed from the death trade, was a relief. OT was a paramilitary organization, so these men were uniformed, and some carried guns, but in spite of this they did not look dangerous. At the concrete plant it was unarmed civilians who supervised us.

We were also greatly relieved by the absence of Askaris, whips, watchtowers, and the whole series of inseparable attributes of an extermination camp. This was a true labor camp. We worked hard there, but we could rest after work, wash ourselves, and even take a bath, which had been absolutely out of the question in Janowska camp. The commander of the Org. Todt camp, Graefe, whose sudden appearance had saved my life some months earlier, was, as mentioned before, a very rare phenomenon in his treatment of Jews.

The inmates from Janowska camp breathed freer here. This sudden transition from Janowska to OT weakened or paralyzed nearly everyone's will to escape into the unknown, where almost certain death lurked. I, however, was one of those very few who decided not to give in to this sleep-inducing effect of our new abode. I was determined to carry out that which I had previously decided—to escape at the first opportunity. I was also warning everybody and reminding them of what had happened before. I warned them not to forget, under the influence of these better conditions, that this pleasant illusion might vanish the very next day; that, in any case, all was heading toward liquidation; and that this oasis would not be left untouched. It was hard to make up one's mind, though.

I wondered about my family, hoping that Józek and Gina were already safely out of Lwów, perhaps together. I hoped I would soon have the chance to join my stepfather in the hideout at St. Martin's Street.

I was assigned to do hard work in the concrete production yard attached to the OT camp, where I had to carry enormous iron oddments, beams, crowbars, and so on, and I had to work with the concrete mixer. The supervisor, a Ukrainian named Warcholak, who wanted to extort some money from me, ordered me to participate in one of the most difficult jobs—the production of concrete. There were only three of us preparing concrete for four workers employed from outside the camp. These four—two Czechs, one Pole, and one Ukrainian—all worked and were paid by the job. Because of this, we also had to work as if by the job, the difference being, however, that the Aryans would go home after having fulfilled their daily norm, while we were transferred to some other job, often a very hard one.

Thus, for instance, one day when we had already finished our main work, I was assigned to unload a transport of cement. The cement was in fifty-kilogram sacks, and each one had to be transported from the freight cars to the sheds located some forty to fifty steps away. I had never carried heavier loads on my back. Having noticed that one of the inmates, a medical doctor as well, but in favor with Warcholak due to bribes he had paid, was transporting cement sacks on a wheelbarrow, I tried to do the same. Warcholak, who had an eye especially on me, did not allow this. Thus, willy-nilly, I was carrying these sacks on my back. It was extremely hard work for me. In less than one hour, I made nearly eighteen rounds, so that I carried almost a ton of cement on my back in this way. I was afraid that I would collapse.

In a word, I had hard work, but my body adjusted itself to this physical labor. I had, anyway, graduated from the hard school of the autumn of 1942 in Janowska camp. I was withstanding physical hardships here quite well, much better than before, for the environment without SS men affected me entirely differently. If not for the danger hanging over us like the sword of Damocles, the physical work would not have forced me to escape. I would have been able to live with it.

Still another factor that significantly improved my mood was the new human environment, namely the Jews who had been in OT camp before our arrival and still constituted the bulk of those here. Our group from Janowska camp formed only one fifth or one sixth of the whole OT camp, and certainly distinguished itself by its outlook from the rest. There was in our group a small clique of well-clad former brigadiers and foremen, people of no scruples or character, who had been lackeys for the SS men in Janowska camp. They had been beating, blackmailing, and tricking money out of their subordinates, conducting a rakish life for themselves. They had not been missing anything. Drinking, most luxurious eating, and a licentious, debauched life—all this was their unique goal, their only interest. They would not talk of anything else. They constantly uttered the most vulgar words, delighting in this. One could recognize them by their elegant officers' boots, with a cane or a rod put behind the boot top. These rods were used to tame their subordinates.

They had made their way into the *Betonwerke* brigade on May 26, the day of liquidation, through the advice and help of their SS connections, but they were not content with their fate in these new conditions. They longed for their old functions and their old power, and were listening with lively interest to the news of what was going on "there"—that is, in Janowska camp. They expected that through the SS men and people from the office that they knew, they would be able to get back to the camp and regain their good positions.

In the meantime, they entered into good relations with Warcholak, who assigned them the easiest work. They constituted, however, only a small portion of our group from Janowska. Most of the rest, 80 percent, were poor men, badly clothed and poorly fed people accustomed to absolute obedience to the brigadiers and foremen; some of them tried to stay afloat at all cost, stealing from one another without the slightest feeling of solidarity—out of the sheer desperation of their situation, of course, but without offering mutual understanding and assistance to each other. A handful of educated men—one veterinary doctor, one lawyer, two engineers, one teacher, two medical doctors—was readily distinguished from the other two groups and was disliked by both of them. The first group, the former brigadiers and foremen, did not like them because they refused to be debased; the second group, the poor and simple, was envious, for here at Org. Todt these educated men were treated with greater respect by the OT inmates and even to a degree by the authorities.

I would like to add that in the almost eleven months of my stay in Janowska camp and OT camp, I observed how people behaved at such a time of distress and struggle for life, often in a manner quite hard to predict from their education and social status. They showed themselves as they really were, beneath this veneer. There were some from good homes and privileged backgrounds who behaved like animals, not just stealing to survive but blackmailing and profiting through others' miseries so they could have a more comfortable life. Fortunately, such people were few, but they were influential. On the other side, there were people from very simple backgrounds, poor and uneducated, who did all they could to help others at great personal sacrifice and risk. People sometimes acted completely differently than they had before, finding unexpected strength or showing to what depths human beings can fall.

Against the background of the physical and moral poverty of many of the Janowska inmates, the superiority of the "natives," meaning those Jews who had been in the OT camp for a long time already, was clearly visible. They were Jews as if from a different world. They were relatively well situated, for they had had enough time to save, to a lesser or greater degree, something from their previous possessions. Graefe, who was nice to the Jews, had also been able to save his favorites from the SS. His people had in no degree gone through the "pleasures" of Janowska camp. They never had to deal with SS men. Until the very last days, they had had entirely free movement after work. Only after May 26 was the camp closed in. Then the chance of contacting people on the Aryan side, and getting some material help from Aryan friends, was much more constrained.

Because of these conditions, the morale of these natives was good; they had a feeling of solidarity and mutual support, and social links were strongly developed among them. Amoral individuals remained in the shadows. The Jewish manager of the camp—the *Obman*, in camp terminology—a known Lwówian lawyer, Dr. Gelb, was a man who could organize this miniature society. One could not compare him with the brigadiers from Janowska camp. It is understandable that I breathed with relief. I was starting to get rid of the repulsion and contempt that I had had to nurture against that Jewish scum in Janowska who dominated over the thousands of depressed, honest, upset, and resigned Jewish prisoners. I saw these other Jews here, and I could conclude that those in Janowska were just the scum covering the great bulk of Jews, who were noble and good. But regardless of any such favorable conditions in this camp, I felt I must still run away—and do it as quickly as possible.

In the meantime, I got an alarming letter from St. Martin's Street, from my stepfather, sister, and brother (who had not yet left for the country, hesitating from fear and waiting for a safer time). They had been in great despair when the news reached them of what had happened in Janowska camp. They thought I had been killed, for the rumors said that all the Jewish doctors had been murdered. They were very anxious about me. What was I now waiting for? An invitation? They begged me to escape at once and come to them. All right, I answered in my letter, at the first opportunity I would do that. But I could not escape from Org. Todt, because in order to reach St. Martin's Street from the Org. Todt camp in Persenkówka, one would have to go almost through the whole city. I certainly would get recognized on the way and this would be the end. I would wait therefore for an opportunity—when we would go to the city, to the baths, or when some car would go to town with our workers to get some goods—and then I would make off.

On the very next day a friend of Faliński, a Ukrainian named Rudnicki, came to the camp. He had gotten to know and be friends with my stepfather, upon whose request he came to take me with him. But I did not want to expose him to danger, so, thanking him, I declined. I stuck to my plan, but then, as if out of spite, no car went to the city.

On June 3, we received the news that the liquidation of the ghetto was taking place in the city. The ghetto was in flames. Our tension increased to the maximum. After the massacre in the camp, we had expected that liquidation of the camp would take place any day, but, as always, we were deluding ourselves, or, rather, we wanted to delude ourselves. Although we expected it, the news of the liquidation of the ghetto still struck us as an unexpected blow.

Psychologically broken and nervous, we were eagerly catching the news coming from the dying ghetto. News was scarce, though. It was reaching us indirectly, through Janowska camp and from the Aryans. We were told of bloodcurdling scenes. Trucks loaded with victims were speeding one after another to the Sands for executions. The ghetto was resisting in an unorganized, chaotic manner. Individual groups were defending themselves without any organization among them. Having learned a lesson in the Warsaw ghetto, the Gestapo had very meticulously prepared their ground. Through a network of informers the Germans knew about everything, including underground passages to the Aryan quarters. All the exits from the sewers to the river Pełtew, flowing under Lwów, were guarded by German police, for it was down these drains that people tried to flee from the burning ghetto. The iron ring of Ukrainian and German police formed an impenetrable net. Only a few individuals succeeded in running away. For hiding a Jew in the Aryan quarter, even for just one night—as, for example, occurred frequently in the Czacki School near the Lwów ghetto—these "magnanimous" people asked many thousands of złotys, showing how full their hearts were of Christian love for their neighbors.

Liquidation of the ghetto lasted for three days. The Polish and Ukrainian communities looked out at the dying ghetto, which was writhing in convulsions of agony, either with calm and indifference or with the expression of true joy and satisfaction. Many had enriched themselves with Jewish money and things given to them for safekeeping, whose owners were just being killed. Hyenas were prowling about, hoping to make some money, to draw the last penny, together with the last breath, from those who miraculously succeeded in escaping from the burning hell of the ghetto. Every passerby was examined to see whether he or she was not a Jew. In the streets of the city, great posters were put up, signed by General Katzmann, warning against hiding Jews under the penalty of death and promising the prize of five thousand złotys and two liters of vodka for every revelation of a Jew's hiding place. There were many who were willing to earn this money stained with Jewish blood.

After the liquidation of the ghetto, the Ukrainian community organized a spontaneous funeral demonstration for those few Ukrainian policemen who had died, killed by the Jews during the liquidation action. Those damn Jews had had the impertinence to defend themselves and to kill the innocent Ukrainian policemen who were bravely serving the new Europe, great Germany, and free Ukraine. This information I found later, in the July 1943 issue of *Ziemia Czerwieńska*, a local underground newspaper of the Polish resistance movement *Armia Krajowa* (Home Army).

In the evening of the first day of the liquidation, four Jewish policemen appeared in our camp. These policemen had succeeded in escaping from the ghetto and now were trying to hide in our camp. News about it spread like lightning and soon a crowd gathered, hostile to these four. Jewish policemen from the ghetto, in the period 1942 to 1943, had a very bad reputation. They had actively helped the Gestapo in all the actions, and were very eager, even too eager and brutal. They had filled their pockets with money and valuable objects from their victims or from those whom they had blackmailed. It was therefore understandable that this crowd of inmates granted no mercy to them and offered them no refuge. The prisoners were angrily shouting at the four. Seeing this, two of them escaped, while the other two hid in a shed and, through the intermediary of their friends, tried to justify themselves in the eyes of the crowd, simultaneously sending their messengers to Graefe. Under the influence of hard arguments—that is, hard currency, dollars—Graefe accepted them two days later as camp inmates.

The fate of whole detachments of Jewish ghetto police, on the other hand, was much worse. Their members were brought to Janowska camp by the SS to be liquidated. Before the execution, crowds of inmates rushed at the policemen, savagely beating them. These traitors and Judases had earned their punishment at the hands of their own brothers, and their masters' prize for their faithful service.

Our people from the OT camp who had gone to obtain various items at Janowska camp returned pale and deeply shaken. A massive massacre of Jews brought from the ghetto was taking place in the camp. They were so nervous they could not talk to us about it. We did not ask them, for everything could be read in their faces.

After a few days a new selection took place in Janowska camp. Several brigades went to slaughter. The promise made by Willhaus had proved to be valid for not more than ten days.

A new brigade, *Reinigungsbrigade* (cleaning brigade), was specially formed in Janowska camp and sent to the partly burned-down ghetto. (This brigade should not be confused with the brigade of the same name, the street-cleaning brigade, which had been liquidated on May 26.) Its purpose was to secure for the SS everything of any value that was still left in the ghetto—namely furniture, house appliances, clothes, and linen. In other words, anything that could be found in the ghetto. Besides that, it was to search for the smallest possible caches in the walls, floors, and the like, where money, jewels, and other valuable items could be hidden. All that was found was brought back in cars to the camp, where these objects, as well as the things taken off the victims during the executions, were sorted out, the more valuable ones being sent to the Reich as war loot.

When the ghetto hospital had been liquidated, all the patients and staff were exterminated with the notable exception of the director, Dr. Kurzrock. This amazing man, who had used his good standing with the SS commandants of Janowska camp to help so many inmates find medical treatment, was again spared. In fact, he was not even sent to Janowska camp proper, but was named by Willhaus chief of the camp hospital and lived outside the camp in separate quarters with his family in one of the villas.

Meanwhile, I was getting no news from the hideout in St. Martin's Street. I was anxious, but I assured myself by thinking that there were fires in the ghetto, that all kinds of police were mobilized and were patrolling and searching in and around the city, and that therefore contacts had to be temporarily broken for the sake of security and precaution. I must wait until everything calmed down, I told myself, and anyway there was no car going to town. I had obtained a promise to be taken to the city as soon as such an opportunity arose, but as of now nothing of the sort was happening. Meanwhile, the ground beneath my feet was burning. News from Janowska camp was bad. Every few days some executions occurred. From the provincial towns, people brought information about the liquidation of camps in Gródek Jagielloński, in Jaryczów, in Mosty Wielkie, and in other small towns around Lwów.

The wave of liquidation grew bigger and bigger. Soon we would find ourselves washed over by it. And I could not break away. Oh, if I could, damn it, finally be there, in St. Martin's Street, in that safe hideout with my family. Every few days Willhaus's limousine arrived in our camp like a deathly apparition. Willie was visiting his friend, Graefe, coming to chat, and using the opportunity to illegally fill up his tank with gasoline. His every visit incited a wave of anxiety and fear. Was it now? Everybody was nervous, and people would look toward the black limousine with alarm. When the limousine drove away from the camp, we sighed with relief. Rumors were going around that SS men would be coming to our camp. This, of course, terrified everyone, except the scum, the former brigadiers and foremen, who did not conceal their satisfaction. You will see, they assured us, how quickly we will get on good terms with them.

It was Saturday afternoon. We had just come back from work. In Janowska camp, after work there were always "vitamins" and other pleasant supplements. Here, however, all of us washed and, having put our clothes in order, sat down to eat. There was one table, and only a few places, so most of us sat on the bunk beds. The room was alive with conversation. Some singers were found to be among us. Soon they were surrounded by the others. There were three of them, each singing solo. Their program was composed entirely of Jewish songs from the good old times—and the camp songs, of course. In a short time, neighbors from other rooms and barracks gathered to listen to these songs. We wanted to forget this sad, tragic reality and be transported with these songs to the past, enveloped in the aureole of happy and sinless years. One song from Jewish folklore followed another, and all of them made us sentimental. The singers were putting all their hearts into singing, all the pain of the present reality and the sorrow for all that would never, ever come back. Most of the listeners had tears in their eyes, listening to the words in Yiddish.

Oj wi nemt men curik di juren, Mojszele majn frajnd,
Nuch jene szejne jinge juren benkt majn herc noch hajnt.
(Oh, how can one bring those past years back, my
        friend Mojszele;
My heart still longs for those years when we were
        young).

Kinderjuren szejne carte blumen, curik cu mir wet ir
        szon mer nicht kumen
(My childhood years, beautiful delicate flowers,
        you will never come back to me).

Alas, those years will not come back, those years of childhood in your parents' home, when everybody dearest to you was near and you did not
know yet this enormous evil that lurks in the human being, when you had
no idea of the human beast, when all people looked equally human, when
we too were looked upon as human beings.

This confrontation of the past with the present was so painful to our
hearts and minds . . . The song titled *"Majn sztetl Słuck* [My little town of
Słuck]" was now sung, telling the life of a shtetl on a Saturday night. We
were aware that even if anything of Jewry were by some miracle saved,
those little Jewish towns would certainly not come back, for they had
already disappeared from the surface of the earth, as had their pious
inhabitants, with their beards and side curls and their long coats and
schtramles. The German beast had liquidated those little townships, beautiful even in their ugliness and poverty, filled with mysticism and the
unworldly brightness of the sabbath candles seen through the windows of
low houses on Friday evenings. These Jewish *Kleinstetl* ("little towns")
lived their separate life, vibrant and tumultuous on weekdays and on
every Saturday giving to the Lord all that belongs to God.

Centuries had passed and the life of Jewish shtetls had not changed,
but now it had disappeared forever. And knowing that this was so
increased our sorrow for the old Jewish little towns hundredfold.

I must admit that in the old times I had not liked the small Jewish towns,
nor did I like the Yiddish language, except for Yiddish songs. But though I
liked these, if they had another, Hebrew, version, I would prefer them much
more. I always considered the Yiddish language a jargon and, along with the
shtetls, a symbol of Golus, something one must break away from forever. I
was not alone in thinking like that. To the contrary, such was the general
opinion of the nationally conscious (Zionist) part of the Jewish community
in Lwów. In the academic Zionist spheres there, people would either speak

Hebrew or Polish; this was completely different than in Warsaw or in Wilno, where academic Jewish youth would generally use Yiddish.

So had it been long ago, but now, when I listened to those songs in Yiddish, I felt how close this language was to me; I felt the blood of my blood, I felt in those songs Jewish soul—my soul. And I felt guilty, like an unfaithful son.

My thoughts were interrupted by another song, "*Majne jidisze mame* [My Jewish mother]." Tears trickled down my face. "*Majne jidisze mame* . . ." Where are you now, my mother? Your life was a chain of sacrifices for your children, as usual with Jewish mothers. If a mother is everywhere a figure of love and sacrifice, of careful kindness and suffering because of her children and for them, then the Jewish mother is the best-known expression of this ideal. I see before my eyes the images from childhood, always the same face full of kindness and compassion, suffering when something hurt us, anxious when we were ill, proud of our primary and secondary school successes and of our progress at the university, stinting herself for us when poverty looked into our home because of the anti-Semitic boycott of Jewish businesses. And sometimes, when things were very bad, she would shed tears sitting somewhere in the corner, when nobody could see her. And later, when I was already a doctor and had my own family and household, I would go almost every day to visit her for at least half an hour, and because my financial situation was better than hers I would help her financially. Still, before saying good-bye she would disappear for a short while to the neighboring little shop and would come back and slip something into my pocket—a chocolate, a piece of fruit.

The heart of a Jewish mother, of my mother. And then war came, and then the Germans came, and then the August action of 1942 came. On the first day two of her daughters went to Bełzec, and me, her son, to the slaughterhouse of Janowska camp. Two days later her beloved sister was taken to Bełzec, and the following day her second son went to Janów. And thus, without a break, in the mornings and in the evenings, my mother's swollen legs traveled from the ghetto to Janowska camp or to my workplace in order to see me, to bring something to eat for us, her starving sons. She did not care about the dangers or about the shootings by Askaris and SS men. She was beaten several times on her back with a rifle butt, but she was always there beside the road along which I was returning from work to the camp.

I have now before my eyes the same beloved face, as she brought food for me to the HKP caserns at Pieracki Street. There was once a big blue spot under her left eye. Tears constantly flowed down her cheeks. These were tears of the sorrow of an insulted, abused woman—a mother. A

Ukrainian policeman had given her a blow in the face. And then I saw her for the last time in the ghetto, on January 3, 1943, where I was sneaking illegally to see her. She was very worried. There were rumors about a new action to come. And two days later she was taken in the so-called January action to the transport to the Bełzec gas chambers. On a frosty day in January, barefoot, in only her shirt, she jumped out of the transport near Rawa Ruska, with others. A boy among them, a distant relative, pitied my mother and offered her his shawl. After a few days, the boy managed to get through to the Lwów ghetto to his family, and told the story.

We were hoping that perhaps our mother would also be able to return to the ghetto. She did not come, alas. Somewhere on the way some "good people" killed her mercilessly. Somewhere on the way her beloved body was lying like the corpse of a masterless dog. "A *kadisz noch der mame* [prayer for the dead pronounced for the mother]"—the singers sang this prayer in our room. My heart bled and was torn to shreds. Jews, pray kaddish for a Jewish mother.

The song had barely ended when those who were sitting next to the window jumped up to their feet as if thunderstruck. All of us became silent in terror. Look, look! We approached the windows. Suddenly there was a shot, and after a short break there were more shots, one after another. We dispersed, running to our rooms. Anxiety and fear overtook us. What happened? A motorcycle passed by along the road. After an instant, someone rushed in and told us what had happened. In our camp there was a group of skilled Jewish workers employed by NSKK, the motorized military organization, belonging to the Nazi party itself but attached to the Wehrmacht. The Germans liked them a lot. Recently, four of them obtained—for a heap of money, of course—a promise from the Germans to facilitate their escape and to bring them to Dniepropetrovsk in eastern Ukraine, where they would be able to work as Aryans. Everything was arranged. They were to leave that day. Just as they were making the last preparations, the very same Germans informed the *Frontleiter* (a high-ranked officer in Organization Todt, a supervisor), who had just come to the camp, about this.

The *Frontleiter*, with his pistol in hand, accompanied by OT men from the camp, ran into the barrack of the four and screamed, "Hands up, go out," and drove them toward the guardhouse. The four victims, walking with their hands up, escorted with rifle barrels and the *Frontleiter*'s pistol, were aware that their path from the guardhouse on led straight to Janowska camp, to the gallows or to the Sands. When they were just by the guardhouse, located near the gate opening out to the highway, they started to run away. Shots rang out. One of the escapees fell down on the ground at once, dead; the second one staggered and tumbled into the ditch after a few steps. The other two escaped. The *Frontleiter* mounted a motorcycle and, shooting blindly, rushed after the runaways. They had soon disappeared into the nearby thicket.

The *Frontleiter* came back to the camp upset. We soon heard shouts. "Roll call, roll call." We stood in rows with our hands up. The *Frontleiter*, still with his pistol, bustled in front of our rows as if crazy. "Count off!" After counting, it turned out that only those two were missing. With foam on his mouth, the *Frontleiter* was shouting out something, waving his pistol and threatening with it. "Dismissed!"

We ran into our barrack. Nervousness and anxiety as to what would happen now were reigning everywhere. At the *Frontleiter*'s order, the bodies of the killed and the wounded prisoners were brought in and put down in front of our barrack. The wounded prisoner, whose name was Metzger, and who was liked and esteemed by all of us, was lying in a pool of blood. His abdominal cavity was shot through. He was writhing in terrible pain. OT men guarded him. He begged them to shorten his torment and kill him off. But the *Frontleiter* sharply forbade this. Metzger clenched his teeth; finally he tried to bite through the veins on his hands. To no avail. After a while the *Frontleiter* approached. He obviously wanted to satisfy himself with the view of this Jew writhing in agony. He bent over the victim. Metzger's face took on an implacable expression.

"What more can you do to me? I despise you!" he blurted through his squeezed lips. With his last effort he raised his head and spat in the *Frontleiter*'s face. The *Frontleiter*, furious, smashed the prisoner on the head with the handle of his pistol. The head dropped down inert. Shortly afterward Metzger moaned in a low voice. In the meantime a pit in the ground was dug out. Upon the *Frontleiter*'s order the dead body, together with Metzger, was put in it. Already lying in the pit, Metzger asked us to send his regards to all his friends and comrades. After a while the OT men killed him off. The pit was filled up.

We could not sleep the whole night under the impact of these events. We expected also that the insulted *Frontleiter* would not be satisfied with just two victims. We listened until dawn for the sounds of SS men from Janowska camp coming to get us.

CHAPTER 20

DESPAIR AND ESCAPE

In this atmosphere of uncertainty, when we expected the unexpected to occur every day, my nervousness and rage became even more pronounced. After all, the hideout was waiting for me while I was uselessly risking my life and fighting anxiety in the camp. Tomorrow, or the day after tomorrow, it might be too late. And I was still receiving no news from St. Martin's Street. It had been almost a week since the ghetto was liquidated. I started to worry. Did anything happen to my family? Probably not. But still my anxiety grew.

There was a Polish family living by the *Betonwerke* plant. The inmates from OT camp would sneak there from time to time and buy something to eat. There was an eight- or ten-year-old boy there, who for the "postage" of ten złotys would carry letters from our people to Aryans in the city. I sent this boy to Faliński, who was helping my family to hide, and with whom we were keeping our money and precious objects. The boy returned with nothing. Faliński was not at home. I sent him the very next day to Faliński's friend, Rudnicki, who was also in touch with the hideout. But Rudnicki was gone somewhere—that was the answer I got.

On the third day, I again sent the boy to Faliński, with a letter in which I asked him to write back with information about what was happening with my family. I received the answer that he had been away from Lwów for a few days and that he would come to me himself. On the next day I was called away from work. Someone had come to me. I jumped up, joyful, and ran to the wire net separating the concrete plant from the sidewalk. From a distance I saw Faliński, carrying a package. My heart was filled with happiness and excitement. I squeezed myself through a hole in the fence and came close to him. His face was strangely pale. He handed me the package.

"How is my family?" I asked, taking the package without thinking.

"Captured," answered Faliński. And his head sank.

"Who?" I moaned desperately. The package slipped out of my hands.

"All."

"O God, what . . ." I could not finish the sentence. Something started to choke me, my blood seemed to leave my heart and go to my legs. There was darkness before my eyes, I thought the earth was moving away from beneath my feet. My head reeled. I leaned against the fence, supporting myself with my right hand. No word would come out of my throat. A stream of tears came down from my eyes.

"Someone apparently informed on them," continued Faliński. He told me that when the Ukrainian police came it turned out that there were almost thirty Jews in that building. He, Faliński, had personally intervened with people he knew and with the police, especially on behalf of my sister Gina, who had Aryan papers. He paid here and there and finally they agreed to let Gina go free, but she refused to go without her father and brother. Faliński begged her to come away. She wanted to at least save Józek, and said she would come if he too were let go. The Ukrainians would not agree to this, so she decided to go to her death with her father and brother. All this happened on Thursday, June 10, 1943. They were kept the whole night at the Ukrainian police post and then were transported to Janowska camp.

Faliński was telling me that he had done all he could. For him too there was no purpose in living now, since Gina, whom he loved so much, was no more. He had brought me a little linen and food. Did I need something? Should he bring me all the money? At first I did not answer. I was completely broken, I was dizzy. I did not know what to do. If I had had a gun, I would have ended this damned life. But a gun I did not have.

"What do you intend to do now?" asked Faliński.

"Me?" I answered mechanically. After a while I became aware that not only had I lost my beloved ones, but also the possibility of saving myself. My thoughts were chasing one another at lightning speed. The hideout, which had been my ultimate goal, had ceased to exist. Faliński did not mention any other hideout. It was senseless to demand this of him anyway—he had no obligations to me. Therefore I did not ask him about it.

What then? Must I wait together with the other inmates for martyrdom, let myself be taken to the Sands like a sheep to slaughter? No. I did not care for my life, I had no one to live for, nothing to live for. I could not stomach hanging myself, and I did not have any other means of suicide, but I would not let them lead me to the Sands. They would never see it; I would flee blindly, without a goal, but I would not go to slaughter.

"What do you intend to do?" asked Faliński again. "Should I bring everything to you?" he repeated.

"What do I intend? I don't know—I will escape, I don't know where to. Please bring me only a part of the money to take with me, in case I am robbed somewhere on the way, so that I would still have something left. When will you come?"

"In four days," answered Faliński. "On Tuesday."

I returned to the shed to continue mixing cement, sand, and gravel, to sprinkle it with water and turn it with my shovel, and suddenly I burst into spasmodic weeping. I stood in the corner of the shed; my whole body trembled. My last ones were taken from me. Tears trickled down my face, choked me in my throat. Lord, oh Lord, are there no limits to human torment? Why? Why? What was my guilt?

I drank my cup of bitterness to the bottom, to the very bottom. I did not have anybody anymore. The murderers took my last ones. I was left as just one, terribly lonesome. Greek mythology describes the sufferings of Niobe, who, before she perished, had to witness the deaths of her seven children, a representation of the highest degree of suffering for a loving person. And me—my God, I was being tormented in this place of torture for almost a year. I was experiencing the martyrs' deaths of my dearest ones for more than the seventh time. My sufferings were greater in quantity and in quality than those of Niobe. And blows were falling upon me not just at once, but slowly, time after time, spread over the year.

On many occasions I had read in the newspapers that when the death penalty was given to a group of criminals, then the last one to be executed was the worst of them. Let him see how the others perish, let him experience his death longer. Had I really sinned so much, had I committed a crime so heavy, that the most severe punishment was what I deserved?

I have no one, no one. This awareness is so acute, so brutal, that I feel that I am losing my senses. I see before the eyes of my imagination the last of my family being executed. I think I will go mad. I am ready to strike my head against the wall. And then I break down in spasmodic crying again. This brings me some relief.

My companions started to comfort me. "It can't be helped, nothing can be done, this is our fate. All this awaits us as well." These last words sobered me up. What? No, I would not go like a sheep to the Sands, I would break away!—not to live, for I did not care for living anymore, but I wanted to live in order to avenge the blood of the innocent ones, to pay for my mother and stepfather, for my sisters and brother, for my wife and child, for my relatives and friends, for all of them. I must live to tell the world of the deeds of this German *Kulturvolk*, the so-called cultured nation; I must tell people of the human beast; I must tell Jews of the fate of their brothers and sisters, mothers and fathers.

And I knew that only a few would believe me. I knew, for I would not have been able to believe all these horrors myself, had I not lived through them.

So what to do? Escape. But where to? The best would be to become a guerrilla. It would be easier, then, to seek revenge. Yes, but there were no guerrilla groups in the vicinity. There apparently had been such a group before, but its members were recently caught by the Gestapo. So where to? Perhaps to Hungary. Jews there still had the right to live. But how to get there? The Hungarian border was strongly guarded on both sides. Roads leading to the border were frequently patrolled, especially now, during the liquidation of the ghettos.

After liquidating the Lwów ghetto, the German and Ukrainian police surrounded the city with a cordon. Highways, forests, and fields were searched through and monitored. But no matter. I began openly discussing my wish to escape and looking for a partner. There were quite enough people willing to break out with me. I chose Mechel Pfeffer, whom Józek had become close to when he was in the Betonwerke brigade. Pfeffer was a man of more than forty years of age, wise, with a good-natured face, physically strong. He had some time before been a farmer and a merchant in the vicinity of the town of Złoczów. I felt sympathy for him because of my brother. In spite of a significant age difference they had gotten along very well working together. He loved my brother. He often spoke with me about him. I felt that I could rely on him, that he would be a good companion in the escape.

Pfeffer was very poor. My brother had helped him, and after my brother's escape I continued to do the same. Presently I got the money I had asked for from Faliński. It would be enough for both of us. On that same day I proposed a plan to Pfeffer for our escape. He was pleased. He was ready to go anywhere with me. But he advised against going to Hungary. While working in the garden of the engineer Lewicki, who directed the work in the concrete plant, Pfeffer talked with Lewicki's wife. She liked him a lot and she told him that her brother had recently been near the Hungarian border and had seen that it was very strongly guarded. There was no possibility of getting through this border.

Pfeffer proposed to escape toward his native region, to Biały Kamień, a small Polish village near the town of Złoczów, which is seventy kilometers east of Lwów. He knew a lot of farmers there. They were good people. For money, if I had some, they would hide us. And even if they refused, in the park in Biały Kamień were the ruins of the palace of King Jan Sobieski, dating from the seventeenth century. In the ruins were deep cellars and tunnels. People avoided these ruins, for it was said that they were haunted by the ghost of the king. We could hide there and go to farmers at night to get food. We could obtain anything for money. Since Jews in this area had been liquidated a long time ago, the Germans would not look for us. In a word, it would be best to go there.

The only problem was how to get through to that region, how to sneak across the police ring around Lwów, and how to avoid surprises on the way. Pfeffer knew the way only starting from Kurowice, a small town about halfway between Lwów and Złoczów. Our journey would be about five kilometers from the OT camp, on the southern edge of Lwów, to the road leading east from Lwów, then about seventy kilometers east until just before Złoczów, and finally ten kilometers farther, northward, to Biały Kamień.

After a short hesitation I agreed. The next day Pfeffer came with a new suggestion, or rather a request. He wanted to take with us a young twenty-year-old boy, who also came originally from Biały Kamień. His name was Icek (Icchak) Hoch. He had escaped from a group that was being brought to Janowska camp from the Lwów ghetto. He had wandered about for three weeks already and was now trying to gain admittance to OT. Pfeffer pointed to a tall young man with a slim and strong constitution, blond hair, and blue eyes—that is, an Aryan appearance. I looked at him. He did not seem too sympathetic to me.

"He will not be a burden to us. He will manage by himself there," added Pfeffer, thinking that my hesitation was caused by apprehension about supporting one more man.

"No, it is not a question of money," I answered. "If it is enough for two, it will also be enough for three. All right," I decided after a while. So now we put together our plans as a group of three. Icek, who had worked in the military barracks before, was to obtain a gun for me, at least one pistol, for which I was ready to pay six thousand złotys. Pfeffer was to buy food for our travel.

A few days passed. I had received the money from Faliński. He promised to bring, on Saturday the twenty-sixth, more money and a wristwatch, which could be of use in our march.

We could not get any weapons for any price. We had to wait. And time was running out for us. In Janowska camp, there was something new going on every few days. Recently, Dr. Kurzrock, the director of the camp hospital, Willhaus's favorite, had been liquidated. Dr. Kurzrock had prepared for himself, with the help of Germans he knew, appropriate papers, and had meant to go together with his family to Dniepropetrovsk, in German-occupied Ukraine. Here he would work as an Aryan. The very same good Germans who had taken money from him, and were to have helped him, had delated him to Willhaus, who personally shot Kurzrock dead. Only a week before his death, while visiting the OT camp, Dr. Kurzrock had warned us that the "final solution" was coming soon and that whoever could should try to escape soon. Indeed, this helped me decide to speed the timetable for my own escape.

Rumors indicated that Willhaus would be replaced by SS Obersturm-führer Warzog, commander of the camp in Lacki, near Złoczów, who was similarly notorious for his dreadful deeds. People were also saying that several new SS men were to come to our OT camp in the next week. The commander's post was to be taken by SS Scharführer Kolonko from Janowska camp.

The liquidation of Jewish camps in the countryside proceeded. On Wednesday, June 23, Pfeffer came to me. His pale face expressed nervousness. The wife of the engineer Lewicki had told him, in strict confidence, that her husband had received a secret letter saying that he should try to employ Aryan workers as soon as possible, for he would not be enjoying his Jewish workers much longer. This was to happen any day now.

In view of such a state of things, we decided not to wait for the money and for the watch from Faliński, nor for weapons, and break away the very next day after work.

In the morning of June 24, I dressed in the WC so that nobody could see that I put on three shirts, two pairs of long underwear, and two pairs of socks. In my physician's bag, which I left standing on my bunk, I placed my white patch with its number and the yellow triangle. When I escaped, the other inmates would be able to give someone else this patch with the number 1455, and thus hush up my escape so that the authorities would not know, thereby avoiding unpleasant consequences.

There were many candidates for this patch. Many Jews wandered about in the neighborhood—those from the ghetto who did not die with the others and for whom getting into the OT camp would be considered salvation. Thus, number 1455 would still exist for the authorities. Meanwhile, with our patches and dog tags removed, we would be inconspicuous, dressed as any other worker. Pfeffer left his number with Mrs. Lewicki, to whom he confided the secret of our escape. She promised to transmit the number to the brigade foreman. She blessed him for the way and promised to pray for us. We were touched by this rare expression of humanity.

We went to work as always. We planned to rendezvous after work by hiding behind the tractor that stood aside in the yard of the concrete works. The weather was beautiful, but our work, as if in spite, was harder than usual on this day. Dressed in three shirts and in two pairs of long underwear, I sweated terribly. My anxiety, due to the desperate step ahead of us, reinforced me in my work, though.

At four P.M., when our work was finished, rain was pouring down. Workers marched in a disorderly fashion back to the camp. The three of us hid behind the tractor. We observed those leaving the plant; they had not noticed our absence. It was still too early to break away. We waited until five-thirty P.M., and decided to get to the nearby forest, wait there for dusk, and then move on. We decided to go one by one at a distance of some twenty steps from each other.

At five-thirty we said a short prayer and set out. First we had to get out of the concrete works. The camp was surrounded by a metal wire net that had barbed wire on top. On the northern side of the camp there was a broad gate through which the railway track led going to Persenkówka station. It was through there that trains passed bringing from Persenkówka to the camp such goods as gasoline, cement, sand, gravel, and other materials. This was the only way to leave the camp without passing by the main gate and its guards. The railway gate was closed, but between the rails and the lower edge of the gate there was a very narrow space. We had to sneak through there. This was a hard task, the more so insofar as we had to do this quickly, not to be noticed by passersby. And it was still before sunset.

After a short rainfall, the sun started to smile at us again. With our nerves as tense as could be, we started to crawl under the gate—first Pfeffer, then me, and Icek after me. Nobody noticed us. Now we were marching at the previously arranged distances, heading toward the forest, which was some one and a half kilometers away from the camp. We felt like running with all our strength, but we had to go slowly, calmly, so as not to catch the attention of passersby returning from work. We were clad just as the other workers, and so nobody paid attention to us.

At one of the gates to the Org. Todt camp two boys pasturing cattle saw us. One of them shouted, "O, *Wajiwrach!* [They're escaping!]" and pointed his finger in our direction. We were terrified. Pfeffer gestured to the boys to keep silent. We nervously marched on. We were afraid that the boys might inform somebody in the camp of our escape and that the chase after us would start. We did not look back in order not to cause suspicion. Soon we passed by the German military barracks. A German soldier walked out of the guardhouse, an officer or a noncom, looked around, and his attention was drawn to Pfeffer, marching about twenty steps ahead of me. Apparently we seemed suspicious to him, because he didn't lose sight of us. Pfeffer did not notice this, but Icek and I did. Icek was frightened and retreated a little, while I proceeded, with my heart in my throat but with a steady pace, following Pfeffer.

Suddenly, there was a storm and heavy rain started to pour down. People on the road started to quickly run to their homes. The German officer hid from the rain in the guardhouse, and taking advantage of the situation, we started to run as fast as we could in the direction of the forest. When we reached the forest, Pfeffer and I waited for Icek, who was still far behind. Soon he joined us. We decided to rest, wait until dusk, and then go on. We were wet through, but our spirits were high. Our anxiety and fear disappeared. We were absolutely happy—for we were free.

After an eleven-month stay in the torture house of Janowska camp (and OT camp), I had broken away from the "care" of the SS; I was free—so it seemed to me. I had an indescribable feeling of liberation, and there was constant music in my ears, as if I were at some concert. But the road to freedom was, alas, very long and very thorny. This was Thursday, June 24, 1943.

In 1945 I discovered how close my escape had been. I met a former bunkmate from Org. Todt who had also managed to survive. From him I learned that a few weeks after our escape the OT camp was suddenly surrounded by SS and Ukrainian police. All inmates were forced onto trucks and brought to Janowska camp for execution in the Sands.

CHAPTER 21

ON THE RUN

We planned to go toward the Biały Kamień region, near the town of Złoczów. There was a highway that ran from Lwów to the east, past Złoczów to Tarnopol, a wide road that had strategic importance for German military movements. Obviously, we did not intend to go down this road, but only to get near it and move parallel to its course, through the woods, which started at this point and continued almost without a break eastward. We decided to march during the nights and hide during the days in the forest, and if this turned out to be impossible, to hide in the fields of grain, which already grew quite high.

The most important problem was to get to the eastern side of Lwów, for the road we wanted ran eastward, but we were now south of the city. I became the astronomic guide. Knowing where the Polar Star was, I knew which way was north, so we could determine the way east.

We went down the field roads and paths, far from inhabited places and villages, so as not to let anybody see us, for any Pole or Ukrainian would mean danger. We, of course, were afraid of being delated to the Germans. We marched all through the night, sometimes passing by Ukrainian patrols, from which we had to hide. Finally, we reached this Tarnopol highway and set out along it down the field paths. We reached the locality called Winniki. We knew that Winniki was a place located to the east of Lwów, and at dawn we hid in the forest. It turned out, though, that we were not safe in that forest, because farmers were coming there to steal wood, so we had to run away. Dogs barked after us.

We went farther to the east, waited again during the whole day, and at nightfall we pressed on. This was our second night without sleep and food, and we were extremely tired. Because we left quickly we had only been able to take half a loaf of bread and some marmalade each, so we tried to conserve our food as long as possible. While marching during this second night, we saw a haystack that looked like a knight on a horse. It seemed to us that this haystack, or knight, was moving. Suddenly, we noticed a round light in the sky that was moving as well. We were convinced that this was antiaircraft artillery, which was searching for airplanes. We assumed that that meant there was a German antiaircraft position nearby, so we decided to go around it. And we walked a wide circumference around the area. After a few hours, we said to each other that we had come back to the same place where we had previously been, and we suddenly noticed the very same knight on a horse.

Dawn was coming. All of a sudden Mechel Pfeffer shouted, "It is him, it is the Err!" Err was, according to a peasant legend, a knight who made people err on their way. Mechel threw himself on the ground and decided not to move at all, because, he said, when this Err appears, one should lie down and not move until the morning. Icek did the same—he prostrated himself on the ground. I tried to convince them that this was just a haystack, and not any knight on a horse. Nothing doing; they refused to get up and continue our march, despite the danger that farmers could notice us during the day and give us away to the German police. Finally, when my efforts to persuade them failed, I also had to lie down on the ground. We stayed that way until dawn. Of course, it was a haystack. And we also saw then that the light that we had noticed in the sky was just the moon, and not German antiaircraft artillery.

We were exhausted, so it seemed to us that the light was moving. In our minds it was the antiaircraft artillery searchlight trying to find airplanes. As it turned out, though, we had tried to go around the moon!

That day, we hid ourselves in the growing corn. It was raining and we were very hungry. We were eating unripe corn kernels and waited until evening to move out. Just as we left the cornfield behind, bullets started to whiz by us. It was probably a Ukrainian policeman, who had noticed us. We seemed suspect to him and so he started shooting in our direction. We ran quickly into the bushes, into the forest, through a small rivulet, and went on our way. Mechel, who was a farmer, and knew the forest and field paths the best, was marching first, with me following him and Icek bringing up the rear.

Later that night we suddenly stopped when we saw a young man on horseback ahead of us on the field path we were on. He stopped also. We were afraid he was a policeman. We saw no weapon, however, and guessed that he might be afraid of us, who outnumbered him. So we cautiously approached and told him we were Poles escaped from a concentration camp, and asked for directions to the main highway. We had, in fact, become a bit lost in the meandering field paths. We then got into a friendly conversation and he told us that he was a Pole also, a farmer, and had feared that we might be partisans who would confiscate his horse for our needs. He directed us to the highway, but failed to mention what we would find there.

We now decided to go to and cross the highway. We knew we would have to do this eventually anyway, and our adventures so far had convinced us that sooner was better than later. On the other side there were forests that continued over tens of kilometers eastward. There we could proceed with fewer "obstacles," since the forest was unpopulated, and we could be hidden while staying close enough to the highway to not get lost.

We came out of the fields onto a side road that led to the highway. Near the highway, when we could already hear the traffic, we approached a sharp curve to the right. Around the bend we suddenly saw just in front of us two armed Ukrainian policemen, chatting flirtatiously with a girl, in front of a small building that was probably a police post. There was quite a big dog with them. We were perhaps some thirty meters away, completely exposed, for here there was only short grass by the side of the road, nothing to hide in. But they had not noticed us.

We lay down flat on the ground and decided to wait it through. Maybe we could get out of this, maybe they wouldn't notice us. In fact, they didn't notice us, but they would not move from the spot and were still chatting with this girl. We were afraid to move. Suddenly the dog noticed us and started to slowly approach. The dog came up to me. I was convinced it was the end. I was never lucky with dogs, for from my childhood on they had always barked at me. When this dog came close to me I knew that if it started to bark, the two policemen would immediately see us and kill us on the spot, or bring us to the Gestapo. We had not the slightest possibility of running away.

The dog slowly sniffed me over and went away. I thought then that not only was this a miracle, but that a dog is better than a human being. When the dog went farther away, we gave each other a signal, "Psst," and slowly started to retreat, crawling. But Mechel would not move at all. I don't know what the cause was for this. Icek and I crawled backward some hundred meters, after which we stood up where the Ukrainian policemen couldn't see us any longer, and started to run. We ran another hundred meters and stopped, waiting for Mechel. But Mechel was not coming. Suddenly we heard the dog barking, a shout, a shot, all this lasting a few minutes, and then silence. We hid in the corn by the side of the road there and waited twenty-four hours for Mechel to come. But he never returned.

Afterward, after liberation, I learned from a man I met in Lwów, a prisoner from Betonwerke with whom I had shared a bunk bed and who managed to survive as well, that rumors circulated in the camp that we had been caught and executed. Most probably it was Mechel who had been caught and executed. We never heard from him again.

So, two of us were left, Icek and myself. Icek was frightened by the situation in which we found ourselves, and decided to return to Lwów. It was ironic that he, who had come from a small town, from Biały Kamień, and not from Lwów, wanted to do this, while I, who was an urbanite, who had lived my whole life in Lwów, did not want to go back there. I knew there was no chance of saving myself there.

We spent much effort trying to convince one another of our different points of view. This haggling lasted a long time, but finally Icek agreed to continue toward Biały Kamień and not go back to Lwów. We both decided, in view of the experience we'd just had, to avoid settled areas and side roads. We would risk going on the highway itself, and duck into the adjacent forest (or into a ditch if rushed) if we heard a car or horse approach. We would continue to travel during the nights and to hide in the corn or in the woods during the days. And so we did.

After seven days we came close to Złoczów, not far from our destination. On our way, we passed by concentration camps in Kurowice, Jaktorów, and Lacki. We had to be very careful, for often when we passed, someone would shoot at us. Apparently this would happen whenever they saw some vague silhouettes dragging themselves down the road during the night.

A bit before Złoczów, we turned to the left to the village of Pociapy, still going toward Biały Kamień. There were swamps in the vicinity of this village. We fell into them and could not get ourselves out. The swampy waters were already up to our breasts. It was a dark night. The situation was desperate. We were trying to find some solution with every means possible, but to no avail, and still we had to get out before dawn, at any price, or we would be noticed and turned over to the Ukranian or German police.

Our efforts lasted I do not know how long; it seemed ages. Just before sunrise, though, we finally succeeded in getting out of the swamp and went quickly toward Biały Kamień, to a Pole whom Icek knew very well and who had some obligations to Icek's parents. We knocked at the door. The host came out, was frightened, and became speechless at seeing us. He did not know what to do. His wife, a Ukrainian, started to shout at us to go away immediately, for otherwise she would call the Gestapo. We asked them for some food, because we were very hungry. We had marched seven days since our escape, with only half a loaf of bread for this whole time. His wife, however, refused to even let him help us in this way. But he promised to bring us some food, and told us to hide in the ruins of the old Sobieski palace. We concealed ourselves in the thicket by the ruins, near the pond, and waited for this Pole, named Szamborski. It rained intermittently. We covered ourselves with what we could, and waited for Szamborski the whole day, dreaming of a slice of bread. But Szamborski didn't come.

Night came, so we hid in the caves of the Sobieski palace and tried to sleep. It was biting cold and damp there, and we were completely wet and all covered in mud from the swamps and daylong rain. Our teeth chattered so loudly that we could be heard from several meters away. We sat with our backs together so as to warm ourselves a bit.

When it got fully dark, Icek decided to look for help from another Pole, whose name was Zawer. Icek praised him, saying that he was a very honest and helpful man. Perhaps he would help us? Zawer was the manager of the electric power station in Biały Kamień. This station was located in an old mill, which had belonged, before the war, to nuns of the order of the Sisters of Charity as part of a farming estate. When the Russians came to Biały Kamień in 1939, they nationalized at once the whole estate with its mill, alcohol distillery, and electric station. In 1941, the Germans had taken it into their own hands as an SS estate, we were told. The distillery and the mill itself were not working at that time, for they had been damaged due to an explosion during military actions. The electric station alone, supplying the neighborhood with electricity, was still functioning, and Zawer was its manager.

Icek went into the darkness of the night to Zawer's house; he knew him personally very well. I waited in the ruins, trembling with cold and anxiety, hoping that Icek would return with some results from his expedition. I was upset and enormously disappointed. According to assurances from Icek, and previously from Mechel, the biggest problem was escaping from the camp and getting to Biały Kamień. From then on we would have no serious troubles. We had succeeded in escaping from the camp; we had succeeded, after a few ups and downs, in reaching Biały Kamień, but our situation seemed to remain hopeless.

My heart thumped when I suddenly heard our watchword. "Psst, psst." Icek returned with nothing. He told me that he had approached Zawer's house, but had seen light inside and feared that there was somebody strange in the house, perhaps even a German. Not daring to even knock on the door, he returned to the ruins.

Upon hearing this, out of stress and hunger, I fainted. Icek promised to go to Zawer the next evening. Still hungry and cold, we remained in the ruins the whole day. Outside the ruins, though, there were some wild gooseberry bushes, and we tried to at least partly appease our hunger and thirst by eating what we could find there. We often had to run quickly back to the ruins when we heard footsteps of people passing by.

Before our escape from Janowska camp, Mechel and Icek had told me that people from Biały Kamień avoided the ruins of the Sobieski palace because of the alleged ghosts haunting the place. Evidently, people had ceased to be afraid of these ghosts.

On the following evening, Icek again went furtively to the house of the Zawer family. I stayed back in the ruins. I was in the utmost despair. I felt that the fight for my life was coming to an end, that it was hopeless, and that I must give myself up to cruel fate. And hunger was biting mercilessly; it was unbearable.

I decided that the very next day, if we didn't get help from somewhere, I would voluntarily go to the Ukrainian police and ask them to give me something to eat. After that they could do to me whatever they wished.

In the silence of the night, I suddenly heard our watchword, "Psst, psst!" It was Icek coming back. He came up to me and pushed a key into my hand. I did not know yet precisely what this key meant, but I knew that this must mean good news and my heart beat with joy. Icek told me that he had finally dared to enter the house of the Zawer family. They were happy to see him. Icek told them that he was with a physician from Lwów, with whom he had escaped from Janowska camp. Mrs. Zawer then told her husband, "Florjan, we have to help them. We absolutely have to help them."

They told Icek that we should hide in the attic of the mill containing the electric power station. Zawer gave Icek the key to the back door of the mill and warned us to enter the mill very carefully, for there was a young Ukrainian man named Vasyl who was on duty in the station during the night. On the second day Zawer would visit us there and bring us food.

Our joy was without limit. Once again, as after our successful escape from the camp to the woods, I constantly heard a beautiful music in my ears, as if I were at some concert. Happily, we quickly started to sneak in the direction of the mill.

CHAPTER 22

THE MILL

We entered the mill silently through the back door, tiptoeing, avoiding all noises, up the staircase, and reached the attic. The mill was a high building of four stories, with walls of brick, at least in the lower part. The stairs were also built of brick. Once we reached the attic, we fell asleep.

On the next day, Zawer visited us and brought us bread and butter as promised. After a few days of hunger, we could finally fill our stomachs. We had a short talk together, whispering, so that nobody could hear us. We had to be careful because a large group of Polish and Ukrainian workers was working in the electric station in the mill. The latter ones could be very dangerous to us. Zawer admitted to us that he belonged to the underground Home Army. During our stay there, he would from time to time bring us the illegal underground newspaper *Ziemia Czerwieńska*, published by the Home Army of the eastern Małopolska (Little Poland) region (that is, eastern Galicia), as well as the regular official bulletin of the AK (Home Army). Besides that, he would bring us news about what was happening in the world, especially on the fronts.

We were very happy to read one day in *Ziemia Czerwieńska* a notice warning Poles against helping the Germans track down Jews, telling them that those who were doing this would be judged in court in the free Polish Republic after the war. This was in refreshing contrast to the behavior of the Home Army forces in western Poland, where they actually helped the Germans kill Jews! The different policy of the Home Army in eastern Galicia was perhaps due to the fact that here the Jews and Poles had the Ukrainians as a common enemy.

The garret where we were hiding was quite roomy, but the glass windows were broken. We made a hideout for ourselves in the corner. At the beginning, Zawer came every day for several days in a row with a small packet of food for us, but after a few days it turned out that the employees working in the mill were starting to observe him. Thus, he decided to come irregularly and not every day. We did not blame him for that. We had full understanding for his behavior. We were afraid for his fate no less than ours.

During the whole period of our hiding, we felt that we had no right to jeopardize the life of this exceptionally good man, who was risking his own life and his family's, saving people strange to him for no gain. We were the condemned ones, who were trying to run away from death, alone and without families, while he had a wife, two little children, a father and brother. Therefore, we decided to do everything we could not to jeopardize the life of our host, especially since, from time to time, news reached us, often published in the press, that such and such Poles were publicly shot dead or hanged for helping Jews in hiding or for supplying Jews with food. The purpose of this, of course, was not only to punish those particular Poles for what they had done but to frighten away others from doing the same.

Thus, we arranged it in such a way that Zawer would not bring us food anymore himself and would not come to us, but instead would leave bread at his place, in the stable. Icek would go and get it once a week during the night. We decided to make a hidden exit for ourselves from the mill. During the night we went down to the cellar surreptitiously, sneaking past the room where a young man was on night duty. We pulled a few bricks from the wall, in order to have a hole for getting out of the mill. Through this small hole we would go out once a week. Icek, who knew all the roads in his native little Biały Kamień well, would sneak to the stable for the bread while I kept watch at the hole.

When he returned, if it was safe, we also washed ourselves in the nearby river at these opportunities, and each filled a bottle with drinking water for the whole week. Also, of course, we were stealing anything we could find to eat in the surrounding fields, namely green tomatoes, cabbage, unripe cucumbers, and so on. What we stole we partly ate then, putting the rest aside for later. Going outside also made it possible to relieve ourselves more conveniently. At other times we had to use a variety of subterfuges to relieve ourselves without leaving traces that might arouse suspicion.

Having returned to the mill through the hole we had made, we would close it back up with some bricks to conceal the suspicious crack in the wall. Zawer was coming to our place from time to time to talk to us, to learn what we were doing, and to share with us the political and military news. Information from the front was favorable. The German armies were retreating everywhere. They had been beaten in Kursk, Orel, and Kharkov. This news was really joyful for us, and our hopes for liberation increased.

All this, however, was still insufficient. The progress of the Allies in the west, and of the Russians in the east, seemed slow. They were still very, very far away, while the Germans were near and around us. Icek and I killed time together, talking about the past, the present, and the future—if we should live to see it. We discussed family histories and our hopes and dreams. I taught Icek various subjects. We also rehearsed two anthems, to be prepared for liberation by either Americans or Russians.

We were still hungry, for the food supplied, or rather left, by Zawer was not enough. For security reasons, he was afraid to leave larger amounts of food in the stable. We did not want to insist that he leave more, for we were afraid that he might give up helping us. We were, after all, neither his relatives nor friends, nor was he taking money from us for hiding us, so he had no obligations whatsoever, while risking his life and his family's. Needless to say, we were grateful for whatever he did for us.

Icek was sneaking, as I mentioned, to Zawer's stable once a week, but never on moonlit nights, which meant that he went out either during the new moon, or before moonrise, or after moonset, and during the full moon only if the sky was completely clouded. I functioned as the astronomer, and calculated the precise times of moonrise and moonset, and when would be the safest time for Icek to go to the stable. It was also my task to guard the hole in the cellar wall, through which Icek went out and came back. The bread we received was meticulously divided up so as to suffice for at least seven days.

Soon we learned that we had partners in the consumption of our modest portions of bread—namely, mice. All our attempts at concealing the bread from these uninvited partners were unsuccessful. These mice proved to be smarter than we were. One day we hung our small sack of bread on a long cord from the cross beam. The mice climbed up to the beam and then descended down the cord to the sack. They bit through the sack and took a share of our bread. On another occasion, when we tried to hide bread under the sheepskin jacket under our heads, mice would run over our heads during the night to get it.

One time, we got a small jar of butter from Zawer. We ate part of this butter at once, but we decided to leave the rest in the jar next to our pallet. I was awakened during the night by a light knocking sound. I did not pay much attention to it and went back to sleep. When we got up the next morning, the jar was no longer there. It had disappeared. I am sure that rats or mice had taken the jar and run away with it. However, Icek was convinced that I had stolen his butter, and no amount of discussion could dissuade him.

One day Icek announced that he knew some people in Biały Kamień from whom he could buy some bread. I was very happy with that. I gave Icek a large sum of money, for he had not a penny, while I had both U.S. dollars and occupational bank notes (złotys printed by the German occupational government); these latter were in the form of 500-złoty notes, commonly called "mountaineers" because of the picture printed on them. I had received this money from Faliński before our escape and again afterward, via a messenger that Zawer sent on my behalf. Icek tried several times to set out on this expedition, but he would always chicken out, frightened, and delay the date. And I thought that I was not entitled to press him or even talk him into searching for food, since it was, after all, risky. Let him decide for himself whether and when he would go to those acquaintances of his. I told him to keep the money I had given him.

Later I even gave him additional money, in both dollars and mountaineers. I told him that I wanted him to have money in case something happened to me, or in case we were separated during escape or something like that. Icek expressed his gratitude to me and noted that he wouldn't have been able to manage without it, for Zawer used it to buy bread for us from German soldiers—he had ceased giving us his own bread, in case we were found and the bread was traced to him. My money was therefore necessary, but Icek emphasized that Zawer was his acquaintance, so that I also needed him. Icek was very annoyed when Zawer came to us, for Zawer almost always talked with me, rather than him, on subjects such as politics and the war situation.

Icek was not a very intelligent or educated person. His formal education had ended with grammar school, but he hadn't picked up much even from there. Since fate had brought us together for long months, I tried to give him some knowledge from various domains. Icek was not stupid and he was very shrewd, but he was an egoist. He loved only himself and loved to eat. Any kind memories of his parents embraced only his mother, who had fed him well.

Icek hated his father, especially because of one thing. His father was a respected merchant in Biały Kamień, and was a pious Jew, apparently liked by his neighbors and other people. When the Russians took Biały Kamień in 1939, Icek got a job in some state institution. He soon noticed, as he told me, that the young people who belonged to the Communist

Youth Organization, Komsomol, had much more say in this institution than even its director, who had to reckon with them. He therefore became a member of Komsomol, although he had no idea about politics, communism, or economics. The local Poles, Ukrainians, and Jews were scandalized and outraged by the fact that a son of a *Pejsach* belonged to Komsomol. Because of this, frequent altercations occurred between Icek and his father. When the Germans marched into Biały Kamień in 1941, the Ukrainians organized—as in all the other localities—anti-Jewish pogroms, looking especially for Jewish Communists, those who had held positions under the Russians, and of course, Komsomol members. It was then, especially, that quarrels between Icek and his father were frequent, and Icek fled from home to Lwów. He hated his father to the extent that he was not at all interested in his father's fate. He knew that his mother had been killed either by the Germans or by the Ukrainians.

One day Zawer brought the news that he had seen Icek's father in the ghetto or in the labor camp in Złoczów. I proposed to Icek then to let his father come to our hideout. I felt that Zawer would agree to that. But Icek absolutely would not agree. I don't know whether this was because of the hatred he still felt toward his father or because of the fear that it would be more difficult to survive as three than as two. I was shocked by Icek's position—to not want to save his own father? At that time period, even the greatest enemies among Jews, who hadn't talked to each other for years, now having to face the deadly dangers of the German occupation, forgave mutual guilts. But Icek was unyielding.

Time passed slowly and monotonously in our hideout. Day after day of waiting for salvation. We hungered, then stuffed our stomachs with the unripe cucumbers, green tomatoes, and cabbage from our expeditions in the fields by the river. It was a surprise to me that just one bottle of water for each of us was enough for a week, most probably owing to those unripe tomatoes and cucumbers. We also had problems with concealing all traces of our existence—especially physiological ones—from people employed in the mill, and had to invent very diverse methods of concealing any evidence we might have left.

After a few weeks of our stay in the hideout up in the attic, we had a small shock. One day, at noon, the door to the attic opened and Vasyl, the young Ukrainian man, who was usually on duty in the electric station of the mill only at night, appeared in the door. We froze in fear. He looked around, standing in the door, as if looking for something. We were hidden in the far, dark corner of the attic, and he did not notice us. When he went out, we gave a sigh of relief, but we were also overtaken by anxiety in the anticipation of his return, and we saw that our hideout was not as safe as we had hoped.

The Germans, meanwhile, were suffering defeat after defeat on the eastern front, and they started to retreat from the Soviet areas they had previously taken, referring to this in the military announcements as "taking up new strategic positions having inflicted heavy losses upon the enemy."

As the Soviet armies progressed, guerrilla detachments appeared in our territories. Some of them were commanded by Russians who had parachuted over the frontline, while some others belonged to the Polish Home Army. Likewise, Ukrainian guerrilla detachments appeared when they saw that Hitler would not keep his promise of establishing an independent Ukrainian state.

Simultaneously, fighting and mutual killings between Poles and Ukrainians started. Executions were ordered by the Polish Home Army for Ukrainians collaborating with the Germans. A Jew named Katz, who was said to have served before the war as a corporal in the Polish army, gained local fame for his fearlessness in carrying out these orders. It was told that some guerrilla fighters were even so bold as to publicly appear during the day in little towns and villages. The Germans then decided to end this, so one day a Gestapo detachment arrived in Biały Kamień. The Germans went from house to house searching for the underground fighters. They even came close to our mill. We were frightened. There was no possibility of escaping. We saw them through the window. They turned around. Then they surrounded the woods and flared some prey there.

When evening came, the Gestapo returned to the mill. We were utterly scared. Suddenly we could hear that they had organized a feast just by the mill. They started to eat and even put on a gramophone record with marches, obviously German ones, to make the picnic more pleasant. We kept a lookout, feeling very tense. After some time, when silence fell at dusk, we understood that they had gone away, and we breathed a deep sigh of relief.

Autumn came and it became very cold in our attic with the broken windowpanes. It was frequently freezing during the nights. One day in late September Zawer came and told us, "Listen, you won't be able to stand being here in the attic come winter; you won't endure it. We must find a solution."

On the very next day, he came with the news that there were guerrilla groups in the nearby woods, with whom Jews also served, and promised to put us in touch with these groups. We were very happy with this and waited impatiently for good news. A few days later, Zawer came with the sad information that the Gestapo detachments had come, and the group was exterminated. We had a bit of luck in avoiding this fate. But what would we do now?

We decided to build ourselves a hideout in the cellar of the mill. We snuck silently to the cellar during the night and dug out a hole there, which we covered with various rags and straw. We pulled out bricks from the staircase and from other places, and constructed a false wall out of them, so that our winter hideout would not be visible to a person entering the cellar. Since, however, the bricks were not stuck to each other, even a light blow would send the wall tumbling down.

We also decided, for the winter, to provide ourselves with cabbages, which were still growing in the fields. One night, when I was coming back from an expedition for cabbage, carrying a heavy sack of them, the sack fell from my back and I felt a sharp pain in the right side of my chest, as if I had broken my ribs. I barely reached our hideout. Having a thermometer and a stethoscope, which I had taken, among other things, when escaping from the camp, I found that my fever was above 39° Celsius (102° Fahrenheit). Having examined myself and listened with the stethoscope, I concluded that I had a pleurisy on the right side with massive exudation (fluid in the cavity between the lungs and chest wall).

I was in despair. No medical aid was available, and no possibility of hospitalization. I wrote a prescription on a piece of paper, using a fictitious doctor's name, made out for Zawer, and asked him to buy me this medicine in the town. Zawer brought me this medicine and, additionally, a bottle of hot tea with milk. For the first time in many months, I enjoyed the pleasure of drinking something warm. The fever lasted for about six weeks. The exudation in the right pleural cavity slowly disappeared, but I could also hear pleural friction quite distinctly. After six weeks, I could stand up and walk. We then decided to go down to the hiding place we had prepared in the cellar.

We lay in the cellar during the days, sometimes visited by the big, fat rats, who somehow seemed to thrive there. The fleas would never leave us alone. We also still had body lice, though not as badly as in the camp. Still only once a week, Icek would sneak out to the Zawers' to get food, and sometimes Zawer would come himself and throw the pack of food on the cellar staircase.

In December 1943 I read in the newspapers and Home Army bulletins, brought by Zawer, that the last concentration camp in eastern Galicia, the Janowska camp, had been exterminated. There were now neither concentration camps nor ghettos in the region. It was then that General

Katzmann, the chief of police and SS in District Galicia, reported to Hitler: "*Galizien ist judenrein* [Galicia is cleansed of Jews]." The tragic fate of the Jews of eastern Galicia was now complete, one and a half years before the end of World War II.

The front was coming nearer and nearer to us, and there were more and more Germans in our small town, as well as the Russians who fought side by side with them against the Soviets. These Russians were called "Vlassov troops," named after a Russian general who had surrendered to the German army and agreed to fight on its side. His troops continued to serve under him as a unit in the German army, in German uniforms. The name became a term for any deserter from the Soviet army who fought for the Germans.

One day, one of them came into our cellar as if looking for something, knocking against things with some steel object. We froze in fear. We heard his steps approaching our hideout. He was already just in front of our artificial wall. We heard his breath, when suddenly a voice called from outside, "Vanya, Vanya, where are you, what's going on with you?"

"Wait, wait," answered Vanya. He defecated by our wall and went away. Again we sighed with relief, but this was not for long.

Because the front was approaching, the Ukrainians started to build shelters in order to hide and to defend themselves against the Russians. They knew what awaited them for their collaboration with Hitler. They came to the mill both during the day and at night, tearing bricks away with a jimmy to build shelters for themselves. They were destroying the walls of the mill, and getting closer to our hideout.

It was January 31, 1944. A hole appeared from the outside of the exterior wall, beneath our legs. The situation was becoming dangerous for us. A few days later, we heard knocking against the wall again. Someone was inside the cellar trying, with a jimmy or with something else, to pull bricks out of the wall. We were even more frightened. The knocking we heard was getting closer and closer. In an instant, a blow hit our artificial wall, which fell down, and through the hole a surprised human head squeezed in, and beside it a hand with a lit candle. It was the night watchman, Vasyl. We retreated as much as possible, and so he probably did not see me, but only Icek, whom he recognized. He fled at once. Icek grabbed his sack and fled. I was left alone in an unfamiliar locality where, other than Zawer, I didn't know anyone, and, additionally, I was exhausted by the disease I had just gone through.

Again, I was in despair. I must flee, I told myself, for certainly either the Ukrainian or German police would come to search this uncovered hideout and find the people who might still be staying there. Where should I escape to? I did not know; I did not even know the way to the Zawers'. I was looking desperately for a place in the cellar where I could hide. I noticed a large chimney and decided to push myself in there, but the hole was too small and it was too difficult for me to get in. Because I was afraid of choking myself in the chimney, I decided to try to force myself in there only when I heard the footsteps of Ukrainian or German policemen.

Meanwhile, I was standing and listening, and I prayed in despair. Time passed. There was silence around me, but my hopeless situation remained unchanged. After a long time, I suddenly heard the footsteps of a single man—and our watchword, "Psst." It was Icek, who had come for me. He told me that he had escaped to the woods, and in the evening had snuck into Zawer's house. Zawer told Icek that Vasyl had come to him and informed him that there were Jews hiding in the cellar and that he had recognized Icek. Vasyl wanted to run to the German military police post and inform them of his discovery. But Zawer put Vasyl off from doing this, saying that this could not possibly be Icek, that those people could not be Jews, but rather deserters from the German army, Germans or Russians, and one should be careful with them, for such a deserter could shoot him.

In view of our desperate situation, Zawer had proposed that both of us hide in his stable. We waited until it was completely quiet outside of the mill, and then we went out, and, wading through the snow, we snuck into Zawer's farmyard and hid in the loft of the stable. It was freezing cold outdoors, but we, hidden deeply in the hay, did not feel this. We were comfortable. In addition, we were now less hungry, because Zawer brought us, almost every day, some cooked food, which we had not had for a very long time. It was cooked millet with sugar beet syrup, which tasted like the best cakes to us.

The German-Soviet front was getting closer and closer. The Russians had already taken Kiev and were progressing quickly forward. They had already reached Tarnopol and Brody, both located not far from Biały Kamień. The German troops were by now in the whole area around us. We often heard Germans in the vicinity of our stable.

One day, we learned that the Russians were only twelve kilometers away from us. We could already hear their artillery, which sounded like beautiful music to us. Our heartbeats quickened in the expectation of our approaching liberation.

And suddenly, at the end of March 1944, the Russian guns fell silent. It turned out that the Russians had stopped their offensive, and even retreated a few kilometers.

In the meantime, the Ukrainians decided to settle their accounts with the Poles. They presented the Poles with an ultimatum, requiring them to move west of the San River, the border between western and eastern Galicia, within a week. They threatened those who stayed after that dead-line with death. Most Poles refused to leave eastern Galicia, however. Thus, Ukrainian squads started to circulate and kill Poles. The Poles were, on the other hand, organized in the Home Army, and their detachments avenged these murders by killing Ukrainians. Every evening in our area there was a local mass migration, in opposite directions: the Poles were leaving their homes and going to Biały Kamień to hide in the church, which they made into a small fortress, while the Ukrainians also left their homes and concentrated themselves in the village of Kawareczyzna Górna, the headquarters of their squads. Poles or Ukrainians who stayed in their houses after dusk could pay with their lives. In the morning, most of these people returned to their homes for the day. The Germans were not intervening, for it was to their advantage that the Poles and Ukrainians were fighting each other, rather than against them.

These Ukrainian squads in the neighboring village belonged, inciden-tally, to the Banderian organization. Its leader was Stefan Bandera, broth-er of the engineer and mayor of Stryj who had given Norbert and me our apartments there. Stefan Bandera had assassinated a Polish government minister. His organization worked underground in prewar Poland, with help from Germany. After the Germans invaded, however, Bandera's hopes that they would soon set up a Ukrainian state were not realized, and he eventually went underground against the Germans as well. After the war, Bandera continued his nationalist underground activities against the Soviets, but ended up fleeing to the West. Later, he was himself assas-sinated in Munich, presumably by Soviet agents.

The front, meanwhile, continued to be completely silent, only about fifteen kilometers away, and our situation was more and more dangerous. The Germans were everywhere in the neighborhood, and some German officers were even quartered in Zawer's house.

One day, in early April, Zawer told us that the danger of our being dis-covered in the stable by the Germans was very high and that we had, alas, to leave. He was very afraid of the peril to his life and his family's, and for their security, which was quite understandable. He advised us to return to the attic of the mill or to hide in the stable of the parish priest in Biały Kamień.

We decided to go back to the mill. Our decision turned out to be the lucky one, for a few days later the Gestapo came and surrounded the stable of the parish priest, looking for guerrillas. They didn't find anyone, and we, luckily, weren't there.

Hiding in the attic of the mill, we listened all day for weeks, hoping that the Russian artillery would resound at last. But nothing. The front was not moving. April of 1944 passed and May began. There was still silence on the front. It was at that time that numerous Jews, who had been hidden by Poles or Ukrainians, were killed. Their hosts, Poles or Ukrainians, out of fear of the Germans, who were now everywhere in this area, felt they couldn't hide them anymore. These Jews had to abandon their hiding places and search for new ones, and so would fall into the hands of the Ukrainian or German police.

One day, the door to our attic opened and a Russian in a German uniform, a Vlassovian soldier, came in. He looked about, then started to walk slowly around the attic, apparently searching for something, and finally came to the corner where we were hidden in the dark. He noticed us and was terrified. "Sit, don't worry," he shouted, and quickly fled.

Icek quickly ran away as well, and I was again left alone. I decided to flee also, for I had no doubts that the German military police would soon come for us. When I hurriedly left the attic, I noticed that many steps were missing in the staircase, and that one had to jump down. I fled to the cellar, but I did not know what to do next, for I had nowhere to go. I knew only one thing—that I had to run away, for they would come looking for us.

Around fifteen or twenty minutes later I suddenly heard, in the room above me, the sound of soldiers' boots. There were at least two people moving about up there. The Germans were most probably looking for something or for somebody. I decided to risk it and go out. I was dressed in a sheepskin coat, tightened with a belt, and with a cap on my head, and a sack on my back, in which there was a priceless piece of bread. There was a large gap in the cellar wall toward the courtyard, on the side away from the river. It had apparently been made by Ukrainians taking bricks. I walked out, with fake self-assurance, through this big hole in the cellar wall, into the cool May air. I looked like one of the workers who were busy in the yard, and no one, it seemed, paid attention to me. I decided to go across the road, get to the nearby wood, wait there until evening, and then go to Zawer—perhaps he would be able to help me in some way.

Since Icek was not with me, I had to act on my own. When I reached the road, I saw a detachment of German soldiers marching on the road. I passed calmly and assuredly at a distance of one hundred meters in front of them, toward the fields, where there were several boys pasturing their cows. I noticed that those cowherds were observing me, but I still went steadily forward, not turning my head, so as not to seem suspect. My shoes were corroded by cement from the time I worked in the concrete plant in the camp, and they were hurting my heels. My socks were torn, and blood trickled from my injured heels, but in spite of the pain I went on without stopping or turning back.

When I had walked a few hundred meters, I finally looked back and saw that the cowherds were still watching me. I went farther in the direction of the wood and hid at its edge. I decided to wait until evening.

As dusk fell, the daily migrations started. I saw a great many people fearfully going in opposite directions: the Poles flocking to their armed church, and the Ukrainians to the village of Kawareczyzna Górna. I made up my mind to go to Zawer when these wanderings ended and ask him to leave the stable open, if he would agree to it.

I went through the park, where the ruins of the Sobieski palace, in which we had stayed before, stood. I glanced around to see whether anyone noticed me, and saw that a Ukrainian woman with a small girl was following and observing me. I went out of the park, therefore, and when I saw that there was nobody around, I quickly went to the house of the Zawer family.

When I entered their home, they were very scared. They asked what I was doing there, what had happened, and requested that I immediately hide in their attic. I told them that I did not want to jeopardize their safety, for someone could have, after all, noticed me, but I asked them to leave the stable open. Meanwhile, I would now go to the ruins, wait there until midnight, and only then, during the night, go to the stable. If, however, someone noticed me leaving their home, they should say that it had been some worker from the Organization Todt who worked somewhere for the German army, and who came in order to exchange something for bread, butter, eggs, or some other food staple.

They agreed, and I quickly went out to go to the ruins. I hid there and waited. Suddenly, I saw German patrols on bicycles, and I heard shooting. They were shooting all around. They also passed by the ruins, but did not enter. After some time the shooting ended. At about midnight, Icek appeared in the ruins and told me that he had been at the Zawers' after I had left there, and saw them kneeling in front of a holy picture. Zawer and his wife were nearly fainting from fear, Icek said. It turned out that after I had gone away, some Ukrainian woman had come to them and told them that she had seen a guerrilla fighter or bandit in the park, and that she was going to the German military police post to inform them about it. The Zawers tried to persuade her not to do this, but she decided to go anyway.

After a while, a German patrol on bicycles and motorbikes appeared. They surrounded the park, shooting, searching for the hypothetical bandit. No German had the idea to enter the ruins where I was hiding. They searched around, and finally they went away without their prey.

The Zawers, however, were terrified and desperate, for they were at first convinced that the Germans had caught me and would force me to admit who had helped hide me. Even after they guessed that this had not happened, they still feared that it might yet occur. They told Icek they could not, alas, hide us any longer. They gave him bread and marmalade for us, and the Lord's blessing, too.

We faced the question, then, of what to do next. Zawer had told us a few weeks earlier that going northward along the river that flowed through Biały Kamień, one could find, after about ten kilometers, an old, abandoned mill, which had some time ago been managed by his father. Since the mill was located in a deserted area, swampy and humid, Zawer thought that there would be no Germans there, and that we could hide in the mill.

Icek suggested that I go to this deserted mill, while he would go to some people he knew and try to find a hideout or at least food that he could buy for us. Judging by the tone of his voice, I gathered that Icek did not intend to come to me at this mill if he found a place to hide. Indeed, it was much easier to hide alone than in twos, and Icek had my money, so he did not need me anymore. I therefore asked him to assure me that he would come for me and not leave me alone in an area I didn't know at all.

Icek did not want to give his word on this. I was surprised at his cruel lack of scruples, but I could do nothing. We had been hiding together for almost a year already; we had been colleagues together, and he had been making use of my money, with which Zawer had been buying us food. I thought about the money I had given Icek some two months before: a large sum, in dollars, and all of the Polish occupational banknotes that I had received from Faliński. I told Icek, "I already see that you plan to leave me to my fate. I cannot force you to come back to me. But I want just one thing from you. I gave you dollars and Polish banknotes. You can keep the dollars, but give back the Polish banknotes. You know someone to whom you can go, while I do not. If I went to a farmer with dollars, he would know at once that I am a Jew and might give me away to the Germans. I didn't keep any Polish banknotes for myself, so please give those back."

The answer Icek gave to this was a categorical no. When I told him this was, after all, my money, he hesitated a little, then added that he could sell me the Polish money for dollars and proposed a very high sum.

"Aren't you ashamed?" I said. "You are selling me my own money for a profiteer's price?"

Icek did not change his resolve. I waited for a while, thinking that he would perhaps realize how dirty his conduct was. But nothing like that happened. We went in opposite directions.

The day was May 10, 1944. I went up north along the river, bitter and desperate. I was carrying a sack on my back in which there were my stethoscope, syringes, and shaving equipment, as well as half a loaf of bread and the marmalade that the Zawers had given us. It was a beautiful moonlit night. A full moon. It was bright as daylight. I went along the river on its right side. To the right of me there was a plain, with wide meadows, and a wood in the distance. To the left, across the river, were dark bushes and trees. From time to time a light wind blew.

Suddenly, the wind brought some voices to my ears. They seemed to me to be talking in German. I stopped, I listened, but nothing. Silence. I started to wonder. Germans here? Didn't Zawer tell us that there would not be any Germans in these swampy areas? What should I do? Go on or not? But I didn't have anywhere to return to anyway. I was all alone in a countryside that was unfamiliar to me. I decided to continue my march northward. I went perhaps twenty meters more when suddenly I heard a shrieking voice: "Halt! Password!" There were Germans on the other bank of the river, which was easy to cross. The water would be up to the waist, at most to the breast, and its width was fifteen to twenty meters here. The Germans were invisible to me in the dark bushes, while I was in the full moonlight against the meadow, visible all too clearly. The Germans were so close to me that there was no point in running away. I was lost. My first thought—there is no way out, I have to give in. "Halt, Parole!" repeated the German soldier.

I changed my mind in a flash. No, I will not give in. Let them shoot me; I will not give in. And I started to run away from them, southward.

I was running in zigzags, falling down, getting up, and running on. The Germans started to shoot chaotically. I didn't know how many they were, but I could distinguish at least two kinds of shots—one of a machine gun, and the other of a regular rifle, but a very noisy one. Bullets whizzed by my ears. I was convinced that some bullet must have hit me, but that out of stress I didn't feel it, for it seemed impossible for them not to hit me from such a short distance.

Although I was running wildly, I didn't throw my sack away, because I didn't want to waste the bread. Exhausted, I soon had no more strength to carry the sack, but even then I didn't leave it; I dragged it behind me. The Germans were still shooting after me. I survived only by a miracle. I was

hearing bullets whizzing past my head constantly. Some fifty meters farther, the river made an abrupt turn. I jumped into the water and hid
myself behind its steep bank. I was completely exhausted from running,
especially since I was still weak from the long-term illness I had gone
through just a few months before. I started to pray. I was convinced these
were the last moments of my life. The Germans were only about fifty
meters away from me, and if they had approached me, I would not have
had the strength to raise my hands. But they were not coming. They were
still shooting without a break. Perhaps they were afraid that this was some
kind of guerrilla group.

I was lying in this shallow water, waiting for God's mercy. Suddenly,
clouds started to cover the sky, and after some time they covered the
moon, so that it became darker. The Germans were still shooting. When it
got even darker, they shot out a few flares—one, two, three—but they
didn't notice anyone, so they started to shoot less and less frequently,
most probably just to scare away this someone in the dark, and after half
an hour the shooting stopped.

I decided, then, to go back to Zawer's, because I didn't see any other
way out. I crossed the river, the water up to my chest, and set out toward
his stable. Dawn was coming. When I marched, my cement-ridden wet
slacks gave out such loud noises that I was afraid someone might hear me.
The stable wasn't closed. I crawled up to the loft over the stable, to our
old place, and covered myself with hay. I was lying, exhausted, and I was
feeling at that moment that I didn't have any more strength or will to
fight for my life. I was ready to commit suicide.

At dawn Zawer seemed to sense that someone was in the stable. He
came out of the house—I saw him through the cracks between the roof
tiles—and went up at once to the loft and found me lying behind a stack
of hay.

"Mr. Zawer," I said, "if you can't or don't want to hide me, I don't have
the right to ask this of you, that you risk your life and your family's for me.
I would not have a grudge against you. If you can help me and will keep
me, I shall never forget this. But if you cannot, then I beg you, here is all
my money, buy me a pistol, and if you cannot get me a gun, then
cyanide."

Zawer looked at me, stood a while, said nothing, and went away. I
noticed through the crack in the roof that his wife came out of the house
and Zawer went up to her. Both of them, standing in front of the house,
talked in low voices for a few minutes. Then they went back to the house.
My fate was at stake.

After a short time, Zawer came to me in the loft and brought me a pot of hot coffee and bread. I had tears in my eyes. I was really deeply moved. What wonderful people! They had two little children, a father, and a brother; Germans were staying in their house; and in spite of all this they decided to take the risk and help me. "Mr. Zawer," I said, "I will not forget what you are doing for me till the end of my life."

After a few days, who but Icek should appear in the loft. Apparently, he had had no luck in the other places. He was furious at me, that I myself, without needing his mediation, had contacted Zawer and made arrangements with him. As long as the military front was far away, Icek had needed me, for I had money; and in return he really did try to take care of me. Presently, though, the front was very near. Germans were around everywhere, and farmers didn't want to hide or help Jews even for large amounts of money. Besides this, Icek already had a large part of my money, clearly enough to last until the Russians arrived, so that I was now a burden for him. Indeed, Icek didn't make it a secret that he would like to get rid of me, and even threatened to strangle me if I didn't go by myself. "You have no right to be here, to endanger Zawer," he told me. I replied, "If you try to kill me, you are stronger than I and could do it, but I will resist and scream, and the Germans will hear it and you will not survive either." Most probably it was only this resolution on my part, and his fear of Zawer, that kept Icek from following up on his threat.

And so we lived together in the hayloft of Zawer's stable, and Zawer brought us something cooked to eat every day.

On May 17, 1944, Zawer announced that, alas, we couldn't stay in his stable any longer, for the danger of being found out by the Germans was becoming greater and greater. There were more and more Germans living in or coming to his house, and they were often going to the lavatory, which was in the stable just beneath our hideout. Our movements, even our talking in low voices or snoring in our sleep, could give us away.

He advised us to hide in a large stable located about eighty meters from there, one he had suggested to us earlier and that belonged to the parish priest of Biały Kamień. The next day we went there and got in through the back of the closed stable. The parish priest didn't know about us. We snuck into the storage room of a granary and from there climbed up to the loft, where we made ourselves a hideout in the hay, of which, unfortunately, there was not too much at that time of the year.

In the evening, when the people who worked on the priest's farm were returning home, we started to look for something to eat in the stable. We were hungry, for Zawer could provide bread for us only once a week. He left the bread in his stable in the back bin next to the dungstead. It was getting harder and harder to sneak into his stable, because German patrols were going around during the night. Sometimes two weeks would pass before we could go and get the food. He also asked that only Icek should go on these expeditions, since Icek knew all the paths and field balks well and could more easily get to the stable. Sometimes Zawer would visit us and bring bread, but this was rare, because he was afraid of being noticed.

We couldn't find anything edible in the parish priest's stable, except for dried-out old beans and old, dusty honeycombs, just wax in which there had been honey some time before. We ate the beans and got diarrhea. We took the honeycombs and beat the dust off them and tried to stuff our stomachs with them, to fend off hunger. We took a few of them with us to our hideout and put them in the hay under the roof.

One day in June, the sun was shining brightly, and, being hot under the roof, we took off our shirts and were half-naked. Suddenly we heard a monotone hum, as if a number of airplane squadrons were approaching us. It turned out that some bees started swarming over, attracted by the smell of honey from our honeycombs. Some flew closer in and started to fly around over the roof under which we were hidden. The humming of the bees came nearer and nearer, and all of a sudden they began an invasion of our hideout through the cracks between the roof tiles. We could not run away, or even make much noise, for fear of attracting the attention of the people working below us who knew nothing of our existence. We tried desperately to brush the bees away from our naked chests with our caps, in spite of the fact that we knew this might excite the bees even more, and that they could sting us to death.

Our struggle with the bees lasted a few minutes and suddenly the insects started, as if upon an order, to retreat by the same route they had come in. We sighed with relief, but decided to get rid of all the honeycombs in our den in order to avoid another attack.

Meanwhile, the danger that our hideout would be discovered by the people working in the stable was increasing. We tried all means possible to prevent our being found. During the day we wouldn't talk, or even whisper, and we didn't move from our den until evening. We also had to conceal the traces of our evacuations. We urinated in the stable at night, where the horse stood, and we mixed our feces with the cow dung using a rake, or dug out holes near where rabbits were kept, and having filled them, we would cover them with earth and hay on which the rabbits would rest and sleep.

The situation with the hay with which we covered ourselves in the hideout became worse. At that season, in June, there was as yet no new hay, and every morning the stablekeeper would take hay from above our heads for the cattle, and since there was less and less hay, there was the danger that if there was no new supply of hay, one day the rake might strike our heads.

Time passed, and the front was still silent. But from time to time the Russians bombed German positions in our area. During the bombing, we had to jump down from the hayloft to save ourselves, for the whole stable trembled from the explosions. We were then afraid that someone could notice us. Fortunately, they had all left the building.

My relations with Icek remained cold. When we were very hungry one day, Icek had the idea to milk the priest's cows a little. Not too much, of course, because the farmers milking them might notice that someone had already done so and then would try to find the offenders. One night we went down from the hayloft to the cows below, bringing a glass we had found in the attic. Icek said that he would not milk a cow for me. He would milk one cow, and leave another for me. He knew how, and quickly obtained a glass of milk for himself. I had never done it before in my life, and so I tired myself and the cow without any effect. I was convinced that the poor cow, whose udders I pulled again and again, would lose her patience and kick me. But the creature was very indulgent, and perhaps she had pity on me. Anyway, I did not extract a single drop of milk from her and returned to our den with nothing. Icek did not give me even a drop of milk.

Icek announced on another day that he wouldn't go for bread to Zawer's for us both anymore and that I should go for my bread myself. One week he would go get bread for himself only, and the next week would be my turn to get bread for myself. On one occasion, when it was my turn, as I was sneaking to Zawer's stable, a watchdog in the neighboring farmyard belonging to a Pole named Bojko started to yap and bark so loudly that this caught the attention of a patrol of German soldiers. They used their flashlights to search around, and the path I was on also came into the light, but luckily they did not notice me. When Zawer later heard what had happened, he got mad at Icek for endangering all of us by sending me.

Meanwhile, the Ukrainians went after the Poles in the surrounding villages and were killing as many as they could. One day several Poles, who had escaped from the Ukrainians, arrived in our stable. The parish priest's farm had become the place of hiding for Poles. Among them was a Pole named Czesnykowski, whom Icek knew from before the war. He was a very honest and rich peasant whose wife was a Ukrainian. One day a Ukrainian squad stormed the house in which he and his brother lived with their families, in the village of Kawareczyzna Górna, and murdered his brother and his brother's wife. He managed to escape. His wife said she was a Ukrainian and, to save her life and her children's, renounced her husband. In this manner she survived, while Czesnykowski was now at the parish priest's farm with us. When he happened to come into the stable attic alone one time, Icek contacted him. He kept our presence secret, visited us in the stable when he could, and even brought us the leftovers from the parish lunches. He also brought us news of what was happening in the area. He said that the front was still quiet, but that a new Russian offensive was expected any time.

A day after Czesnykowski first came up to our attic another of the Poles who had sought refuge with the parish priest came upstairs and saw us there. We said we were also Polish refugees like him, but he suspected that we were Jews. Icek spoke Polish with a strong Jewish accent, which made it harder to keep up the pretense. The Pole strongly advised us to leave and not endanger the priest like this. We said we would, but in fact we stayed, and luckily nothing ever came of it.

CHAPTER 23

LIBERATION

In the middle of July of 1944, the Russian offensive suddenly took off. After only a few days it seemed clear that the Russians had cut off the Germans' withdrawal route toward Lwów. Through the cracks between the roof tiles, we could see tanks and German artillery retreating to the west down the fields and side roads. Soviet artillery could be heard nearer and nearer. The Germans, cut off from the west, decided to dig in and resist the coming Russians.

To our shock, we noticed that a cannon was located next to our stable. It was a large cannon, covered with branches and leaves so it would not be spotted by Soviet airplanes. We were terrified by this, because we knew that if the Soviets attacked this artillery position, the whole stable would go up in the air, together with us. The front was approaching and was only a few kilometers away. Germans were pulling together all their forces in our direction. "Attention, two tanks from up front," I heard a German officer say.

Suddenly everything fell silent. There were no shots, no explosions anymore. The Germans were hastily building entrenchments for themselves, preparing for a stationary fight. We slept a bit, exhausted, but were awakened abruptly by shouts and by children crying; by sounds of horses, cows, and goats; and by an immense turmoil. It was not fighting, but an evacuation of all civilians. Under cover of the confusion around us, Icek ran to Zawer's to learn what was happening. He returned to the stable with Czesnykowski. We found out that one or two German divisions were already surrounded by the Russians, who had presented the Germans with an ultimatum to surrender. That was the reason for the silence on the front. The Germans rejected the ultimatum and decided to fight. It was important, therefore, for them to evacuate the whole civil population from Biały Kamień, to secure their battle positions from any interference from people they didn't trust. They ordered everybody to move to Kawareczyzna Górna, the village that was the center of the Ukrainian Banderian fighting squads. It was from there that these armed squads had been going out, first to murder the Jews and then, more recently, the Poles.

Czesnykowski lived in that village. We were in despair and didn't know what to do. Those who stayed in Biały Kamień and refused to evacuate would be shot on the spot, according to German orders. If, however, we went out of the hideout, local people would at once recognize Icek, for he was, after all, a native of Biały Kamień and everybody knew him. And me, as a strange man, I would also be suspect. What were we to do? Czesnykowski advised us to mix with the crowd at dusk. We might go unrecognized. We could pretend to be driving cows from the priest's farm, or mask ourselves in some other way, because people were moving out together with their cattle, cows, goats, and all the belongings they could take with them. Czesnykowski promised that when we reached Kawareczyzna Górna, he would hide us.

We jumped quickly down from the loft. It was early evening. Icek took one of the priest's cows by the cord, and I did the same with another one. Together with people employed at the priest's farm, and others, we went in the direction of the village of Kawareczyzna Górna, located deep in the forest. German soldiers surrounded our procession by forming a lane along the road, lighting the way with their flashlights, and they were watching that everybody marched in the right direction. There was no possibility of turning right or left. We—Icek and myself—were afraid that the Germans could at any moment take all or part of this group for trench digging, and then, in the light of day, people would recognize us as Jews and give us over to the Germans to be liquidated.

We marched in fear. So far nobody had recognized us; everybody was preoccupied with their own troubles. People were in despair because they had to leave their homes. When we approached Kawareczyzna Górna, the Germans didn't guard us anymore, so that upon a signal given by Czesnykowski, we slipped out of the crowd and went toward his house. Here Czesnykowski situated us in the attic of his stable, where we could still see bloodstains that remained from when his brother had been discovered and murdered. We hid in the hay. A few hours later the bombing started. It was a true hell on earth. Wave after wave of Soviet airplanes were dropping bombs. The whole local population was in the shelters or in ditches. Nobody stayed at home; it was too dangerous. We were lying in this attic and were afraid to go down, for we might get noticed by the people in the ditches. Especially in this village, the center of the Ukrainian fighting squads, this would be a great risk.

The stable trembled with explosions from the bombs. The roof was showered with the soil thrown into the air by these explosions. This hell lasted for several hours. The Russians bombed without a break. There was wave after wave of planes. One could not hear any antiaircraft defense.

Later, the bombing fell silent and then the Soviet artillery started its activity. We had to stay in the attic while the stable again shook from explosions and was showered by earth. This lasted a longer time. Night came. After some time the artillery stopped shooting and the infantry's turn came. We could hear machine guns and, from time to time, shouts— "Hurrah! Hurrah!"—from the Russians.

When dawn came, silence fell. We looked through the cracks between the roof tiles, and both of us exclaimed in joy, "The Russians have come!" When I had seen them the last time, in June 1941, the Soviet soldiers had given me the impression of being utterly scared. But now I saw them proud and self-assured. In spite of their closeness to the front, they marched without helmets, with their sleeves rolled up, automatic guns hanging from their shoulders.

Upon seeing the Russians, Icek jumped down from our high attic, without a word to me, and joined them. Local Ukrainians recognized him at once and started shouting in dismay, "Pejsach's son, Pejsach's son!" They were terrified, because every Jew who survived was a witness to all the murders committed by the Ukrainians. So, once again, Icek had left me alone.

When Czesnykowski heard the shouts and learned that Icek had run away, he came running to me and asked me not to move for a while. He said that he would come for me when it became possible. He was probably afraid that the Ukrainians might find out that he had been hiding Jews. He also brought food for me to have during my wait.

On the next day, Sunday, July 23, Czesnykowski came at dawn to the attic and brought a ladder so that I could get down. I decided to go back to Biały Kamień, to the Zawers'. Czesnykowski guided me up to the forest so the Ukrainians would not see me, and told me the way to take to get to Biały Kamień. I thanked him for his help and went on my way. I was blinded by the daylight, which I had not seen for so many months. I was marching happily, for I was finally free after three years. Going through the forest I said the *Hallel*, the thanksgiving prayer, which I had known by heart since my childhood.

There were masses of German corpses lying around, and dead horses. Here and there I saw young Ukrainians searching through the dead Germans for weapons, ammunition, and other military materials.

I went first to the parish priest's stable, where I had left my sheepskin coat. The stable was completely destroyed; the coat was not there. Then I went to the Zawers', and they were very happy to see me. I was also very happy to see them, and expressed my deep gratitude to them. I repeated that I would never forget what they had done for me. In addition, I gave them some money.

For the first time since I don't know when, I took a bath. Mrs. Zawer gave me fresh underwear and some old slacks, and I went into the daylight as a free human being. I slept in a bed in their house, a very nice one-story house with an attic. I shared a room with two Russian soldiers, officers or noncoms. They were very friendly to me. And for the first time in almost three years, I ate at a table, as others did, with Zawer's entire family and the Russians. However, my digestive tract was long unaccustomed to normal food, and so I immediately got diarrhea. A few days later I had a cough and a fever had started.

I went out into the yard and from there onto the road in order to expose myself to the sun a little. In front of the house there was a bench where neighbors and some Home Army colleagues of Zawer's would come to sit and discuss the political and military situations. The front was still not far away. We heard shots and explosions at a distance, but we could gather that military activities were moving away from us.

The Russians located the *Trofeynyi Batal'on* ("Spoils Battalion"), which busied itself with gathering spoils won from the Germans, such as military equipment, weapons, sanitary equipment, and medicines, in Biały Kamień. When I was walking along the road, enjoying the fresh air, a Russian officer came up to me and ordered me to prove my identity. I appeared suspect to him. I told him that I was a Jew and therefore I could not have any official identity document. This wasn't enough for him. I showed him the certificate of the Polish Red Cross, stating that in 1939 I had taken a course in antigas defense for medical doctors, and the photograph of myself with other doctors of the Internal Medicine Clinic in Lwów, in which I was an assistant (see photo, page 7). All that I had with me was not sufficient for the officer, and he brought me to the military police post. There he told me to sit down on a bench and ordered two soldiers with bayonets on their rifles to keep an eye on me. These soldiers, having learned that I was a Jew, started to ask me about my fate with sympathy and interest. Our talk was suddenly interrupted when the officer who arrested me noticed this while going out of another room and started to shout at these two soldiers not to befriend me and not to talk to me at all, for I was a suspect.

After a while a Vlassovian soldier in a German uniform, caught at the front, was led in and seated beside me. Later, soldiers escorted in a civilian, a Pole. Suddenly I became aware that I was accused and that after all I had gone through during the German occupation, I was still a victim. First the Russian in the German uniform was called out for interrogation. After ten to fifteen minutes he was taken away to be executed.

After that the Pole was called out and then conducted away after about fifteen minutes of interrogation, but I don't know anything about his fate. Then my turn came. I was interrogated by a Soviet major and my explanations were written down by a female military stenotypist. I was speaking in Russian, a language I knew well then. This major seemed sympathetic to me, for as the interrogation went on, he was showing a lot of compassion for all I had gone through. He finally announced that I was free but that I could not move around without identity documents, and so I should apply to NKVD (the Soviet security police, which was succeeded by the KGB) to get some document, or to the army, for I was anyway subject to conscription. I told him that I had already decided long before that I would volunteer for the army if I survived. I wanted to avenge my dearest ones. It is true, though, that I had thought of the Polish army, not the Russian army. The Soviet major answered, "Perfect, for we need medical doctors," and he gave me a piece of paper and directed me to appear with it in the Woyenkomat (army recruitment office) in Olesko, a town not far from Biały Kamień. News of me, apparently the only Jewish survivor in the area, spread among the Russians. They would come to me in wonder, as if to a museum, to see this rare human specimen.

I had a visit from, among others, a Russian officer named Turski. Turski was a Russian Jew whose ancestors were said to have originated in Poland. He was a captain or a major in the Russian army. He told me that he was a member of the Communist party and that he had recently been at a meeting of some Party committee in Moscow, at which the known writer Ilya Erenburg described terrible German crimes. He admitted that when listening to Erenburg he didn't want to believe it, deeming that it was either exaggerated or a piece of propaganda. Only after hearing my experiences was he convinced that Erenburg had not exaggerated, but to the contrary, that the reality was even more horrible. He sat with me for hours for several days, listening to my stories. It was he who also arranged for a car to take me to Olesko.

I reported to the Woyenkomat, and its commander, a major, was very happy to see me when he learned that I was a medical doctor. There was a lack of physicians in the whole area, for Jewish doctors had been murdered, the Ukrainian ones had fled westward fearing the Soviets, and the Polish doctors had fled to the west as well, being afraid of the Ukrainians.

The major, a tall man with a good-natured face, and with a prosthesis replacing his amputated right arm, also asked about my past, about my war experiences, and so on, and exhibited a lot of sympathy and compassion for me. He ordered his aide to conduct me to the military canteen for something to eat, and gave me a letter to the NKVD for a checkup, assuring me that this was just a trifling affair, a mere formality. He also gave me a paper that stated that I was employed as a medical doctor for the Woyenkomat.

The next day I reluctantly went to the NKVD office, also in Olesko. The Woyenkomat provided transportation for me. When I arrived, I met Icek, who was now working there! Icek warned me that for the NKVD the fact that I was a Jew was neither a privilege nor an advantage, but the contrary. It was difficult for me to believe this after all I had gone through, and knowing that the Russians were already well aware of what the Germans had done.

I went in, and met two NKVD men with bandits' faces. They looked at me, read the letter that I had brought with me from the Woyenkomat, and told me to go wait outside. I was running quite a high fever then and felt very exhausted. I waited rather long before I was called for interrogation. They started to ask me very rigorously about everything since my birth, and especially, in detail, about my experiences during the German occupation. From time to time they interrupted me, posing additional questions. These questions, and the tone in which they were addressing me, hurt me painfully. I expected that the Russians, the ones who had freed me, would extend compassion, pity, and assistance to a man who had survived by a miracle—a sick man who was physically and spiritually wasted, a homeless man who had lost his whole family—but here I had the impression that I was accused of being alive.

Something began to rebel inside of me. When my very long interrogation ended, one of them then told me to write down everything I had explained verbally. I answered them that I had a high fever, and that it was out of the question for me to write down all that I had said during almost two hours. So they asked me to write down only my autobiography. I agreed to that. Suddenly one of them stood up and said, "You know that the Germans were doing what they wanted to everybody."

"Yes," I answered.

He went on. "This means that if you're alive, it may not be just by accident."

This I couldn't tolerate. I got up and shouted indignantly, "How dare you speak to me in such a stupid way!"

They both were surprised. They were not accustomed to people daring to speak in a loud voice to them. Those who were interrogated by them were usually fearful and terrified. But I didn't even care if they shot me for lack of respect for their authority. After all I have gone through, I thought to myself, these are my "liberators"? They saw my anger and one of them turned to me reassuringly and said, "Well, we are not saying that you personally are suspected, it is only that for us every Jew who stayed alive is suspect."

They told me I could go, but didn't give me any certificate, informing me only that their decision would be sent directly to the Woyenkomat. This interrogation was an unexpected and painful shock for me. I decided then to try by all means possible not to serve in the Soviet army.

I still had a high fever, and a cough as well. I made up my mind to go to a doctor. According to information I had, there was only one physician in the vicinity, a Dr. Bielecki, a Pole, in the town of Złoczów. There was no means of transport, though, and unlike my two trips to Olesko this one was unrelated to my enlisting with the Woyenkomat. The Russian soldiers stationed in Biały Kamień, however, who knew me and liked me, helped by driving me to Złoczów in a military car. Dr. Bielecki examined me, expressed his compassion, and gave me medicine for my cough. My problem now was how to get back to Biały Kamień, where I was living at the Zawers'. In order to get on a military truck, one would have to be helped by the *regulirovshchiki* ("regulation men"), who were, in fact, Soviet women soldiers controlling vehicular traffic at the crossings of major roads and who would stop a car if someone needed transport. This was mainly meant for the military, of course.

I came up to one such woman soldier, showed her my paper from the Woyenkomat, which stated that I was a doctor serving in the army, and told her I wanted to go back to Biały Kamień, where I was temporarily living. She declined to help me, stating that I had to have the permission of the town commander. I went, therefore, to the commander. He would not see me. Finally he said that if I belonged to the Woyenkomat, I should have gone to their office in Złoczów. By that time it was already late afternoon. I went to the Woyenkomat, but the officer I addressed did not want to talk to me, saying that he was in charge of the first division of Woyenkomat, while I belonged to the third division. I went to the head of the third division. He listened to my request and said, "During the German occupation, when you were in the concentration camp, you could march even forty kilometers by foot, couldn't you? If so, you can now walk the thirteen kilometers from Złoczów to Biały Kamień."

I was shocked by this answer. I responded in anger that he was not only unhelpful but also indulged in stupid remarks, and I left his room, indignant.

I went out into the street, helpless, not knowing what to do. It was almost evening, and I was unable to march thirteen kilometers to Biały Kamień by foot, both for security reasons and because of my health. I didn't know anybody in Złoczów, nor where there might be any surviving Jews there, for they were as yet not showing up in the streets at that time, still in fear of the Ukrainians. There was nowhere to go, to spend the night, but if I wandered in the streets at night I could easily become the prey of Ukrainian squads. I was in despair, walking without purpose through the streets.

Suddenly I heard "Doctor, doctor." I looked back and saw a Russian who was stationed in Biały Kamień. He was now driving a small tank, and had recognized me. He asked me what I was doing there. I told him that I wanted to go back to Biały Kamień. "Then sit down here," he shouted, and pulled me into his tank. So I luckily returned to Biały Kamień, having had one more bitter experience, yet another disappointment.

CHAPTER 24

THE BITTER CUP

The next day I learned that Lwów had been taken by the Russians. I was very happy. I went to my superior, the major, the local commander of the Woyenkomat, and told him I was ill and had to go to a hospital. There was no hospital in the area, but there were several hospitals in Lwów, as well as the University Clinic, in which I had worked some years ago. I wanted to go there.

The major grudgingly agreed to this and gave me a permit, under the condition of my return on August 2, 1944. On July 29, 1944, I was driven in a military truck to Lwów. I got off at Łyczakowska Street. My fever had already lasted for several days and I could barely stand on my legs. I was pale, thin, in ragged clothes, and with shoes worn to the point of having holes. Passersby looked at me, and I didn't know whether it was with compassion or just curiosity.

I dragged myself to the University Clinic of Internal Diseases. There I met some of my old colleagues and a Jewish classmate from medical school, Dr. Zosia (Sophie) Rosenkranz. I could not be admitted to the clinic, for it still had to be put in order after having had war damage, so I was advised to go to the clinic of lung diseases at Kurkowa Street. I was also told that there was a Jewish Committee in the process of being formed at Jabłonowska Street, where Jews were meeting and where every Jew who survived was registered, so that relatives and friends could find each other. (Religious and even national groups were generally illegal under Soviet communism, so this Jewish Committee was asking for special permission, in light of the unusual circumstances of the Holocaust. This permission was eventually granted.)

I went to this office. With quickened heartbeat I looked through the list of the registered. I still had some faint hope that I could find somebody I knew on the list. Alas, I did not find anyone. Neither from the close nor from the more distant family, nor even friends. Pain, sorrow, and depression overtook me. I was now not only physically, but also psychologically, broken. I registered myself and put up a notice stating that I was going to a hospital, giving its name and address, and imploring any friend or relative of mine who saw the notice to come visit me there.

I went to Faliński, for he was the only acquaintance of mine left in Lwów. He received me very cordially. Since I last saw him he had married a Polish woman, a very nice lady, full of humor and goodness. They invited me to eat with them. Mrs. Faliński knew that he had been very much in love with my sister Gina. He gave me a picture of Gina that he had, and repeated the story of her last day, how she went to her death with her brother and father despite Faliński's pleading. He also told me that he had been burglarized, and that all my money and other possessions that were still with him had been stolen.

I told them I was going to the hospital in Kurkowa Street. Mrs. Faliński promised to visit me there. I was admitted to the hospital, completely exhausted, not having the strength to stand up, to sit, or even to raise my head. I was practically paralyzed. My fever was very high.

On the second day, when the primarius, the head of the medical department, was making her rounds through the ward with her assistants, she just waved her hand with resignation when passing by my bed, as if to say, "No hope for this one."

I was also the only Jewish patient in this hospital. There were no Jewish doctors at all. Many patients would come to my room to see the Jew who had survived. Every day a Polish priest came to me. He was there visiting Polish patients, but he would especially sit down next to my bed, asking about the things I had gone through and showing great compassion. He came every day. The nurse in our room was a nun who said that she had a lot of sympathy for me, because she had worked in the Hospital of Social Insurance at Kurkowa Street, where I had also worked before the war. One day this nurse-nun told me, "Doctor, you are aware, I think, that your hours are counted? Please, save your soul, get baptized."

I answered her, "Sister, I lived and suffered as a Jew. I will die as a Jew."

She quickly responded, "Please, Doctor, do not understand me wrongly. . . ."

I told her, "Sister, I understand you very well. I repeat: I lived and suffered as a Jew and I will die as a Jew."

Her face reddened and she went out of the room. After this conversation, the Polish priest stopped visiting me.

Soviet food supplies for the hospital were astounding, simply scandalous. Our daily diet consisted of a bowl of soup, a clayey bread, and nothing else. All the sick people in the hospital were provided with food by their families, who were bringing things to eat every day. I didn't have a family, and now, after having been freed from hell, I would have died of hunger under the rule of my Soviet liberators were it not for Mrs. Faliński, who came to the hospital every day, as she had promised, bringing me a perfectly prepared lunch with meat, rolls, compote, and other treats. She really saved my life.

In the West, having liberated the victims of the Nazi occupation, the Allies provided them with food, clothes, and other necessities, and sent the sick to well-equipped hospitals or to sanitoriums. The Russians did not care about us, even to the least degree. As I found out later, a number of young Jewish survivors of the Holocaust were immediately inducted into the Soviet army and sent to fight on the front in Germany.

I was visited in the hospital several times by two women who were also patients there, Jews, who had Aryan papers and who were still afraid to admit being Jewish. They told me about it in secret, whispering. They also told me that I was a frequent topic of discussion among patients, as the only (known) Jew there, and there were several Poles who were disappointed that I still lived.

One Polish woman, a nurse, was said to have announced that she was waiting impatiently to drive the nail into my coffin. It gave me a reason to live, out of spite. I would disappoint them; I would not die for them. Slowly, my health started to improve. When this nurse heard of this, she allegedly said, "If he should come down here [into the garden courtyard with benches where convalescing patients came] to sit, I will leave." So, as soon as I was able to walk, I did go down, and took a seat next to her! However, she did not get up.

I soon received another and better reason for wanting to live. I had been depressed by my lack of visitors, and feeling very lonesome, for I knew that I really had nobody left. But after six weeks I finally had an unexpected joy when I was visited by my cousin Teresia (who had given me that piece of cake on Yom Kippur when I had typhus). Then I had visits from two other cousins, Anda and Bronia, and then learned that still two more cousins, Milek and Salek, had survived as well. All of them, except Teresia, were living together in one apartment. I was happy that, after all, after this great disaster, there were some people left in my family.

Milek (Samuel), in fact, had always been my favorite cousin, even though we were not actually blood relatives; his uncle was my stepfather. Anda was Milek's niece. Teresia, on the other hand, was a second cousin on my mother's side, while Salek (Saul) and Bronia (Bronisława) were the children of my natural father's brother, Zygmunt (whom I had seen taken for execution in Janowska camp).

One day in the hospital I was accidentally noticed by the secretary of the recently created Jewish Committee in Lwów. His name was Gutwirth. When we had been together in the HKP brigade in Janowska camp, I had helped him, for which he was very grateful. We had no time to speak then, for he was on his way to have X rays taken, but when he got out he set about doing what he could to help me.

Soon afterward I had a call from a very nice older man who had heard about me from Mr. Gutwirth and who, although he had never heard of me before, visited me very frequently and brought me four slices of bread with butter and marmalade every time. Also, after leaving the hospital, I was invited by him for dinner and, seeing my torn shoes, he presented me with some shoes from one of his surviving sons.

My health improved a lot in the meantime. It now was mid-September. I had been in the hospital since July 29. When Teresia had visited me, after six weeks, I was just starting to get up and walk each day. Now the doctors wanted to discharge me from the hospital, but I didn't have an apartment. I didn't have anywhere to go—I was homeless. My home was occupied by Poles, refugees from Volhynia who had fled from the Ukrainians. The Russian authorities assigned free flats in the city specifically to Russian Ukrainians, whom they were bringing in from the east in order to make Lwów, which had been a Polish city—with a predominantly Polish population, a significant Jewish minority, and a smaller number of Ukrainians—into a Ukrainian city. It was paradoxical that there wasn't a place for me in the very city of my birth, where I had lived all my life and where I rightfully owned an apartment house. I therefore stayed in the hospital and looked for a way out of my desperate situation.

The Jewish holidays of Rosh Hashanah and Yom Kippur (Jewish New Year and Day of Atonement) came. I learned that there was one single synagogue left in Lwów, the only one that had escaped destruction by the Nazi barbarians. This synagogue was located in the old Jewish quarter at Węglowa Street. It was a small synagogue, very poor, and primitive. All the other synagogues, and there had been many of them in Lwów, some very beautiful, had been destroyed and burned down by the Germans.

I decided to go on Yom Kippur to my first *Yizkor* (prayer for the dead) since my liberation. It was September 27. Although it was rather far from the hospital to this synagogue on Węglowa Street, I didn't take the street-car but instead went there by foot, in accordance with Jewish religious law. When *Yizkor* started, I began to weep and wail, crying so much that I thought my chest would break. I was afraid I would go out of my mind. It lasted a long time before I calmed myself down. Some years ago I would have spent these holidays of Rosh Hashanah and Yom Kippur with my beloved family, but now?

At the synagogue I happened to meet my cousins Anda and Salek. They were living, together with Milek, Bronia, and others, in an apartment on Kadecka Street that had previously been lived in by Germans. They found it just after the Germans had left the city. There were eight of them staying in the apartment already, not all from our family. When they heard that I was in need of a place to stay, they offered me two square meters in a corner of their kitchen to stay in. I took advantage of this offer and left the hospital. I had been examined prior to this by the Soviet military medical commission and released from military service.

When living in Kadecka Street, from early October 1944 to June 1945, I often went to the Jewish Committee, which had been transferred from Jabłonowska Street to the synagogue building in Węglowa. Those of us who had survived went there to look for registered names, still searching for our close relatives and friends. We hoped that, since the last time we had checked, someone we knew might perhaps have been registered as being still alive. We waited for a miracle, and told each other stories of what we had gone through during the Nazi occupation.

I learned from the Jewish Committee that only about 700 survivors of the Holocaust were registered at that time. The Jewish population of Lwów before the German invasion in 1941 had been around 160,000. The number of surviving physicians registered was 17. I remember very well that before the August action in 1942, when I was working for the Sanitätsamt (Health Center) of the Lwów ghetto, there were 520 Jewish physicians registered there.

Shortly after I left the hospital, I met a man on the street in Lwów; his name was Rudolf Reder. I had known him fairly well before the war. He had lived on the same street as I, and we often met. He owned a factory that made soap, candles, and the like, and also had a wholesale store that sold these products. He had been in his sixties at the start of the war. He told me his story, which was also published at the time by a Jewish historical commission in Poland. During the August 1942 action he was taken to Bełzec, and was on the same train with my wife, Frania, and her mother and grandmother. After arrival in Bełzec, all the people were herded out of the train. The commandant gave a short speech to the newcomers,

In early 1945, a few months after my release from the
hospital.

telling them that nothing bad would happen to them, they would be sent
to various places in Europe for work, but that first they would have to
have a thorough cleaning in the showers. He showed them a barrack that
bore the inscription "BADEHAUS" (bathhouse), decorated with flowers. A
number of men were taken aside for work, and Reder was among these.
The remaining inmates were ordered to undress, and to each put all his or
her belongings in a pile labeled with his or her name. The women had to
have a haircut, ostensibly for delousing purposes. The undressed people
were led into the bathhouse, and were pushed in if they hesitated. Then
the door was hermetically sealed. Soon after, Reder could hear screams
and weeping, which lasted a few minutes and gave way to silence. The
door was opened, and Reder's group had to remove the bodies and bury
them; this was the work for which he had been spared.

This routine was repeated daily. Many of the workers tried to escape
Bełzec in various ways, with no success. It was virtually impossible to get
out. They knew that in a few weeks they would be killed and be replaced
by workers selected from a new transport. One day, an important boiler
used by the SS broke down. The camp commandant asked the workers if

any of them knew how to fix it. Mr. Reder stepped forward, explaining that he was familiar with such boilers, having used them in his factory. After he had inspected the boiler he told the commandant that he could indeed fix it, but needed some spare parts. He said that he knew where in Lwów these could be found. The commandant reluctantly agreed to send him to Lwów, and assigned three SS men to escort him there and back. When they came to Lwów the SS men put Mr. Reder in the Gestapo jail for the night while they went out to some nightclubs. The next morning they came for him and went for the parts. On their way back they stopped on the main street next to a famous delicatessen. They left the driver in the car while the other two went in for some food. Mr. Reder soon noticed that the driver, possibly as a result of his carousing the previous night, was snoring, and his rifle drooped. Mr. Reder realized that this was his chance, and very slowly opened the door and crept out, always watching the driver carefully, for he would surely be shot at once if he was seen trying to get away. He crossed the street and watched for a while to see if his escape had been noticed. When he saw that it was safe, he ran away, heading for the house of his former servant, a Ukrainian woman. She agreed to hide him, and in this way he survived until liberation.

Mr. Reder's amazing story provided a firsthand verification of what went on at Bełzec, and for me personally it was a confirmation that Frania indeed had been killed. With the image of how she died now so vividly in my mind, I was filled with despair and outrage beyond words. It was hard to want to go on living.

I didn't have anything to live on. The Soviet authorities didn't care about the fate of the surviving Jews. Although I was not quite healthy yet, I had to look for a job. In the meantime, I was visiting Mr. and Mrs. Faliński daily, even slightly before my discharge from the hospital. They had invited me for dinners, and I gratefully accepted their offer. I continued in this way until I got my job.

Being a physician, I got a job easily. There was an enormous shortage of doctors in Lwów, even though before the war our city had more doctors than any city in Poland, except Warsaw. I also had it easier finding work because I was known to professors and assistant professors of the University Clinic.

On November 15, 1944, I took the post of doctor of internal medicine in the IInd Municipal Polyclinic at Brajerowska Street. The clinic's chief doctor was Dr. Rajski. (His name before the war had been Reiss, and he had changed it when hiding under Aryan papers.) When I got this job, and waited for my first paycheck, I learned from the Moscow newspaper that the trade union of doctors and employees of the health care institutions in western Ukraine, which meant Lwów too, had decided, out of gratitude to the Red Army, to give it their next three months' pay. So it meant I would work for nothing during these three months, with only very modest food rations.

Luckily, I could earn some money privately as a doctor after official working hours, and thereby help myself a bit. Under Soviet rule, socialized medicine was available to all, but one had no choice of whom to go to, and the quality of care could be very poor. Those who could afford to do so would go outside the system and pay a doctor to see them unofficially. Several months passed before I could buy myself some old, patched-up clothes. Fortunately I had gotten slacks from Faliński previously, and an old winter coat from the Jewish Committee.

When I looked for work, I did not even attempt to resume the career I had begun, as a medical researcher. I felt like an eagle whose wings had been clipped. Before the war, I had been full of idealism, and also believed I could do anything I set myself to. My dream had been to find a cure for cancer. But now, after all I had seen, I had lost my idealism about the human race and was bitter at this loss. I did not want to sacrifice and postpone my own needs for the sake of this humanity. Instead, I would work as a doctor and live for the moment, enjoy life so that someday I too could say "I have lived."

The Russians soon started to issue passports. In Soviet Russia a passport was not a document entitling one to travel abroad, as it is in the democratic countries of the world. In Russia it was an obligatory personal document that one had to always have in one's possession. Whoever didn't have a passport was immediately arrested. In 1939 the Russians had been issuing passports good for five or ten years, but now in 1944 they issued them for only one year for the "nonsuspect" persons, and for only six months for the "uncertain" citizens. After taking over Lwów in July 1944, the Russians combed through the city during the night for a period of several months. They very often searched through houses looking for "suspect elements." Many people who had these six-month passports were then arrested without cause and sent away to do heavy labor in the mines of Donbas, in the eastern Ukrainian coal basin. (This was the same town to which Polish workers had been enticed in 1939, believing it a model of fine worker conditions!)

When I reported to the passport office in Lwów, the Soviet clerk asked me for my German document, the *Kennkarte*. I answered that I was a Jew and that Germans had given these ID cards only to non-Jewish citizens. The clerk repeated sharply, "Do you have a *Kennkarte* or not?" I answered him again, that being Jewish I could not have this ID card. . . . My sentence: a six-month passport.

During the same period, the NKVD was carrying out a *proverka*, meaning a political inspection in all institutions. One day a middle-aged woman, with a babushka on her head, came from NKVD to make a political investigation of our Polyclinic. When I was taken for interrogation, this NKVD woman, having listened to my personal data, such as date and place of birth, nationality, education, profession, and so on, requested a detailed description of my experiences during the German occupation.

During my explanations she suddenly interrupted and asked me, "How long have you been with the Banderians?" I looked at her in disbelief. How could I be with the Banderians? It was commonly known that they were a radical nationalist Ukrainian fighting organization responsible for many mass murders, that they were murdering Jews, and that they were anti-Semitic extremists. I explained this to her. "All right," she said, "go on." I went on describing my experiences, but after ten minutes she interrupted me again and asked, "And how long have you been with the Banderians?"

I answered her again with irritation, "But I told you that as a Jew I could not be with the Banderians."

"All right, go on," she said. I continued the description of what I had gone through, and in a few minutes she suddenly asked again, surprisingly, for the third time, the same question: "How long have you been with the Banderians?" I repeated my answer in an impatient tone. The interrogation finished, at last, and she went to speak to other employees of the Polyclinic. This hag was not too clever.

A worse incident occurred during her interrogation of an elderly doctor, Dr. Lewenheck, who was an assimilated (Polonized) Jew. When she asked him for his nationality, he answered, "Polish."

"You are a Jew," said the NKVD woman. "Isn't that so?"

"Yes," replied Dr. Lewenheck. "I am a Pole of Jewish origin."

To which she shrieked, "Immediately change the nationality in your document to Jew!"

"I will not change it," answered Dr. Lewenheck. "I feel Polish."

The NKVD woman started to shout, "You are a Polish nationalist, a Fascist!"

Then Dr. Lewenheck asked her, "Tell me, do you abide by the same racist rules as the Nazis?"

She reddened with indignation, ran for the telephone, and called the police to arrest him. It was only due to the efforts of the director of our

Polyclinic, Dr. Rajski, who turned for help to higher authorities, that Dr. Lewenheck avoided prison.

People joked and laughed in the clinic afterward that out of several dozen people working in the clinic—Poles, Ukrainians, and only four Jews, all medical doctors—the hag had found only two suspects. Both were Jews, one suspected of being a Polish nationalist and a Fascist, the other a Ukrainian Banderian fighter.

Not far from our Polyclinic, just a few blocks away at Jachowicza Street, was a prison. The Russians put all those arrested during the nighttime and daytime roundups there, for eventual transport to the east, apparently for hard labor in the mines of Donbas. From time to time two Russian policemen with bayonets on their rifles would come to our Polyclinic in order to take a physician and medical assistants to the prison to examine sick prisoners. We gave the prisoners medicine or dressings, whatever was needed, and when the disease was more serious the doctor could send the prisoner to a hospital. For a prisoner, getting out of the gloomy, primitive, overpopulated prison cells to be sent to a hospital, to a clean bed, to be taken care of there, was like getting out of hell and going to heaven. None of the doctors wanted to go for these examinations in the prison, for we did not want to appear to be helping the NKVD in its oppressions, but we had to go when ordered to.

I somehow succeeded in evading this function, but one day, when the armed policemen came to the director of the Polyclinic, I was just speaking with him about some medical matters. They needed a doctor and I couldn't refuse the request. I went with the policemen, and brought along a nurse, a hospital attendant, and a pharmaceutical assistant. When I got to the prison, the Russian policemen opened the doors of the cells and I could see prisoners lying or sitting on the straw, packed like sardines in a can. Prisoners who reported sick were conducted out of their cells to the corridor, where I examined them and gave out medicine.

At a certain moment an SS man, who had escaped from a transport of prisoners, was brought to me. He had been shot in the right elbow, caught, and put in this prison. I looked at him. He had the face of a murderer. I asked the nurse to take his temperature. He had a fever. The wound on his elbow was stinking of pus, which was oozing out of quite a big wound. I issued an order to send him to the hospital. My co-workers from the Polyclinic, all of them Poles, looked at me in astonishment. "Doctor, what are you doing? After what you have gone through, after the loss of your whole family, you direct an SS man to the hospital?"

I answered, "Alas, at this moment I am a doctor and this is my duty." I was angry at myself, dissatisfied, but I knew and felt that I could not do otherwise. My assistants shook their heads. They couldn't understand my behavior.

A few weeks later one of my friends told me that he had been at a reception hosted by a Polish family who did not know me. During this reception the host and the guests stated that Jews didn't know how to take revenge. They had heard that some Jewish doctor had pulled an SS man out of the prison on Jachowicza Street and sent him to the hospital to be cured.

At the end of 1944, Poldek Zawer, the younger brother of Florjan Zawer, visited me and told me that his brother Florjan, my benefactor, was dead. A detachment of Soviet soldiers had marched into Biały Kamień. It later turned out that this detachment was in fact a group of disguised Ukrainian fighting squads who had put on Soviet military uniforms. These Ukrainians went to the houses of Polish families and took the men to the post office. The Poles didn't suspect anything, and didn't resist. At the post office, the Ukrainians shot all the Poles, took their shoes and documents, and then informed the wives of those killed that they should come and take their husbands' bodies. I was shocked and bitterly saddened by this news. I felt as if it was someone from my close family who had been killed. After all he had done, this good man had become the victim of such a horrible crime. I expressed my condolences and put together a package for Mrs. Zawer, with whatever I could manage to give, for Poldek to take back with him. After a few months Poldek Zawer was also killed by the Ukrainians, during a battle. I lost contact with Mrs. Zawer; she and her children were forced, together with the other Polish families of Biały Kamień, to leave and relocate to western Poland.

CHAPTER 25

STRANGER IN THE HOMELAND

The apartments around us at Kadecka Street became occupied by Russians and by Ukrainians from eastern Ukraine, and those Jews who had found a home here after the Germans had fled were now forced by the Soviet authorities to leave the flats. We were given hints that we would also have to leave our apartment, but we were left in peace for the moment. We made friends with our Russian neighbors who had military or civilian jobs. They were very friendly and hospitable to us.

One day they invited me to a party. There were many guests there, mostly officers. People spoke about the political and military situation. At one point, a guest said that rumors were circulating that during the upcoming summit meeting in Yalta, President Roosevelt would ask Stalin to let Soviet Jews emigrate to Palestine. I was surprised to notice among the Jewish officers an overt interest in such a possibility.

In December 1944, while I was at work in the Polyclinic, two armed NKVD men came to our apartment and left a paper summoning me to come to Smiersh (from *Smiert' shpionam*—"death to spies") to be a witness. Smiersh was the notorious department of the NKGB, the national state security commissariat. (The NKGB, eventually known as the KGB, took over some of the functions of the NKVD.) It turned out that a Jew named Szpilka—who had been with me in Janowska camp in the same HKP brigade, Opel-Damke, and had been a cabdriver before the war—had recognized a former Askari from Janowska camp. He had seen him walking down Copernicus Street, dressed as a Russian noncom and armed with an automatic gun. Szpilka, without hesitation, caught hold of the Askari's automatic rifle and started to curse him. The Russian got frightened and tried to escape, but Szpilka would not let him go until the Russian military police arrived and arrested him. Szpilka named me, among others, as a witness. I didn't know how he knew that I had survived or what my address was then.

I went to Smiersh. The offices were in a villa, surrounded by barbed wire, at the end of Kadecka Street. When I reported at a broad counter, two noncoms on duty asked me for my passport, my ID document. When I gave them my six-month passport, they both gave me such a suspicious look that I felt uneasy. They called some superior of theirs on the telephone, and told me to go to one of the upper floors. Big glass doors closed behind me. I wouldn't be able to get out of there if not allowed to. I entered the room indicated to me. I was happy to see Captain Kagan, whom I had met not long before at the party in my neighbors' apartment. He was to interrogate me now. I smiled at him, but his face was serious and official. He started to interrogate me in a very bureaucratic manner. After that, the accused Askari was brought in. I didn't recognize him, but then he had belonged to the group of Askaris whom Willhaus, no longer trusting the Askaris who had been there, brought to the camp when the massacre and the final camp liquidation were imminent.

I told Kagan that I had escaped from the camp soon after this new group of Askaris came, and so I couldn't recognize him, but I told him that I had learned from other ex-prisoners that the new Askaris particularly tormented the inmates. At the end of my interrogation, I went down to the exit door, which was closed. I had to wait until those who were guarding the exit obtained the telephone order to let me out. I left the Smiersh building with relief.

I was extremely disappointed about the attitude of the Russian authorities toward the Jewish survivors of the Holocaust. The Soviet government–controlled newspapers, the Polish *Czerwony Sztandar* ("The Red Banner"), and the Ukrainian *Wilna Ukraina* ("Free Ukraine"), described the atrocities the Germans had committed in Janowska camp, stating that in this camp people of many nationalities—Ukrainians, Poles, Russians, Gypsies, and so on—perished. At the end, Jews were mentioned, despite the fact that over 90 percent of the camp inmates had been Jews. I noticed that the Soviets were not interested in the truth, only in what could serve their propaganda. They formed several offices for investigating German crimes, but I didn't go there to testify because I wanted the truth, and not to be used for their propaganda.

In March 1945, I returned with a group of survivors from Janowska camp to the site. It was a bitter experience when we came to the place where a few years ago inummerable thousands of people had been tortured and killed. There was now a unit of the Russian army stationed there. We went to the commanding Russian officer, who lived in what had been Untersturmführer Willhaus's villa. We introduced ourselves as former inmates of the Janowska extermination camp, and we asked him for permission to visit the grounds. He politely agreed to it and was even interested enough to come with us. The huge grounds were almost empty. The barracks where we had lived were burned down, and the places where people were forced to work, and the gallows, had disappeared. All that remained was the latrine in which the floor was completely covered with hardened human excrement from which many shoes, among them children's shoes, were protruding. Depressed and disgusted, we left the latrine.

In Western Europe, they preserved the former concentration camps for history, as a warning symbol of human cruelty and bestiality. They built monuments for future generations. Here, though, not the slightest effort was made on the part of the Russian authorities to preserve this place of martyrdom of so many thousands as a historical monument of inhumanity. We then went to the Sands, and other places of execution, where we collectively said the prayer "El Mole Rachmim" ("O God of Mercy") for the people who were murdered there. It was a very painful experience for us.

At that time I was informed that before the final extermination of Janowska camp the SS had formed a special brigade there called the Death Brigade. Because the Russians were moving victoriously westward the SS wanted to erase all traces of their crimes. The work of this brigade had been to dig up the mass graves and burn the corpses using gasoline on wooden logs. The bones were then crushed by machines similar to a cement mixer. The fine bone dust and ash were strewn in the neighboring fields, and the pits, after being filled back in, were seeded.

Some time after this visit to the site of Janowska camp, it was announced that on the basis of an arrangement between the Polish government in Lublin and the Soviet government, Poles and Polish Jews could register for repatriation to Poland. (Lwów was to become a part of the Soviet Union, due to agreements signed by the three powers after World War II.) At that time the German-Soviet front crossed the whole of Poland, and the only Polish freed territories were the region of Lublin and a belt between Przemyśl and Rzeszów. I was one of the first to register to go to Poland. I didn't want to stay in this slavish Soviet system, and besides that, my city of Lwów was only a cemetery for me, where I had suffered so much and lost all those I loved, everything of mine. I couldn't live there any longer.

There were numerous people who wanted to register but were afraid that it was a new Soviet trap. Several colleagues came up to me asking me whether I was aware of what I was doing. They recalled that in 1940 the Russians had organized a registration for those who had fled from western Poland and who wanted to return to their homes and families in western Poland, which was at that time under German occupation. A few months later, all those who had registered were arrested and sent to Siberia (or to Middle Asia). In spite of this, I didn't want to change my decision. I didn't care.

After a short period of time, I was called to appear before the chief doctor, a woman, in the regional health care department. She announced that she had been informed that I had registered for repatriation to the west. Why was I doing this? she asked. They respected me very highly and a splendid career was ahead of me, she said. She also said that there was anti-Semitism in Poland, and insisted that I change my decision. She was very friendly, trying hard to persuade me, but I stood firm in my resolve.

About a week later, two armed NKVD men came to our apartment, again when I was at work, and left an order from the Soviet authorities saying that I should leave Lwów and go to Poland in seven to ten days. I accepted this order with indifference, but the director of our Polyclinic was terrified. I was the only doctor in the Polyclinic who was a specialist in internal diseases. The clinic wouldn't be able to function without me unless it found another internist, but this was extremely difficult. So, the director started to appeal to various higher offices, and finally obtained a delay in my forced expulsion. It turned out anyway, soon afterward, that even if I had tried to go to the west, it wouldn't have been possible by any means, for this happened just before the new Soviet offensive against the Germans. All roads, and all trains, were overfilled with Soviet army troops. The authorities who had ordered my immediate expulsion certainly knew that. They simply wanted to scare me.

I continued my work at the Polyclinic until June 1945. I lived to see the dreamed-of moment when the Germans were at last completely defeated and had to capitulate unconditionally. When this happened it was already expected, but still I was extremely joyful and felt a certain completeness. The news was broadcast thoughout the city by public loudspeakers, and there were fireworks that night.

I had won, but it was a Pyrrhic victory, or even worse. On June 24, 1945, I was evacuated to the west on a truck with a group of other people from Lwów. There were several such trucks on that day. We were transported in the direction of Kraków.

I was leaving behind Lwów, my beloved city. In my childhood and young adulthood, long ago, whenever I left the city for vacations, I longed, after just a week, to return, and I was always happy when I was coming back. Lwów was where I lived in the warm atmosphere of family life, surrounded by my close ones, whom I loved so much, and where I had so many friends, and where I passed so many happy years.

And now I was leaving this city behind, with pain in my heart; the city where I suffered so much, and where there was no one left for me. I was leaving Lwów forever. I recalled the words of our great Polish poet Adam Mickiewicz:

> My tears poured down,
> tears pure and abundant,
> over my childhood idyllic and holy,
> over my young years lofty and cloudy,
> and over my years of manhood,
> years of calamity.

EPILOGUE

One week prior to my departure from Lwów I married Alicja (Alice) Samet, whom I had briefly met before the war through my cousin Milek. She was now also a Holocaust survivor who had lost her family during the Nazi persecution. She had come to Lwów from her native Warsaw, fleeing the Germans, in 1939. Soon after the Germans captured Lwów she took on an Aryan identity and lived in the Aryan section. She did not have the proper Aryan papers, however, and felt unsafe, so she moved to Kraków and finally got these papers. Meanwhile, she successfully hid Milek, Anda, and two other Jews in her Lwów apartment, starting before her move to Kraków.

In August 1943 she was jailed and beaten in the notorious prison in Lwów at Łąckiego Street, under suspicion that she was Jewish because she had tried to help a Jewish woman. She was released after two months when the Gestapo came to the conclusion that she was not Jewish.

Many years later, when the United States State Department organized a World Gathering of Rescuers from the Holocaust in the fall of 1984, Alice received an invitation to be among those honored in Washington. She replied that since she was herself a Jew this invitation must have been a mistake. They answered that she was risking herself doubly, both in hiding Jews and in risking being discovered as a Jew, and therefore should indeed come, which she did.

In January 1945, when Milek learned that Kraków had been liberated by the Russians, he went there and brought Alice to Lwów to join our group. In this way I came to know her closer. Alice changed my life dramatically. When I met her after the war I was depressed and destitute,

Alice in a 1943 photo taken in Kraków.

having lost all whom I had loved. I was without a home and pitifully frail. I had no desire to live. I had not wanted to be killed like a dog; I wanted to live to see the Germans defeated. But after that, with none of my dearest left alive, I wanted to commit suicide and was mad at myself that I couldn't carry this out, that I still clung to this pointless existence. Alice brought a new light into my life. We fell in love with each other. I found a purpose to live and be happy. I wanted to build a new family. We decided to leave Poland (and Soviet rule), to try to get to the West.

We moved to western Poland, to the territories that had been annexed from Germany, and in September 1945 settled in the town Wałbrzych (formerly Waldenburg) in Lower Silesia. We found a large apartment and were later joined by Milek (and his fiancée), Anda, Salek, Bronia, and two other cousins from my stepfather's family who had survived: Wanda and Jadzia. Alice and I shared our apartment with them. I had a medical office adjoining our apartment, and also worked in the City Health Center. But as Jews came under increasingly frequent and violent attack from the Polish ultranationalistic, anti-Semitic underground, we all felt we must leave Poland immediately. Applying for an official exit permit would entail at the least a long wait, and quite possibly expose us to the government's suspicion and harassment. What convinced us beyond all doubt to leave quickly was that pogroms were even happening in several towns, among them Kielce, where a number of Jews who had survived the Holocaust were killed!

Together with some friends, our entire group illegally crossed the Polish-Czechoslovakian border in June 1946. There we joined a large group of Jewish refugees who were being helped and guided to freedom by two Jewish relief agencies, Joint (American Joint Distribution Committee) and Bricha (a settler group hoping to bring Jews to Palestine). Going disguised as Greek repatriates, we passed through the Soviet zone of Austria (which at that time was still partitioned and occupied) to the American zone. Here we were helped by the U.S. Army, which brought us in freight trains first to a transitory camp in Puch, near Salzburg, and one week later to Landshut in Bavaria, in the American zone of Germany. During our brief stay in Austria I again saw how little had been learned from this disastrous war. The farmers near the refugee camp refused to sell their produce to Jews, even at very favorable rates, saying they would rather see their fruits rot than go to a Jew.

In Bavaria I was employed by UNRRA (United Nations Refugee Relief Administration) as an internist in the Displaced Persons Hospital in Bad Reichenhall, and later by the IRO (International Relief Organization) Resettlement Center, Medical Division, in Munich.

In 1947 our son, Severin, was born in Munich. During this time, I received a medical license to practice in Germany. I worked at the Medical University Polyclinic in Munich and later opened a private practice as a specialist in internal medicine.

In 1956 I emigrated to the United States, joining my wife and son, who had already been there for a year. We lived in Brooklyn. I had to start over, working (in a position allowed those with foreign M.D.s) at Menorah Hospital and Home for the Aged while studying for the New York State Board Examination. In 1959 I took and passed this exam, and subsequently received a license to practice medicine in New York State.

In 1960 I opened my medical office in Manhattan and was associated with Jewish Memorial Hospital in New York. At the same time I was working for the German Consulate in New York examining Holocaust survivors for their restitution claims for damage to their health sustained during the Nazi persecution. I had some initial hesitation about working for the German government, but I felt that it was sincere in its desire to atone for the crimes of its countrymen, and I knew that I could give a most sympathetic hearing to these survivors, as one of them. In October 1991 I received a high award from the president of the German Federal Republic, Von Weizsäcker, for contributing through my work to strengthening the relations between Americans and Germans.

In March 1992, after fifty-five years of medical practice, I retired, but I continue my work for the German Consulate.

My son, Severin, graduated from Bronx High School of Science and then from Cornell University, where he received degrees in mathematics and in teaching. He has been teaching mathematics at Ithaca High School since 1973. In 1982 he married Pamela Rozelle, a fine arts graduate of Kalamazoo College in Michigan and SUNY Oswego. In 1984 our first grandson, Julian, was born, followed in 1987 by our second grandson, Nathaniel.

Alice and I today, with our grandsons Julian and
Nathaniel, our son, Severin, and his wife, Pamela.

Mrs. Zawer (with members of her family) between Alice and me during our visit to Wrocław, Poland, 1976.

After the war I had to fulfill some obligations, both of duty and love. First among these was to show my appreciation and gratitude to Mrs. Zawer, who with her husband, Florjan, had saved my life; they selflessly risked their own lives and the lives of their children, for a stranger. We lost contact with each other when I left Lwów, while Mrs. Zawer and her two small chidren were forced to leave their home some time after her husband had been killed by Ukrainian nationalists. I tried for several years, but with no results, to find her address through different organizations, such as the Red Cross and the Polish State Repatriation Office, as well as through friends who remained in Poland. Only after I came to the United States did I succeed in getting her address, with the help of the Polish Embassy in Washington, D.C. She was living in the city of Wrocław (previously Breslau). We were very happy to find each other. When I asked what to send her I received the following answer: "Dear Doctor, don't send me anything. You don't owe us anything. We did our human duty." This answer was all the more remarkable as she was in real need, supporting her family herself amid the bleak conditions of Communist Poland. Despite her answer I have helped her with money and packages sent several times a year. She has been very grateful to me for it, especially as she has gotten older and sick. She is now eighty-three years old. In 1976

Alice, Severin, and I visited her and her family at her home. It was a joyful meeting for all of us.

In March 1989, as a result of my efforts, the Special Commission for Designation of the Righteous, at Yad Vashem in Jerusalem, conferred upon her and her husband its highest expression of gratitude: the title of Righteous Among the Nations. They received the medal, a certificate of honor, and the privilege of having their names inscribed in the Garden of the Righteous in Yad Vashem. Because of her poor health, Mrs. Zawer could not travel to Jerusalem. Instead, the Israeli Ambassador and his secretary went to Wrocław from Warsaw to hand Mrs. Zawer the award. The ceremony was shown on Polish television in Wrocław, and included the mayor of the city.

My second duty, which I owed to the martyrs of Lwów, particularly those of Janowska concentration camp, I fulfilled by testifying in German courts against SS murderers, namely in 1967 in Stuttgart and in 1977 in Saarbrücken. In Stuttgart in the so-called *Lemberger Prozess* (Lwów trial) over seventeen SS men were tried for participating in the mass murder of almost half a million Jews in Galicia. After 144 days of trial, the verdict of the jury represented a travesty of justice. These SS men, accused of murdering innumerable men, women, and children, got away with small sentences—from two and a half years to nine years. In each case about two years were deducted from the sentence because of time served during and while awaiting trial. Only one SS man received a life sentence. Four were acquitted, among them Büttner and Fox (!), whom many witnesses, including myself, accused of the incredible acts, especially concerning hanging, that were detailed earlier in this book. Several other witnesses described how Fox tortured victims by raising and lowering the rope to considerably prolong the hanging. Among the others on trial were Rokita, who was excused from the trial because of bad health and shortly afterward died in jail there; Kolonko, who received a seven-year sentence; Blum, who received a six-and-a-half-year sentence; and Schönbach, who received an eight-year sentence.

After my return to New York I received a letter from Yad Vashem. They had found out from my testimony in Stuttgart that I had memoirs from Janowska camp written immediately after liberation. They requested that I donate these to Yad Vashem because they were of great historical importance. After I had done so, they asked me to make a tape for them, describing my experiences and observations of Ghetto Lwów and Janowska camp from a medical doctor's standpoint, as well as an account of how I survived.

In 1977 I was called to testify in a court in Saarbrücken against the archmurderer of Janowska camp, SS man Friedrich Heinen. I testified for about four hours. Heinen at no point showed any emotion, acting bored and unconcerned, as if this was someone else's trial. In August 1979 I received a letter from the presiding judge, Franz Priester, telling me that Heinen had been sentenced to life imprisonment mainly because of my very detailed testimony. I was very satisfied that at least in this important case I helped justice be done.

As to Willhaus (who had been a citizen of Saarbrücken), he was not brought to trial for his crimes; I heard from the judge at Saarbrücken that he had died during the war on the Soviet front.

I heard from many sources that SS General Katzmann died in an Italian hospital after having survived on false papers. He allegedly admitted to all his crimes before his death.

The other sacred duty I owe to the martyrs of Janowska camp and Ghetto Lwów is this book, so that they should not be forgotten.

Final note: Dr. Merkel, who in March 1939 (see chapter 1) prophesied the disaster to all of us, escaped from the burning Lwów ghetto during its liquidation in June 1943 to the city sewers and committed suicide there.

INDEX

Boldface page numbers refer to photographs